VOCATIONAL EDUCATION AND TRAINING: IMPACT ON YOUTH

A TECHNICAL REPORT FOR THE
CARNEGIE COUNCIL ON POLICY STUDIES
IN HIGHER EDUCATION

John T. Grasso
West Virginia University

John R. Shea
Carnegie Council on Policy Studies
in Higher Education

VOCATIONAL EDUCATION AND TRAINING: IMPACT ON YOUTH

A Technical Report for the Carnegie Council on Policy
Studies in Higher Education

VOCATIONAL EDUCATION AND TRAINING: IMPACT ON YOUTH
by John T. Grasso and John R. Shea

The material in this project was prepared under Grant No. TPRM 21-06-77-03 from the Employment and Training Administration, U.S. Department of Labor, under the authority of Title III, Part B, of the Comprehensive Employment and Training Act of 1973. Researchers undertaking such projects under Government sponsorship are encouraged to express freely their professional judgment. Therefore, points of view or opinions stated in this document do not necessarily represent the official position or policy of the Department of Labor.

The Carnegie Council on Policy Studies in Higher Education, 2150 Shattuck Avenue, Berkeley, California 94704, has sponsored publication of this report as part of its continuing effort to obtain and present signficant information for public discussion.

Library of Congress Catalog Card Number LC 78-75168

International Standard Book Number ISBN 0-931050-11-1

Manufactured in the United States of America

DESIGN BY WILLI BAUM

BIBLIOGRAPHIC DATA SHEET	1. Report No. DLMA 21-06-77-03-1	2.	3. Recipient's Accession No.
4. Title and Subtitle VOCATIONAL EDUCATION AND TRAINING: IMPACT ON YOUTH			5. Report Date March 1979
			6.
7. Author(s) John T. Grasso (West Virginia Univ.) and John R. Shea			8. Performing Organization Rept. No.
9. Performing Organization Name and Address Carnegie Council on Policy Studies in Higher Education 2150 Shattuck Avenue Berkeley, CA 94704			10. Project/Task/Work Unit No.
			11. Contract/Grant No. DLTPRM 21-06-77-03
12. Sponsoring Organization Name and Address U.S. Department of Labor Manpower Administration Office of Research and Development 601 D Street, N.W., Washington, D.C. 20213			13. Type of Report & Period Covered Final
			14.

15. Supplementary Notes

16. Abstracts

The report examines 1) choice of high school curriculum; 2) relations between curriculum, on one hand, and aspirations, occupational information, and highest year of school completed on the other; 3) psychological reactions to the high school experience of those who have followed various "tracks," and 4) the early labor market and further training experiences of former vocational students as compared with their general program peers with equivalent years of schooling (10-11; 12; 13-15). Multivariate techniques, including path analysis of the educational attainment process, are used extensively. The experience of men and women, blacks and whites, is treated separately. The analysis is based on data from the two youth cohorts in the DOL-sponsored National Longitudinal Surveys (men, 1966-73; women, 1968-72).

17. Key Words and Document Analysis. 17a. Descriptors

Attitudes	Job satisfaction
Counseling-vocation interests	Manpower
Earnings	Negroes
Education (includes training)	Specialized training
Employment	Technical schools
Females	Vocational guidance
Industrial training	

17b. Identifiers/Open-Ended Terms

Vocational Education: How Much? For Whom? (early title)

17c. COSATI Field/Group 5I, 5J

18. Availability Statement Distribution is unlimited. Available from National Technical Information Service, Springfield, VA. 22151. (Also: Carnegie Council, 2150 Shattuck Ave., Berkeley, CA 94704	19. Security Class (This Report) UNCLASSIFIED	21. No. of Pages 255
	20. Security Class (This Page) UNCLASSIFIED	22. Price

FORM NTIS-35 (REV. 3-72) $_____) THIS FORM MAY BE REPRODUCED USCCMM-DC 14952-P72

1286458

Contents

Foreword

In *The Federal Role in Postsecondary Education* (1975), the Carnegie Council noted the paucity of research on the outcomes of occupational training, and urged that additional work be undertaken. We asked John Shea, a member of our staff, and John Grasso, a former colleague of his, to extend and refine some of their earlier work in this area.[1] With the help of a grant from the Employment and Training Administration of the U.S. Department of Labor, Grasso and Shea have provided at least tentative answers to the following important questions regarding occupational education:

- Who gets it?
- Why?
- What difference does it make?

Their work is based on an analysis of data through the early 1970s from two representative national samples of young men and women in the civilian population.

In their earlier work, Grasso and Shea restricted their attention to young men who were out of school by 1969, and who had completed exactly 12 years of school. While they reported some information on the psychological correlates of curricular experiences, most of their work had to do with labor market outcomes. They did not examine: (1) the ways in which curriculum affects educational attainment; (2) the interrelationships between educational and occupational goals on one hand, and curriculum on the other; (3) the relationship between high

[1] Grasso and Shea (1973); Grasso (1975).

school curriculum and labor market and psychological outcomes for former students who left high school early, or who
obtained one to three years of college; or (4) the impact of
curricular experiences on young women.

This report breaks new ground in each of these areas, and
carries forward to the early 1970s Grasso and Shea's analytic
work on young men. This document also reports on an attempt
to examine whether or not vocational studies in high school are
especially beneficial for young people who might be considered
disadvantaged or handicapped. On this topic, however, Grasso
and Shea ran into the serious problem of inadequate sample
cases. Their limited findings are presented in Chapter 6, only
because the analysis may be of some heuristic value.

As Grasso and Shea document in Chapter 2 of this report,
youth in college preparatory programs "stand out" from their
peers in other major program areas in terms of scholastic aptitude, social class background, and in other important ways. The
emphasis here is on a comparison of students from vocational
and general programs. Former college preparatory students
without a baccalaureate degree are as successful as, if not more
successful than, former students from other programs with
equivalent years of schooling—a fact that I believe highlights the
importance of basic skills to career success.

It is clear that major program categories—college preparatory, vocational, and general—hide tremendous diversity. As
Grasso and Shea point out in Chapter 1, "vocational" studies
for boys usually consist of blue-collar, skilled manual training.
For girls, such studies are generally in clerical, office, and sales
work. Major program areas differ from state to state in structure
and in degree of separation from other "tracks," as well as in
the hours or class periods devoted to occupational training versus general studies, basic skills, physical education and the like.
Fieldwork readily demonstrates differences in the apparent
quality of vocational and other programs, as judged by program
content, purposefulness, quality of instruction, physical facili-
ties, and the like. For example, some classes in automobile mechanics are singularly unimaginative programs in which students
do little more than tinker with their cars, while other classes are

carefully organized, and involve extensive diagnostic and repair work on most subsystems and types of automobiles. Well-organized programs often develop a wide range of know-how in parts management, inventory control, accounting and billing, cashier work, advertising, and a host of other skills—many of general usefulness, whether or not a student embarks on a career as a mechanic.

Grasso and Shea have been forced to compare "averages." In doing so, they have made a valuable contribution to our understanding of the impact of vocational studies. Yet it is still true that additional research would be helpful in adding to our collective understanding of curriculum effects, with future emphasis on qualitative differences within program categories.

CLARK KERR
Chairperson
Carnegie Council on Policy
Studies in Higher Education

Preface

This study was undertaken for the Carnegie Council as part of a larger project addressed to policy issues surrounding formal programs of preparation for work, especially federally-assisted vocational education, and employment and training programs. In studying access to occupational training and its impact, we have used an immensely rich body of data generated as part of the National Longitudinal Surveys (NLS) of Labor Market Experience, a project sponsored by the Employment and Training Administration of the Department of Labor, and carried out, in cooperation with the U.S. Bureau of the Census, by Professor Herbert S. Parnes and his associates at the Center for Human Resource Research, Ohio State University. We have used information from two of the four representative probability samples of the civilian, noninstitutional population included in the NLS: (1) approximately 5,000 young men who were 14 to 24 years of age when initially interviewed in the fall of 1966; and (2) an equivalent number of young women who were the same age when first interviewed early in 1968.

We have analyzed data pertinent to many questions that are important for vocational education today. The richness of our data source has permitted us to adduce direct, and sometimes indirect, evidence on many issues. Nevertheless, we recognize limits in the scope and depth of our inquiry, and feel that the reader should be made aware of the more important ones. Our data source is simply inappropriate for answering some questions of importance in any complete examination of the effects of curriculum. To be specific, we say nothing about do-it-yourself activities because there are no measures of such activities in the NLS. The same is true of individual differences in learning styles. On the matter of motivation to learn or to stay in school, our information from the NLS is limited to the subjects that students like and dislike; educational and occupational goals; satisfaction with present job and past schooling; and actual school enrollment. On the question of whether occupational training in school substitutes for (or complements) training received beyond regular school, we have indirect measures consistent with modern theories of human capital.

With respect to other topics, although data are available, we have relied wholly on tabular rather than multivariate regression analysis. On the topic of curriculum differences in unemployment experience, we have relied on tabular presentation, in part because Grasso's earlier multivariate work on this subject (1975) turned up no curriculum differences among young men. In Chapter 4 of this report, however, we show rather consistent differences in unemployment of young women by high school curriculum. Whether these differences would hold up if statistical controls were introduced for years of work experience, mental ability, and the like, must await additional research. Another area where our analysis is less refined than we would like has to do with satisfaction with work and schooling, and with subjects liked and disliked in school. Here the absence of testable models and the relative paucity of information in the NLS about psychological attributes has led us to be more descriptive than analytical.

Despite these caveats, we feel that this report addresses many important questions regarding the kinds of youth who receive occupational training, why, and the difference it makes. To provide an overview of the highlights of our work we have prepared an Executive Summary, which immediately precedes Chapter 1. In Chapter 1, we describe some of the demographic characteristics associated with different major program emphases, with special attention to socioeconomic background and mental ability. Next, we examine curricular choice (or assignment) and its correlates, especially occupational and educational goals (Chapter 2). We then analyze dropout rates from high school and transition rates to college or to other forms of postsecondary training (Chapter 3). In Chapter 4 we examine the relationship between curriculum in high school and various measures of labor market success. In the next chapter, we explore reactions to work and to earlier schooling to see whether curriculum bears any systematic relationship to these psychological outcomes (Chapter 5). We then present information on the question of whether vocational studies are especially beneficial for disadvantaged or handicapped youth (Chapter 6). In Chapter 7, we bring to bear indirect evidence on the matter of benefits of training that may extend beyond the individual to employers. Finally, we discuss some of the implications of our research for education, employment, and training policies, and for further research (Chapter 8).

We wish to thank several individuals and organizations for their encouragement and assistance. For financial support, we are especially indebted to Howard Rosen, Director of the Office of Research and Development of the Department of Labor's Employment and Training Administration, to the Carnegie Council, and to West Virginia University. We thank Ellen Sehgal, a member of Dr. Rosen's staff, who served as project monitor, for her patience, suggestions, and general helpfulness. We wish to acknowledge the suggestions of Clark Kerr and Verne Stadtman of the Carnegie Council staff, and those of Herbert Parnes and Steve Director, who along with several anonymous reviewers of an earlier draft, offered valuable suggestions for its improvement. Needless to say, none of the reviewers is responsible for any remaining errors of fact or interpretation or for the recommendations we advance in Chapter 8. The latter are wholly our own. Finally, we wish to thank Patsy Foster for her assistance with data processing, Steve Archibald for his conscientious and careful research assistance, and Sandra Loris for her skillful typing and secretarial help.

John T. Grasso

John R. Shea

Executive Summary

This report examines access to occupational education in high school, and its impact on eventual educational attainment, post-school training, labor market success in the first few years out of school, and psychological well-being. Answers have been sought to the following kinds of questions:

- Is choice of curriculum closely linked to educational and occupational aspirations? Is it more common for aspirations to come into line with available options and the reality of educational experiences, or is the reverse typical?
- Does high school curriculum influence number of years of school completed, and extent of postschool training (apprenticeship, company-sponsored training, and the like)?
- To what extent are economic outcomes (e.g., rate of pay, unemployment experience) and psychological states (e.g., job satisfaction, retrospective assessments of prior education) affected by earlier curricular experiences?
- When these questions are asked of young women, are the results similar to, or different from, those obtained for young men? Do young women who hold occupations nontraditional for their sex enjoy higher earnings then those who enter sex-stereotypic positions?
- Is there any evidence that disadvantaged and handicapped youth are better served by a vocational than by an alternative curriculum? Is there evidence to support the dual labor market hypothesis—that the jobs available to disadvantaged groups tend to be inferior in various ways?

The study is based on analysis of data from two of four cohorts in the National Longitudinal Surveys (NLS) of Labor Market Experience: 5,000 young men who were 14 to 24 years of age when initially interviewed in the fall of 1966; and 5,000 young women who were the same age when first interviewed early in 1968. The study makes use of interview data through 1972 for women and 1973 for men. Attention is restricted to (1) those who were in high school in the base year surveys, and (2) men and women who were out of school and who had completed 10 to 15 years of school as of each survey year. Whenever possible, the experience of blacks is contrasted with that of whites.

The major variable of interest is high school curriculum, by self-report of respondents, categorized as follows:

- Men: Occupational
    Vocational (largely blue-collar, manual)
    Commercial (largely sales)
    College preparatory
    General
- Women: Occupational
    Business and office (clerical)
    Other vocational (including distributive
    education[1])
    College preparatory
    General

Since many women in general and academic programs take typing and shorthand, some attention is paid to these measures as well.

Both multiple linear regression analysis and tabular techniques have been employed. In examining several labor market outcomes, such as hourly rate of pay and annual earnings, controls have been introduced for scholastic aptitude, socioeconomic origins, geographic location, and several other variables. Former U.S. Commissioner of Education Sidney Marland (1971) and others have argued that all students should be in

[1] The term "distributive education" embraces all facets of sales and marketing work at sub-baccalaureate levels.

either an occupational or a college preparatory program, and that the general program option should be abolished. For this reason, the experience of students from occupational curricula has been compared with the experience of their peers from the general track.

Findings. In the base year surveys (1966 for men, 1968 for women), approximately 14 percent of the male and 20 percent of the female students in grades 10 to 12 were enrolled in occupational curricula. Of women high school graduates from all curricula, 87 percent of the whites and 76 percent of the blacks reported having taken one or more typing courses in high school.

High school students in the NLS from occupational curricula differed from their counterparts in other programs in the following respects:

- College preparatory men and women, on the average, ranked noticeably higher in scholastic aptitude (SA) and socioeconomic origins (SEO) than did either occupational or general students. Differences between the latter groups were minor overall, except that black males in vocational programs displayed slightly higher academic aptitude than did their general counterparts. (Chapter 2)
- Although fewer blacks than whites chose (or were assigned to) an academic rather than a general program, within each third of the SA and SEO distributions, blacks were more likely than whites to be college preparatory students. In other words, the fact that fewer blacks than whites were in academic programs is associated with the noticeably lower scholastic aptitude and social class background of black youth. (Chapter 2)
- Over four-fifths of college preparatory students in the base year surveys aspired to four or more years of college. Among the young men, nearly half the general students and a quarter of the vocational students wanted at least four years of college. Among the women, about one-third of the general and one-sixth of the occupational students held such high aspirations. (Chapter 2)

- Among male students, proportionately more blacks than whites in vocational programs aspired to four or more years of college. In other curriculum categories, more whites than blacks aspired to college. Among female students, blacks held about the same level of aspirations as whites, except that very few white girls in business and office programs wished to attend college. (Chapter 2)
- By and large, occupational goals were consistent with educational aspirations, except that, for whatever reason, many young black men aspired to occupations which, in terms of typical educational requirements, ranked below their hoped-for educational attainment.[2] (Chapter 2)
- The preferred occupations (at age 35) of women students where overwhelmingly sex stereotypic. Altogether, only nine occupational categories out of 297 accounted for over two-thirds of expressed job preferences. Indeed, secretary (code 342), teacher (codes 182, 183, 184, which define levels), and "clerical and kindred (not elsewhere classified [n.e.c.])" (code 370) accounted for fully half the preferences. Except for black females, young men and women in occupational programs were somewhat more likely to want jobs for which pre-employment preparation below the baccalaureate is sometimes available. (Chapter 2)
- Male students in vocational programs displayed less knowledge of occupations than did their general counterparts. Females in business and office studies, however, displayed more such information than did their peers from a general program. College preparatory students of both sexes were more likely to know about different occupations than were either occupational or general students. (Chapter 2)

Aspirations and curriculum assignment are not always con-

[2] Selected characteristics of occupations, including a judgment as to the level and type of education or training required or preferred for each, are presented in Appendix C. For example, if a person aspired to any of a number of professional jobs, such as lawyer or accountant, and expressed an educational goal of at least 16 years, such goals or aspirations are judged to be "consistent." However, if a person aspired to four or more years of college, but wanted to be a draftsman or surveyor, aspirations are said to be "inconsistent." Chapter 2 contains a more complete discussion of the classifications used.

gruent. For example, some vocational students aspire to four or more years of college. Curriculum and goals can come into line through either revision of aspirations or movement between curricula. This pattern of change from year to year is not only important in its own right, but also must be understood in order to judge whether occupational programs enhance the likelihood that students will complete at least high school. Regarding these points, our findings may be summarized as follows:

- Between the base year and first follow-up surveys, fewer than one in ten high school students moved from one major curriculum category to another. The net flow was away from general and college preparatory programs, and toward occupational programs. (Chapter 3)
- Students who moved to occupational programs held aspirations in the base year which, on the average, were higher than those of occupational students in the base year but lower than those of students who stayed in college preparatory or even general programs from one year to the next. Associated with the move to an occupational program was a tendency to report liking school more at the reinterview than in the base year. (Chapter 3)
- Remaining in a program two years in a row tended to raise the already-high aspirations of college preparatory students, but in the case of male vocational students to lower their already relatively low aspirations. (Chapter 3)
- Regarding completion of high school, evidence is mixed as to the implications for boys of being in a vocational rather than a general program. Controlling for SA, SEO, and other background variables, cross-sectional analysis for out-of-school youth seems to indicate that vocational studies enhance completion of high school. There is a positive correlation between having been most recently in a vocational program, rather than a general one, and highest year of school completed over the range from grade 10 through grade 12. However, tracing students from one year to the next suggests the opposite conclusion. That is, if anything, male students in a vocational program in 1966 were more likely to leave school by 1967 than were their general peers.

Some students move to occupational programs as they progress through high school, and this fact may account for our mixed findings. Some vocational courses are offered only to seniors; others, to juniors and seniors only. Thus at any given time there are proportionately more seniors in occupational programs than juniors, and more juniors than sophomores. By itself, the net flow toward occupational studies results in a positive correlation between having been in an occupational program and highest year of school completed over the range from 10 to 12 years. (Chapters 2 and 3)

- With respect to girls, the net flow toward occupational studies is less in evidence, and both the cross-sectional and longitudinal results indicate that women in a business and office curriculum are more likely than are their general peers to complete at least 12 years of school. (Chapters 2 and 3)
- Ignoring aspirations, there is little doubt that, having completed at least 10 years of school, students in vocational and business and office studies are less likely than are those in a general program to complete at least one year of college. Moreover, with the possible exception of students from the lowest third of the scholastic ability distribution, the net effect of pursuing an occupational program is a reduction in ultimate educational attainment of at least half a year. (Our estimates are conservative, since many of the respondents had not completed their schooling.) (Chapter 3)
- Path models indicate that between general and occupational students, the latter curriculum had a negative "effect" on educational attainment, apart from educational aspirations. For some students, low aspirations doubtless precede curriculum choice; for others, curriculum choice probably precedes clarification of educational goals. The addition of aspirations to a path model of educational attainment reduces the direct negative "effect" of curriculum on attainment by only about one-third. Among young black men, but not white, differences in aspirations are largely independent of choice between a vocational and general program. Furthermore, for this group, the addition of aspirations to a path model has little or no effect on the negative relationship between voca-

tional curriculum and attainment. (Chapter 3)

- Postschool training in company-sponsored programs, business colleges and technical institutes, apprenticeships and the like is common. At the most recent follow-up surveys, about two-thirds of out-of-school young men with 10 to 15 years of schooling, and half the women, report having had some post-school training. Attesting to the opportunity afforded by postschool training, SA and SEO are less strongly related to having had some college *or* post-school training than to having completed one or more years of college. Among men, whites were more likely to have had such training than were blacks. However, perhaps because of manpower training programs and affirmative action efforts, the gap narrowed considerably between 1966 and 1971. Among women, racial differences in reported postschool training were slight. (Chapter 3)

✓How effectively do various high school curricula prepare young people for later labor market experiences? To examine this question, we looked at the relationships between curriculum and several indicators of early labor market success, controlling for highest year of school completed, background characteristics (SA, SEO), and other variables conceivably associated with both curriculum and labor market outcomes, such as type of community of residence—rural, small town, or large city. Our principal findings for respondents with exactly 12 years of school are as follows:

- Evidence is mixed as to whether a vocational program, in comparison with a general one, reduces the incidence or severity of unemployment. Unemployment rates at various survey dates are not consistently lower (or higher) for one curriculum group than for another. Analysis based on one of our measures (employment status as of the survey dates) suggests that former students from occupational curricula are less likely to be jobless. However, analysis based on another measure (total number of spells of unemployment from 1966 to 1970) suggests that high school male graduates from vocational programs have had more total spells of unemployment than their general peers. Among white males at least, the average duration of current spell of unemployment was shorter for vocational graduates, and fewer reported having had multiple spells over the entire period.

Among employed young women with exactly 12 years of schooling, business and office students reported less unemployment than did general students, while college preparatory graduates were the most likely to have encountered joblessness. (Chapter 4)

- In terms of hourly rate of pay and annual earnings, only among female graduates is there clear evidence of an advantage to these who completed occupational programs in high school, and the positive effect is as large for young black women as for whites. Among young men, having been a vocational rather than a general student makes essentially no difference: the vocational curriculum coefficient for blacks is generally negative and for whites is positive, but neither of these is statistically significant for hourly pay or annual earnings. At that, having been a vocational student is negatively associated with measures of longer-term career outcomes: change in hourly wage over time; occupational status; and full-year earnings of *all* men in the respondent's occupation (derived from the 1970 Census of Population). Once again, however, the vocational curriculum coefficient is not statistically significant. (Chapter 4)
- Consistent with earlier work (Grasso, 1975), it appears that postschool training may pay off somewhat more for former vocational than for general students. (Approximately equal proportions report training beyond high school.) (Chapters 3 and 4)
- Despite the fact that fewer young black than white men perceive that their postschool training has been useful in their current (or last) job, having had such training makes a positive contribution to early labor market success, and this "effect" is about as great for blacks as whites. (Chapter 4)
- Some vocational educators feel that occupational studies enhance the opportunity for self-employment. Perhaps it is too early to tell, but we find no evidence in the NLS data to

suggest that former vocational students are any more likely to be self-employed than are their general program counterparts. (Chapter 4)

- Job differences among high school graduates from the various curricula were minor, as measured by industry attachment, major occupational group, whether their occupation called for pre-employment occupational preparation, and by extent of job mobility. (Chapter 4)

Considerations of sample size rule out strong statements as to the implications of high school curriculum for the labor market success of high school dropouts and respondents with one to three years of college. Nevertheless, the following observations are worth making:

- Ignoring curriculum, "some college," as opposed to high school graduation only, makes a good deal of difference in pay, earnings, and occupational assignments, and the differences are sizable for each race-sex group. (Chapter 4)

- Between dropping out of high school after grade 10 or 11 and completion of exactly 12 years, average differences in economic performance are, again, considerable. The one exception—and an important one—is that white males who left school early are not at a serious disadvantage, as judged by rate of pay, earnings, and especially their pattern of occupational assignments. For example, about a third of both the white male dropouts and graduates held jobs in the craftworker category. (Chapter 4)

- Among whites, major differences in outcomes emerge for those with some college, as compared to all those with less schooling. For blacks, on the other hand, the major differences are between high school dropouts and those who have completed at least high school. (Chapter 4)

- Employed women in the NLS overwhelmingly held sex-stereotypic jobs in 1972. Surprisingly, the sex composition of an occupation, as measured by the percentage that women represented of total 1970 employment in each occupation, made little or no difference for hourly rate of pay or earnings, especially among high school graduates. Among the high school dropouts, being in a "female job" depressed earnings somewhat, while among women with some college, the opposite was true. (Chapter 4)

• While fewer high school dropouts than graduates reported some postschool training, such training is positively related to labor market outcomes for both groups, and the "effect" of training is as great (if not greater) for dropouts as for graduates. This is true for men and women, and for blacks as well as whites. (Chapter 4)

• Only among the young men is it possible to say anything about the relationship between high school curriculum and labor market outcomes for those with "some high school" or "some college." For rate of pay and earnings of males, having been in a vocational rather than a general program may make a slight positive contribution, but in no case is the curriculum coefficient statistically significant. Among females, occupational (largely business and office) students were unlikely either to drop out of high school or to obtain some college. This factor, plus relatively low labor force participation rates, led to an inadequate numbers of cases to permit comparison with the general track. (Chapter 4)

It may be argued that, regardless of the implications of curriculum for subsequent performance in the labor market, curriculum options are important because they enhance choice, respond to individual differences, and otherwise contribute to psychological well-being. Our findings in this regard may be summarized as follows:

• College preparatory students express greater satisfaction with school than do either their occupational or general program counterparts. Few students in any program are "dissatisfied." Overall, black youngsters express greater satisfaction with school than do whites. Least satisfied with school are white males from occupational programs, but this is not due to their occupational studies. (Chapter 2)

• Vocational and office subjects are frequently cited when students are asked to name the subject they enjoyed the most. Very few youths disliked these subjects. The ratio of responses for subjects "enjoyed the most" to "disliked the most" is particularly high for occupational subjects, especially among students in occupational curricula and among those in the low third of the scholastic aptitude distribution. Black youngsters, however, were somewhat less likely than white to name a vocational course as their favorite. (Chapter 2)

- In terms of the perceived adequacy of their education in meeting their needs in the labor market, respondents from occupational programs were more likely than were their general peers to judge their schooling as adequate. However, this was not true of young black men. Women who have not completed college rate the adequacy of their preparation higher than do men. (Chapter 5)
- Black youths expressed less satisfaction with their jobs than did white. Black men perceived less progress in their work than did white, and felt their chances of reaching their occupational goals by age 30 were not as good, but had equally high desires to obtain more education. (Chapter 5)

Vocational education is sometimes thought to be especially important for disadvantaged and handicapped youth. Inadequate sample cases prevent statements about the "effects" of curriculum on the labor market success of youth with health problems or those who grew up in homes where a language other than English was spoken. Nevertheless, in comparison with all graduates, these two "special needs" groups reported a higher mean hourly rate of pay. (The implications of having dropped out of school before graduation are discussed above.) Related findings include:

- The age-earnings profile for young black male high school graduates is considerably flatter than it is for whites, giving some support to the dualist conception of the labor market. However, the actual change in rate of pay from 1966 to 1971 suggests that the black-white earnings gap for men actually narrowed somewhat in relative terms. We suspect that especially rapid gains in the earnings of young blacks entering the labor market may account for the apparent discrepancy between cross-sectional and longitudinal results. (Chapter 4)
- Young black men in the NLS were less likely than were their white counterparts with equivalent years of schooling to hold

"good" jobs. And, while barriers between "secondary" and "primary" labor market jobs are not impenetrable, black youths—especially dropouts—made less progress than did whites in moving out of "secondary" and into "primary" jobs. (Chapter 6)
- Black male graduates from a general program were more likely than were those from an occupational curriculum to enter the primary sector, or to escape the secondary. The opposite was true for white graduates. (Chapter 6)

A relatively underexplored area of research has to do with the implications of high school curriculum for (1) do-it-yourself activity, (2) the level and nature of post school training, and (3) difficult-to-measure, diffused effects on productivity. The NLS contains no information on the first topic, but permitted us to adduce limited evidence on the other two. Our findings, with some interpretation, may be summarized as follows:
- Postschool training is common; men from vocational programs are as likely as are their general peers to have received postschool training. However, the form is often different. Former general students are more likely to have received school-based training (e.g., in technical institutes); former vocational students more frequently report company training or "other vocational," a category which includes apprenticeship. It does not appear that postschool training to any substantial degree duplicates skills developed in high school. (Chapter 7)
- Both human capital theory and past research suggest that the kinds of occupational skills developed in schools may be socially rational, in the sense that (1) school-based training is more cost-effective, or (2) employers would not have sufficient incentives to develop skills at the work place. Specialized occupational competencies, such as typewriting or welding, are by no means *specific*, in Becker's sense, if these skills are relevant for a large number of employers. Reflection suggests that it is cheaper and probably more effective to teach 25 students how to operate a typewriter in a classroom than to leave the acquisition of this skill to the work place. In general, one would expect smaller firms to be less efficient than large firms in developing skills in the work place.

This line of reasoning suggests that schools may tend to develop skills commonly found in smaller establishment. Our measure of size of firm—an overall average from each industry—is not ideal. Nevertheless, we find that young black men from vocational programs are employed in industries with lower-than-average mean size of establishment. On the other hand, it is consistent with past research that having had some postschool training is positively associated with industry average size of establishment. These findings suggest that hourly rate of pay and earnings may capture only some of the social (economic) benefits that are derived from curricular experiences in the high school. (Chapter 7)

Conclusion and Recommendations. Any conclusions and policy judgments based on the research reported here should be sensitive to limitations implicit in the kind of analysis and data with which we have worked. With respect to the data base, our measure of curriculum is a self-report by students. Major categories (especially vocational) hide considerable variation in content and program duration. A second note of caution stems from the time period covered (1966 to the early 1970s), and the likely improvement in curricula since the 1960s. A third difficulty stems from the "aggregation problem." Vocational programs vary in content, quality, and duration among states and localities, but this study, of necessity, deals with overall "averages." A national sample of 5,000 persons 14 to 24 years of age is simply too small to permit more detailed analysis. Finally, since many (if not most) students select their own program of studies, inferences drawn from a comparison of ostensibly similar students in occupational and general programs may reflect unmeasured variables associated with self-selection.

We hope that the results of our research will be of practical use for guidance personnel, educators, those in charge of employment and training programs, and policymakers at state and federal levels. The research, in our judgment, supports the following recommendations: (Chapter 8)

- Educators and policymakers should judge the "success" of occupational training in high school on the basis of several indicators, not just training-related placement rates. These indicators include: (1) congruence with career objectives; (2) differences in learning styles; (3) satisfaction of non-vocational purposes; (4) psychological well-being; (5) influence on eventual educational attainments; (6) economic benefits to the individual; (7) efficiency at the work place; (8) ability to serve persons with special needs; and (9) overall cost-effectiveness.

- Educators and guidance personnel can improve career guidance by (1) increasing their efforts to inform students and parents of career opportunities and education and training options; (2) avoiding "tracking," especially of young black men, into existing vocational rather than more general programs; and (3) being sensitive to the fact that sex-stereotypic vocational education for women may provide earnings in the first few years out of school that are at least as high as those in fields in which women are less concentrated.

- The allocation of federal and state funds for vocational education to areas with high concentrations of low-income or otherwise disadvantaged youth, or high dropout rates, can be (and, we believe, should be) defended on purely fiscal grounds. Vocational education may or may not be especially helpful to, or especially desired by, youth with "special needs." We were unable, for reasons of sample size, to determine whether vocational studies have been especially useful for young people who are handicapped, educationally disadvantaged, or who grew up in a home where a language other than English was spoken. In the case of young women, blacks who took business and office studies benefited as much as whites. We uncovered no evidence, however, indicating that vocational programs of the 1960s were especially beneficial for young black men in comparison with their general program counterparts.

- Post-high-school noncollegiate training warrants encouragement and support. Such training is received in business colleges and technical institutes, in apprenticeship, in the military service, in company-sponsored programs, and elsewhere. Nonformal education and training opportunities are important for at least three reasons. First, the influence of social class background and mental ability is much less potent when educational attainment is viewed broadly to include both collegiate and noncollegiate forms of training. Second, among the NLS men at least, blacks were less likely than were whites to have had any postschool training in 1966, but the relative gap closed considerably over the next five years, attesting perhaps to the success of equal opportunity efforts and manpower training programs. Finally, postschool training (1) was associated with clear economic benefits in terms of hourly rate of pay; (2) helped close (in relative but not absolute terms) the wage gap between white and black men; and (3) yielded benefits for both men and women at least as great for high school dropouts as for graduates.

Regarding access to and the impact of occupational education and training, we see a need for further research addressed to the following questions: (Chapter 8)

- What kinds of education and training experiences are most useful for young persons who are handicapped or disadvantaged in some way? Is vocational education especially appropriate? Is it especially desired?

- In what way, if at all, do occupational studies influence acquisition of basic skills, such as reading and competency in mathematics? Does a "positive interaction" help to explain the economic advantage accruing to young women from business and office programs, compared to their general curriculum peers?

- Concerning curriculum for boys and their dropout rate from high school, can the divergent conclusions from cross-sectional and longitudinal analyses be resolved? Does experience with a vocational program influence the probability of dropping out? If so, what is the direction of the effect?

- Would a multivariate analysis of high school curriculum and employment of young women sustain the view (based on a bivariate analysis) that an occupational curriculum for female high school students reduces their subsequent unemployment?

- Why is it that young black men in the NLS in vocational

programs had somewhat higher scholastic aptitude scores
than did their general counterparts, and were more likely to
aspire to four or more years of college, but actually attained
less education?

- In the absence of public support for occupational training,
would the volume and mix of occupational training provided
through the marketplace be socially optimal? (On theoretical
grounds, we would say no.) What benefits of publicly-
supported training, if any, are captured by employers and
society at large?

- How important are nonmarket outcomes of vocational education? For example, what is the value of do-it-yourself activities facilitated by skills gained in school?

1

Introduction

How much vocational education should young people have? The answer, we believe, depends on an understanding of the aptitudes and interests of students, the desires of parents, knowledge of the probable short- and long-term consequences of pursuing a vocational curriculum rather than some other option, and the needs of employers.

The Effectiveness Issue To date, evaluative research on vocational education has rarely gone beyond examination of selected economic outcomes, typically ascertained shortly after leaving school, such as labor force and employment status, occupation and its relationship to the training program, and earnings. Even in this limited domain, the evidence is mixed. After reviewing over a hundred studies, Reubens (1974a, p. 318) concluded that the evidence " . . . failed to satisfy the desires of a Wyoming vocational educator . . . for decisive and irrefutable evidence of the labor market advantage to high school vocational graduates."[1] Of course, the fundamental research question is far broader: What would have happened to students had they not participated in a vocational program? Would they have left school earlier? Would they have been less satisfied with school? Would they have entered a different (and less congenial) line of work?

---

[1] Reubens (1974a, 1974b) gave somewhat higher marks to vocational programs at the postsecondary level. She based her conclusion largely on the work of Stromsdorfer (NPA, 1972), and Somers et al. (1971).

The literature is largely devoid of information regarding several of these matters:

- the direction and sequence of change in aspirations and schooling decisions (e.g., whether or not to continue, choice of curriculum);
- the implications of such patterns for subsequent educational attainment and later labor market experience;
- the attitudes and interests of students in various curricula; and
- the labor market and psychological consequences of curricular experiences several years after leaving school.

Longitudinal data from the National Longitudinal Survey of Labor Market Experience (NLS) provides a unique opportunity to learn about several of these relationships.

The Policy Issues. How one views the *effectiveness issue* doubtless depends on vantage point and values. The history of federal involvement in vocational education since the original Vocational Education Act of 1917 reveals several recurrent themes. At various times, emphasis has been placed on:

- reducing unemployment, especially among youth, by developing marketable skills;
- providing a wider array of schooling options, responsive to differences in needs, interests, and abilities (a theme often associated with efforts to stem the dropout rate);
- meeting employer needs for skilled manpower in vocational-technical areas; and
- preparing persons historically outside the mainstream (e.g., the disadvantaged and handicapped) for employment.

In this chapter we comment on each of these themes in turn. First, the reduction-in-unemployment argument is based on the plausible assumption that competencies appropriate to one occupation or to a small group of occupations make persons more employable by providing entry-level skills needed by employers. Since the federal government bears principal responsibility for dealing with unemployment, it should be no surprise that occupational education is promoted as part of overall economic policy. The second perspective, dropout prevention, is related to a belief that students in general curricula are more likely than are those in vocational or college preparatory programs to leave school prematurely. The view is that many such youngsters would be encouraged to stay in school (and would profit from) a vocational education opportunity responsive to their interests and aptitudes. Regarding the third point, training-related placement rates provide an indication of whether employer needs for trained manpower are being met. Such a measure also speaks to the matter of whether students find work related to short-run career objectives. The fourth theme is more recent (advanced from 1963 onward)—namely, that disadvantaged and handicapped persons have all too frequently been denied equal educational opportunity, and vocational programs may be especially important in developing their self-sufficiency.

Despite these recurrent themes, the major expressed purpose of the federal Vocational Education Act has been, " . . . ready access to training or retraining that is of high quality, which is realistic in light of . . . opportunities for gainful employment, and which is suited to . . . [the] needs, interests, and ability [of people] to benefit from such training." The Education Amendments of 1976 expanded the purposes of federal support for vocational education, but reiterate this fundamental goal of increasing the schooling options available to youth and adults.

The Research Questions. We began our research with several overarching questions as to who gets occupational training, why, and the difference, if any, that it makes.

1. Is choice of curriculum closely linked to educational and occupational aspirations? Is it more common for aspirations to come into line with available options and the reality of educational experiences, or is the reverse typical?

2. Does high school curriculum influence (a) number of years of school completed and (b) extent of postschool training (apprenticeship, company-sponsored training, and the like)?

3. To what extent are economic outcomes (e.g., rate of pay, unemployment experience) and psychological states (e.g., job satisfaction, retrospective assessments of prior education) affected by earlier curricular experience?

4. When these questions are asked of young women, are the

results similar to, or different from, those obtained for young men? Do young women who hold occupations nontraditional for their sex enjoy higher earnings than those who enter sex-stereotypic positions?

5. Is there any evidence that disadvantaged[2] and handicapped youth are better served by a vocational than an alternative curriculum? Is there evidence to support the dual labor market hypothesis—that the jobs available to disadvantaged groups tend to be inferior in various ways?

Methods and Procedures. Answering these questions is by no means easy. Research by Jencks (1972), Duncan, Featherman, and Duncan (1972), and others points to the importance of family background, scholastic aptitude, and other factors antecedent to curriculum choice (or assignment) in explaining differences in educational attainment and in later experience with the labor market. We have therefore conducted much of our analysis in a multivariate framework, in order to test explicit theories or models of behavior, or to control statistically for variables thought or known to be related systematically to both curricular experiences and proximate (or ultimate) dependent variables.

In evaulating the outcomes associated with a vocational program experience, a particularly critical problem is the identification of an appropriate comparison or control group. As pointed out in Chapter 2, young people in occupational curricula possess background characteristics that are more similar to those of general than of college preparatory students. For this reason—as well as the policy issue as to whether a general curriculum is inferior to either of the others[3]—we generally compare

---

[2]The proper meaning of the term "disadvantaged," from an educational point of view, has always been elusive, as the discussion in Chapter 6 attempts to make clear.

[3]The comments of Sidney Marland (1971, p. 6) illustrate this point of view. "(The general curriculum is) a fallacious compromise between the true academic liberal arts and the true vocational offerings. It is made up, as its name suggests, of generalized courses, possessing neither the practicability and reality of vocational courses nor the quality of college preparatory offerings. Watered-down mathematics, easier English—such is the bland diet offered in the name of the general curriculum."

students from vocational and general programs, holding constant or adjusting for socioeconomic background, scholastic aptitude, and other relevant variables.

As indicated in the Preface, we make use of data from the two youth cohorts in the National Longitudinal Surveys (NLS) of Labor Market Experience covering 1966 to 1973 (young men) and 1968 to 1972 (young women).[4] In the NLS, blacks were deliberately oversampled relative to whites. In this report, we generally present data on blacks and whites separately, although we sometimes show the total for all races combined, especially where the number of black sample cases is insufficient for separate analysis. When this is done, other races, such as Asian, are included in the total. We have run our analyses using weighted observations, because of differing sampling ratios for blacks and nonblacks. Weighted N's, expressed to the nearest thousand persons, are shown in most tables. An exception is made in presenting regression results, where the actual number of sample cases is shown. As a rule of thumb, one nonblack respondent represents about 4,000 persons in the universe from which the sample was drawn; one black, about 1,000 persons.

In controlling for differences in family background, we use a summary measure, called *socioeconomic origins* (SEO). SEO is a weighted average of five components: level of education of (1) father; (2) mother; and, if appropriate, (3) oldest older sibling; (4) father's occupation when respondent was age 14; and (5) an index of the availability of reading materials in the home at the time. A score was calculated for each respondent for whom at least three of the five measures were available.[5]

The measure of scholastic aptitude (SA) employed is based on pooled test score results reported by school officials in a

---

[4] General findings from the two surveys, under the authorship of several individuals, are reported in *Career Thresholds* (young men) and *Years for Decision* (young women), Manpower Research Monographs 16 and 24, in several volumes. For additional details, including a list of over 200 reports using data from the NLS, see Center for Human Resource Research, *The National Longitudinal Surveys Handbook* (1977).

[5] For young men, 11.5-15.8 defines *High* third; 9.8-11.4, *Middle*; and 2.1-9.7, *Low*. In the case of young women, 11.5-16.2 defines *High*; 9.7-11.4, *Middle*; and 1.1-9.6, *Low*. The precise rules used in the construction of the SEO measure can be found in Kohen (1973, pp. 177-183).

special mail questionnaire survey conducted by the Bureau of the Census in 1968. A questionnaire was sent to each high school attended by one or more of the respondents. The reported test scores were combined into a single measure that is scaled in a fashion similar to intelligence tests, with a mean of 100 and a standard deviation of approximately 15.[6] The index is not represented to be, nor should it be construed to be, a measure of innate cognitive ability. Especially for groups historically kept outside the majority culture, a great deal of measurement error (e.g., cultural bias or lack of test practice) probably exists. We presume that whatever underlying *real* differences remain among individuals reflect a complex set of influences: for example, native endowment, prenatal factors, and experiences prior to high school in each person's home, school, and neighborhood.

The Sample: An Overview. Throughout this report, our principal variable of interest is high school curriculum. In the initial wave of interviews, all youths were asked to name their high school program of study.[7] In subsequent surveys, respondents were asked about any change in curriculum from one year to the next. Our measure of curriculum, then, is a self-report, not an indicator derived from school records.

An "official measure" would doubtless reveal some discrepancies, but is not available. In the National Longitudinal Survey of the High School Class of 1972, a project sponsored by the U.S. National Center for Education Statistics, both stu-

---

[6] For young men, 50-97 defines *Low* third; 98-110, *Middle;* and 111-158, *High.* Among young women, 46-99 defines *Low;* 100-111, *Middle;* and 112-158, *High.* For a detailed discussion of the pooling procedures and the common metric used, see Kohen (1973, pp. 155-174).

[7] Young men were asked, "Are (were) you enrolled in a vocational curriculum, commercial curriculum, college preparatory, or a general curriculum (during your last year in high school)?" For vocational or commercial responses, a further probe was "What did you specialize (are you specializing) in?" Young women were asked, "What kind of curriculum are (were) you enrolled in (during your last year in high school)—is (was) it vocational, commercial, college preparatory or general?" Only for vocational was a probe added: "What are you specializing (did you specialize) in?"

dents and administrators were asked to classify a student's program. Administrators agreed in two-thirds of the cases where students classified themselves as vocational (Fetters, 1975, p. 4). In a personal communication with Grasso, one researcher noted substantial disagreements among three coding procedures: the administrator's report, the student's report, and a course-based measurement system.

In the base year surveys, young women in our study were enrolled in occupational[8] programs in higher proportions than were men (Table 1.1). For instance, approximately 14 percent of the male students in grades 10 to 12, but 20 percent of the female, say they were enrolled in either a vocational or commercial program of study. Women were heavily concentrated in white-collar, clerical programs, while young men were congregated in blue-collar specialties. Relatively few males reported a white-collar curriculum, and for these few, the precise program area is typically distributive education (i.e., sales or marketing) rather than office or clerical work. Because of these differences, as well as for ease of exposition, we maintain the *commercial* designation when speaking of men who report such a program, and *vocational* for the other specialties. We use *business and office* in referring to the white-collar, clerical programs reported by women, and *vocational* for other occupational studies.

The fact that few women report home economics as their program of study (which we feel is helpful to the analysis), as well as the reporting of course work in typing and shorthand, deserves attention. In national program statistics for 1968, home economics had the largest number of secondary-level enrollments in federally-assisted vocational programs—nearly 1.5 million (Simon and Grant, 1973, p. 43). However, a negligible proportion of young women in the NLS report home economics as their curriculum—only 0.6 percent of those enrolled in grades 10 to 12 in 1968. Thus many students take home economics without perceiving it as their *program of study*. Similarly, on

[8]We use the term "occupational" to embrace vocational and commercial (or business and office) programs of study, realizing, or course, that immediate economic and learning needs and vocational purposes prompt such enrollment for many youngsters.

Table 1.1. Curriculum by grade in school, sex, and race:
men (1966) and women (1968) 14 to 24 years old,
enrolled in grades 9-12
(N in thousands)

	Whites				Blacks			
	9	*10*	*11*	*12*	*9*	*10*	*11*	*12*
	Men							
N[a]	840	1,493	1,475	1,315	153	212	195	14?
Percent:[b]								
Vocational	5%	8%	12%	11%	6%	13%	18%	18%
Commercial	2	2	4	3	3	5	4	6
General	57	48	42	39	82	64	48	50
College preparatory	36	43	43	48	9	18	31	26
	Women							
N[a]	1,488	1,780	1,420	1,164	215	229	176	18?
Percent:[b]								
Vocational	1%	1%	2%	4%	4%	7%	2%	2%
Business and office	8	15	19	19	5	15	18	19
General	64	48	32	31	78	54	51	56
College preparatory	27	36	46	46	14	25	29	24

[a]Excludes those for whom curriculum was not ascertained.

[b]Detail may not add to 100 percent due to rounding.

the basis of NLS estimates, approximately one million girls in grades 9 to 12 in 1968 were in a business or clerical program, a number not dissimilar from the 1.1 million federally-assisted program enrollments in the service area designated as "business and office" (*ibid.* p. 43). However, aside from the NLS women enrolled in business and office programs, well over half the remainder—or over 2.6 million high school girls—report having taken one or more courses in typing or shorthand.[9] Nearly all (99 percent) of the high school business or office seniors say

[9]The extent of training in these areas was ascertained by a series of questions asked immediately after the curricular item: "Are you taking (did you take) any courses in typing or shorthand in high school?" If yes, "What courses are you taking (did you take)?" and "How many years have you taken (typing, shorthand)?"

they had such course work; three-quarters of the remaining senior girls also took typing or shorthand (Table A1.1)[10] To this day, substantial training in clerical skills—an area not eligible for federal aid until the early 1960s—almost surely takes place without federal funds.

Young black women in the NLS were less likely than were whites to report courses in typing and shorthand. Nearly all of the difference can be traced to the general track. Black women were more likely than white to be in a *general* curriculum (Table 1.1), and were less likely to have had typing or shorthand when they were. (See Table A.1.)

To complete this brief introduction to the sample, the curricular distribution of nonstudents, as of the NLS base years, is presented in Table 1.2. In later chapters, much of the discussion of curriculum effects is based on the three educational attainment categories: 10 to 11, 12, and 13 to 15 years of school. As we shall see in Chapter 3, it is not appropriate to draw inferences from Table 1.2 on the relationship between high school program and number of years of school completed. The reason is that many 14 to 24 year old respondents were attending college in the NLS base years, and thus are ignored in Table 1.2. This group in postsecondary education is disproportionately made up of those who followed a college preparatory program in high school.[11] Their ultimate educational attainment will be known only with the passage of time.

Attrition. In all longitudinal surveys, sample attrition is potentially a serious problem. As time passes, some respondents refuse to be re-interviewed or cannot be located. Attrition is rarely random and, particularly if sizable, can lead to bias in analysis.

---

[10] Appendix tables are designated as A1.1, A1.2, and so forth, and may be found in Appendix A.

[11] It is likewise the case that out-of-school youths from a college preparatory program with 10 to 15 years of schooling are among the less successful of those from an academic program, in terms of educational attainment. The reason is that among youth 14 to 24 years of age, the more successful are still enrolled in school.

Table 1.2. **High school curriculum (most recent), by highest
year of school completed, sex, and race: men (1966)
and women (1968) not enrolled, who had completed
10-15 years of school
(N in thousands)**

	Whites			Blacks		
	10-11	*12*	*13-15*	*10-11*	*12*	*13-15*
	Men					
N[a]	852	2,514	596	228	323	45
Percent:[b]						
Vocational	11%	16%	6%	13%	17%	3%
Commercial	3	6	2	5	3	6
General	79	59	39	76	70	42
College preparatory	7	20	52	7	11	50
	Women					
N[a]	1,067	4,343	930	261	508	107
Percent:[b]						
Vocational	4%	2%	1%	4%	6%	0%
Business and office	23	39	8	18	21	10
General	65	40	22	75	57	48
College preparatory	9	19	70	4	16	43

[a]Excludes those for whom curriculum was not ascertained.

[b]Detail may not add to 100 percent due to rounding.

In the National Longitudinal Surveys, field work is performed by the Census Bureau, under special contracts with the
Department of Labor. The Census interviewers have been extremely successful in tracking respondents, especially in light of
the substantial geographic movements of young people, and a
prior decision not to interview respondents in the armed forces.
(Efforts are made to reestablish contact upon termination of
military service.) Of 5,225 young men interviewed initially in
the fall of 1966, 76 percent were interviewed in 1971, and 77
percent were reached for telephone interviews in 1973 for the
sixth followup. Nearly half of the total (net) attrition occurred
between the first and second interviews, and entry to the armed

forces was the major reason.[12] Attrition from the sample of young women has been less serious, since few women enter the armed forces. Of 5,159 young women interviewed initially in the spring of 1968, 90 percent were reinterviewed in 1972 (the fourth followup), the most recent year for which data were available when we began our study.

[12] Fourteen percent of the 12th graders, and 12 percent of those who were out of school in 1966, were lost at least temporarily from the sample in 1967. The armed forces accounted for three-fourths and two-thirds of these losses, respectively.

2

Curriculum Assignment
and Its Correlates

In many ways, this chapter is a prerequisite to the next. Here we seek answers to several interrelated questions: First, do systematic differences exist in social class background or scholastic aptitude between occupational and general students? Since these two factors influence highest year of school completed, the answer informs our analysis of curriculum effects on school attainment in Chapter 3. Second, are practical courses congenial? Do such courses attract students and respond to their psychological needs and propensities? If they do, this may support the view that occupational programs respond to individual differences, and therefore might be expected to increase the holding power of the school. Third, is choice of an occupational program informed by greater-than-average knowledge of occupations in general? Fourth, are the educational and occupational goals of vocational students higher or lower than those of their general-curriculum counterparts?

The answers to these questions are important in understanding the implications of curriculum for educational attainment, since many studies reveal a strong correlation between plans and expectations and later achievements.

After considering these matters, we turn to two additional questions: Are curriculum assignments appropriate for (congruent with) goals? How much movement between curricula occurs over a one-year period, and what are the correlates of movement? In seeking an answer to the first question, we examine whether a persons's curriculum is congruent with his or her educational aspirations, and also with occupational goals. Answers to the second question add greatly to our understanding of motivation and attainment, as shown in Chapter 3.

Family Background and Scholastic Aptitude

Division of a group of high school students by thirds simultaneously along the dimensions of scholastic aptitude (SA) and socioeconomic origin (SEO) generates a table with nine cells. If the two variables were uncorrelated and unrelated to the fact of enrollment, approximately 11 percent of all high school students would be in each of nine cells. However, the actual pattern diverges sharply—especially for blacks—from this hypothetical distribution (Table A2.1). One reason for this divergence is that SA and SEO are positively related to each other. But the overall distribution for black youngsters in high school is considerably lower than it is for whites. For example, while one in ten white students is in the lowest third of *both* the SEO and SA distributions, the same is true for nearly one-half of the blacks. At the other extreme, one in five white youngsters is in the top third of *both* distributions, while only about one in fifty blacks is so advantaged.

Being in a college preparatory curriculum is positively related to both SEO and SA. Interestingly enough, within each of the nine cells, blacks are more likely than whites to report being in an academic program (Table A2.2). Thus the reason more blacks than whites are in nonacademic programs is that blacks rank far below whites on measures of family background and mental ability. Stated differently, if blacks were distributed as are whites along dimensions of SEO and SA, a higher proportion of the former would be likely to be in a college preparatory program.[1]

---

[1] Work by Jencks et al., in *Inequality: A Reassessment of the Effect of Family and Schooling in America,* supports this finding. They note that, "When we compared blacks and whites of comparable economic background as well as comparable test scores, we found that blacks were 7 percent more likely than the whites to be in the college track." (Jencks et al., 1972, p. 35.)

For those *not* enrolled in an academic program, are SEO and SA systematically related to being in an occupational as opposed to a general program? Overall, the answer seems to be no (Table A2.3). The pattern is so varied that it defies ready interpretation. Among white males, the highest-ability students are less likely than are their peers to be in an occupational program, except for those from the lowest SEO families. Among the white females, except for the high SEO third, being in a business or office curriculum is positively related to scholastic aptitude. This may be a reflection of the English language and other cognitive skills required by curricula emphasizing typing, shorthand, and bookkeeping. Echternacht's 1975 analysis of the National Study of the High School Class of 1972 also revealed mixed findings: general students ranked slightly higher than vocational students in academic ability, but the difference was not statistically significant.

Attitudes, Likes, and Dislikes

In the base year surveys, respondents were asked their attitudes toward high school: "All things considered, how do you feel about your high school experience? Do you like it very much? like it fairly well? dislike it somewhat? dislike it very much?" Among youths enrolled in grades 10 to 12 in the survey years: (1) students in college preparatory programs were more satisfied than were their counterparts in other curricula; (2) blacks expressed greater satisfaction than whites; and (3) while satisfaction is positively related to scholastic aptitude among white youths, high SA blacks of both sexes were least likely to like school "very much" (Table A2.4). We are not sure what this latter finding means.

Differences in satisfaction between students in occupational and general programs of study stand out only for white male youth. In this group, occupational students are considerably less likely to express high satisfaction: 30 percent versus 37 percent say they like school "very much." In general, few students express dislike for school. For example, only 6 percent of the young men said they disliked school "somewhat" or "very much." (These data are not shown here in tabular form.)

Table 2.1. High school subject "enjoyed the most" and "disliked the most," by curriculum and sex: men (1966) and women (1968) enrolled in grades 10–12, base year
(N in thousands)

	Occupational			General			College preparatory		
	Enjoyed	Disliked	Ratio E:D[a]	Enjoyed	Disliked	Ratio E:D[a]	Enjoyed	Disliked	Ratio E:D[a]
Men									
N	706			2,168			2,032		
Foreign languages	1%	1%	—	1%	4%	—	4%	13%	—
Humanities	13	33	1.0	17	32	0.2	14	27	0.3
Social sciences	14	25	0.4	18	16	0.5	20	13	0.5
Natural sciences	9	9	0.6	14	10	1.2	25	10	1.6
Mathematics	13	18	1.0	20	24	1.4	24	21	2.6
Commercial	7	3	0.7	2	1	0.8	2	1	1.2
Vocational	39	2	2.0	20	2	2.6	8	1	1.2
Other	4	2	22.8	6	2	12.3	3	3	7.9
None	1	7	2.2	2	10	2.4	1	12	0.9
			0.1			0.2			0.1
Women									
N	980			1,983			1,989		
Foreign languages	3%	2%	1.1	3%	3%	1.1	8%	6%	1.3
Humanities	18	16	1.1	28	13	2.2	36	11	3.2
Social sciences	10	33	0.3	15	24	0.6	15	15	1.0
Natural sciences	5	12	0.4	9	12	0.8	15	13	1.2
Mathematics	7	17	0.4	8	26	0.3	15	38	0.4
Commercial	44	7	6.0	18	5	3.3	4	2	2.7
Vocational	3	0	∞	2	0	∞	1	0	∞
Other	9	4	2.0	15	5	2.9	4	2	2.2
None	1	8	0.1	1	12	0.1	b	13	b

[a]Calculated on basis of percentages figured to nearest tenth of a point.

[b]Less than 0.05 of one percent.

Despite the fact that not everyone takes an occupational course in high school, many boys and girls name such a course when asked, "What high school subject have you *enjoyed* the most?" Very few youngsters mention an occupational course when asked, "What high school subject have you *disliked* the most?" As might be expected, students in occupational curricula are more likely than those in other programs to name a vocational, business, or office course as the one they most enjoy: nearly half the boys (46 percent) and girls (47 percent) in occupational programs, compared with one-fifth in the general track and less than one in ten college preparatory students (Table 2.1). The ratio of "enjoyed" to "disliked" is consistently higher for occupational than for other subjects, with the possible exception of young women in the college preparatory program.

Are young people in the lowest third on scholastic aptitude more inclined to enjoy occupational courses than are more academically able students? Among white men in high school, the relationship is clear (although not shown here in tabular form.) More white male students in the lowest SA third report having enjoyed vocational subjects the most. For example, of those in an occupational program, the proportions were 40, 30, and 31 percent for low, middle, and high SA thirds, respectively. Among young black men, an inadequate number of sample cases prevents a comparison except for the low and middle thirds in college preparatory and general programs. In the case of the academic curriculum, a much larger fraction of those in the middle than in the lowest third say they enjoyed a vocational subject the most. Overall, young white men are more likely than black to dislike courses in the humanities and more likely to enjoy vocational subjects. Young black men more often say their favorite course is in the humanities, an interesting finding consistent with black-white differences in performance as measured in the National Assessment of Educational Progress (1977, p. 31). Nationwide, black youngsters achieve higher than whites in three areas: reading habits, music performance, and attitudes toward music.

Career Plans and Occupational Goals

At the initial interview, young men were asked, "What kind of work would you like to be doing when you are 30 years old?" Of those enrolled in grades 10 to 12, about one-fifth said they didn't know, or failed to respond to the question (Table 2.2). Choice of an occupational curriculum (except perhaps for cluster programs) presupposes an occupational or career objective, although career exploration and other motives may prompt many high school students to enroll. Boys in a vocational program are more likely than are other students to name a specific occupational goal; commercial students are least likely. Many commercial programs follow a cluster approach, preparing young men for possible entry into an array of business, sales, or clerical kinds of work. It is interesting that black youngsters in vocational programs are considerably less likely than are whites to name a specific occupational objective, while the opposite inter-color pattern exists among college preparatory students.

Of the male students who mentioned a specific occupational aspiration, a clear majority named one in the professional or technical area: 59 percent of the whites, and 52 percent of the blacks. Students in occupational programs were least likely to aspire to jobs at this high level (about one-third); college preparatory students most likely (nearly four-fifths). The goals of general students lie in between, closer to the pattern of those in occupational than in academic programs.

On the whole, the goals of young men in school are quite high, when one realizes that only 15 percent of all employed men work in the professional and technical group (*Employment and Training Report of the President*, 1977, p. 161). However, young men out of school in 1966, with 10 to 12 years of education, expressed considerably lower occupational goals than those still in high school (Table A2.5). In the out-of-school group, just over one-fifth of those naming an occupation aspire to jobs in the professional or technical category. Nearly one in six hopes to be a manager or official someday. Leaving school before college undoubtedly lowers aspirations, at least for

Table 2.2 Occupation (major group) desired at age 30 (age 35, for women),
by curriculum and race: men (1966) and women (1968)
enrolled in grades 10–12, base year[a]
(N in thousands)

	Total (or average)[b]	Curriculum			
		Vocational	Commercial (or B&O)	General	College preparatory
		Men			
Whites (N)	4,439	429	126	1,842	1,906
Prof, tech	59%	32%	31%	46%	78%
Nonfarm mgr	6	5	11	5	8
Craft	18	43	15	27	4
Other	17	20	43	22	10
Don't know[c]	(20)	(6)	(37)	(23)	(20)
Blacks (N)	574	89	27	304	136
Prof, tech	52%	36%	d	44%	77%
Nonfarm mgr	5	3	d	5	1
Craft	19	41	d	20	7
Other	24	20	d	28	15
Don't know[c]	(18)	(17)	(26)	(21)	(7)
		Women			
Whites (N)	4,364	96	751	1,663	1,830
Prof, tech	46%	d	6%	33%	74%
Clerical	37	d	80	40	16
Service	10	d	8	16	5
Other	7	d	6	11	5
Blacks (N)	584	22	100	312	149
Prof, tech	43%	d	24%	35%	74%
Clerical	37	d	63	40	16
Service	8	d	1	10	8
Other	12	d	12	15	2

[a]Includes "don't know" category; individual percentages are based on number, not shown, who specified an occupational goal or preference, and may not add to 100 percent due to rounding.

[b]Includes small percentage for whom curriculum was not ascertained.

[c]"Don't know" and no data cases.

[d]Percent not shown; base less than 25 sample cases.

professional-technical jobs. Compared to former general students, those who were in occupational programs are as likely (or more likely, in the case of blacks) to have uncertain goals.

Returning to the group of students still in school, vocational men are considerably more likely than are those in the general curriculum to want a job in the craftworker category, while commercial men often aspire to clerical or sales jobs. Within each curricular category, the aspirations of black youth are nearly the same as for white. Because so few black students are in a college preparatory program, however, their aspirations are, on the average, slightly lower than those of whites.

In 1968, young women were asked about their plans at age 35. After a lead-in, "Now I would like to talk to you about your future plans," the interviewer asked, "What would you like to be doing when you are 35 years old?" Respondents who said "working" (one-quarter of the whites; one-half of the blacks) were asked to name the kind of work. Those who said "married, keeping house, raising a family" or the like (two-thirds of the whites and one-third of the blacks) were asked, "Sometimes women decide to work after they have been married for a while. If you were to work, what kind of work would you prefer?" Some young women still did not express an occupational aspiration (for example, "Don't plan to work.")[2]

Among girls in high school, there are essentially no differences by curriculum in intentions to work at age 35. This suggests that, although young women in occupational programs might be assumed to have a stronger orientation to a career than their peers, the influence of other factors on plans at age 35—higher education, marriage, and motherhood—is probably more salient. Enrollment in an occupational program in high school, in other words, simply does not constitute evidence of intention to work several years hence. Those in business, office, and in

[2] For example, of the respondents with 10 to 12 years of schooling who were not enrolled in 1968, only 26 percent of the whites and 43 percent of the blacks planned to be working at the age of 35 (Table A2.6). An additional 54 and 32 percent, respectively, named an occupational preference, should they decide to work outside the home.

other occupational programs may be developing skills primarily for use immediately following high school.

Looking at female students who specified a type of work desired at age 35, it is clear that occupational goals differ by curriculum. While 45 percent of the young women in high school expressed a desire for professional or technical work, including teaching, this was true of only 9 percent of business and office students, but of over 70 percent of those in college preparatory programs. (See Table 2.2.) Furthermore, while 37 percent of all high school females wanted clerical work, including secretarial jobs, this was true of only one in six college preparatory females, but of more than three out of four business and office students.

What about the realism of the preferences of young women, should they work for pay at age 35? Once more, aspirations are high, although more in line with present job market realities than are the aspirations of men. In 1976, 16 percent of employed women worked in professional or technical jobs (*Employment and Training Report of the President,* 1977, p. 161). The proportion of girls who prefer a clerical occupation (37 percent) is nearly identical to the percentage of all employed women (35 percent) in this category.

Young women out of school, with 10 to 12 years of education, hold lower aspirations than do girls in school (Table A2.4). Only 11 percent of the whites and 15 percent of the blacks see themselves working in professional or technical jobs; about half foresee clerical jobs. Black women from occupational programs express preferences higher than those of whites; the reverse is true for out-of-school women from academic programs. The latter finding may reflect plans of many young white women to return to school or college.

In view of these curricular differences, it is not surprising to find differences in several other occupational measures. For example, the jobs desired by business and office students are low-paying in comparison with jobs desired by their peers: 88 percent of business and office students prefer jobs that paid, on the average, less than $6,000 to full-year women workers in

1969.[3] The analogous figures for other vocational and general students are 51 and 67 percent, respectively. Business and office students also lean toward jobs that are stereotypically "female": 69 percent desire jobs in which 80 percent or more of incumbents are women. The same is true for only 57 percent of other vocational and 54 percent of general students.

On the whole, regardless of high school curriculum, the job preferences of the young women strongly suggest occupational segregation. Occupational goals were coded according to the 1960 Census classification scheme. Although there are 297 possible codes, only the nine shown below are needed to account for *over two-thirds* of the job preferences of the girls.

Secretary (Code 342)	21%
Teachers (182, 183, 184)	20
Clerical and kindred, nec (370)	9
Professional nurse (150)	8
Hairdresser (843)	5
Sales clerk (394)	4
Social and welfare workers (171)	2
Total	69%

Are these data out of date, given developments in the women's movement since 1968? The answer seems to be no. In a recent Gallup Youth Survey, the top ten career preferences of teenage girls included secretary, teacher, nurse, social worker, and cosmetologist/hairdresser. The others were "other medical," veterinarian, fashion design/modeling, doctor, and business.[4] At least three of these are nontraditional for women, perhaps suggesting some reduction in stereotyping.

[3] See Appendix C for median 1969 earnings for men and women in the experienced civilian labor force at the time of the 1970 Census of Population.

[4] The top ten choices of boys, in order, were: skilled worker, engineer, lawyer, teacher, professional athlete, musician, architect, farmer, doctor, and military (Gallup, 1976.)

Occupational Information

Reasonably accurate knowledge of the labor market, such as information about occupations and their education or training requirements, should help a person make choices regarding career directions, how much additional schooling to pursue, and what high school curriculum to follow. Students who choose a vocational program in high school presumably have an above-average need for career information, since they are closer than are their peers to the time when they expect to leave school. Because the decision to pursue a vocational program involves considerable choice, the possession of adequate information about career possibilities is a prerequisite for making sound career decisions.

In 1966, young men in the NLS were asked a series of questions under the heading "Knowledge of the World of Work" (KWW). In a multiple-choice format, each respondent was asked to identify the principal duties of workers in ten occupations, and to state the typical education level of the incumbents.[5] Respondents were then provided eight pairs of occupations and asked to identify which one normally yields higher earnings.[6] Answers to all parts of the test were scored from 0 to 56. In 1969, young women in the NLS, who at that time were 15 to 25 years old, were asked to identify the major

[5]The interviewer asked, "I'd like your opinion about the kind of work that men in certain jobs usually do. For each occupation on this card (*Show Flashcard 1*) there are three descriptions of job duties. Will you please tell me which description you think best fits each job? Be sure to read all of the possible answers before you decide." To illustrate, response categories for stationary engineer were: (1) Works at a desk, making drawings and solving engineering problems; (2) Drives a locomotive that moves cars around in a freight yard; (3) Operates and maintains such equipment as steam boilers and generators; and (4) Don't know. For each occupation, a probe asked, "How much regular schooling do you think usually have?"

[6]The introduction was, "Now I'd like your opinion on whether people in certain occupations earn more, on the average, than people in other occupations. By average, we mean the average of all men in this occupation in the entire United States." This was followed by: "Who do you think earns more in a year: a man who is (1) an automobile mechanic, or (2) an electrician?" Space was provided for "Don't know."

tasks performed by persons in ten occupations frequently held by women.[7] Respondents were scored on the number of correct answers (0 to 10). Within both male and female cohorts, blacks scored somewhat lower than did whites.

More than nine out of ten male students were able to identify the principal tasks of an acetylene welder, a draftsman, and a social worker (Table 2.3). At the other extreme, only 13 percent knew the duties of stationary engineers; most young men selected "works at a desk, making drawings and solving engineering problems." Students also frequently misstated the educational attainment of men in various jobs. For example, over half the students thought draftsmen have four or more years of college, and 32 percent were under the impression that social workers average a high school diploma or less.

Only for the item on machinists did male vocational students clearly outscore their general curriculum counterparts. For the three occupations for which graduation from college is the norm, vocational students scored significantly lower. Commercial students, on the other hand, did about as well as those in the general track. College preparatory students were more likely than were those in the general program to know what high-level occupational incumbents do. They were also more likely to be able to identify the principal tasks of hospital orderly, machinist, statistical clerk, and draftsmen. Some of this difference doubtless is a reflection of underlying differences in mental ability (and perhaps in test-taking ability).

A series of regressions for the total score and for the college and noncollege items separately—with statistical controls for scholastic aptitude, socioeconomic background, grade in school, size of community of residence at age 14, and previous

---

[7]The interviewer asked, "I'd like your opinion about the kind of work that women in certain jobs usually do. For each occupation on this card (*hand card to respondent*) there are three descriptions of job duties. Will you please tell me which description you think best fits each job? Be sure to read all of the possible answers before you decide." As an illustration, the response categories for deparment store buyer were: (1) Selects the items to be sold in a section of a department store; (2) Checks on the courtesy of sales people by shopping at the store; (3) Buys department stores that are about to go out of business; and (4) Don't know.

Table 2.3. Percentage of respondents who correctly identified occupational
duties in Knowledge of the World of Work test, by curriculum, sex,
and race: men (1966) and women (1969) enrolled
in grades 10 to 12 in relevant year

| | *All curricula average* | | *Curriculum* | | |
		Vocational	*Commercial (or B&O)*	*General*	*College preparatory*
Men					
Fork lift operator	70%	69%	65%	69%	71%
Acetylene welder	92	88	88	93	92
Hospital orderly	70	67	66	68	74
Machinist	64	70	69	59	66
Stationary engineer	13	16	18	14	10
Statistical clerk	81	61	84	76	90
Draftsman	94	94	94	93	96
Economist	76	57	72	72	85
Medical illustrator	54	38	51	50	60
Social worker	93	86	94	91	97
Women					
Assembler	74%	50%	74%	67%	83%
Key punch operator	68	58	78	65	70
Bank teller	80	68	84	73	89
Department store buyer	73	83	77	65	82
Dietician	80	54	80	75	87
Statistical clerk	44	27	42	40	50
Nurse's aide	92	100	94	90	95
Social worker	93	71	94	90	97
Medical illustrator	52	33	55	48	60
Quality control girl in a bakery	57	43	55	55	61

work experience—reveals that the vocational (but not the commercial) curriculum for men has a (net) negative effect on occupational information. (See Appendix A2.7.)

Among white males, vocational students scored lower on the total KWW index, as well as on the part-score for college-level items, then did students in the general curriculum. Among blacks, vocational students scored lower on the non-college items. Our findings are consistent with those of Decker (1967), who found that vocational high school students knew somewhat less about a variety of occupations than did students from other curricula. They were also more inclined to name mechanic and other skilled trades as the "best" jobs they knew about. Other students were more likely to cite a professional, technical, or managerial job as "best." Decker, however, did not control for background differences.

In contrast to the sample of young men, for a young woman to be in an occupational curriculum is positively related to KWW. The percentage of correct responses is higher for business and office students than for general program students in nine out of ten occupations (Table 2.3). On the other hand, in only two instances is the proportion higher for "other vocational" than for general students. Once again, for whatever reason,[8] proportionately more college preparatory students were better able to identify the duties of nearly every occupation on the list.

Educational Aspirations

Occupational aspirations and educational goals are not always consistent, but for groups as a whole, the patterns are similar. First, the overall picture: 62 percent of the white boys and 56 percent of the black say they "would like to get" four or more years of college; the comparable proportions for girls are 48 and 50 percent (Table 2.4). Nearly one in seven of the boys and one in four girls would like two years of college, a category that grows larger as students move from the tenth to twelfth grade.

---

[8] KWW is highly correlated with general mental ability, and the higher-than-average SA scores of academic students is undoubtedly one reason.

Table 2.4. Educational aspirations, by sex and race: men (1966)
and women (1968) enrolled in grades 10–12, base year
(N in thousands)

| | N^b | Percentage[a] | | |
		12 yrs or less	*college 2 yrs*	*college 4 yrs +*
		Men		
Whites				
Vocational	426	50	28	23
Commercial	144	37	27	36
General	1,833	40	17	44
College preparatory	1,887	3	5	91
Total (or average)	4,405	24	13	62
Blacks				
Vocational	89	48	11	40
Commercial	27	23	22	55
General	303	33	21	46
College preparatory	135	8	6	86
Total (or average)	572	29	16	56
		Women		
Whites				
Vocational	96	c	c	c
Business and office	751	52	36	12
General	1,663	40	30	30
College preparatory	1,830	6	16	79
Total (or average)	4,364	28	25	48
Blacks				
Vocational	22	c	c	c
Business and office	100	35	38	28
General	312	35	22	42
College preparatory	149	4	13	84
Total (or average)	584	28	22	50

[a]Detail may not add to 100 percent due to rounding.

[b]Excludes less than one percent for whom aspiration was not ascertained.

[c]Percent now shown; base less than 25 sample cases.

(These data are not shown here in tabular form.) By curriculum, three observations stand out. First, a very high proportion of young black men in occupational programs (40 percent of the vocational and 55 percent of the commercial students) aspired to four or more years of college—a goal of questionable realism, given the ostensible purpose of vocational studies and the admissions criteria of colleges and universities. Second, black girls within each curricular category express higher aspirations than do white girls in comparable categories. Third, white vocational males and all business and office females are relatively unlikely to desire four or more years of college.

Of course, educational goals are fostered, in part at least, by encouragement and support from parents, teachers, and peers. Young women in high school in 1968 were asked about some of these influences. Those in a college preparatory program seem to have been the beneficiaries of high levels of encouragement and support in comparison with classmates. For example, 77 percent of the white girls and 71 percent of the black girls in academic programs reported that they believed their parents wanted them to achieve four or more years of college. The same was true of only 38 and 52 percent of the white and black girls in a general program, and of even smaller proportions of youngsters in occupational curricula. The figures for young men, although not reported here, conform basically to what has been said of the young women.

Boys and girls were also asked how much education they actually expected to get. Between 10 and 20 percent reported expectations lower than aspirations, the difference being somewhat greater for blacks than for whites. Reasons offered for expecting less differ little by race or by curriculum. However, 67 percent of black girls versus 50 percent of white girls who reported this discrepancy between educational expectations and aspirations cited "lack of funds" as the reason.

The Appropriateness of Curriculum to Goals

We turn now to the matter of how congruent curriculum choice (or assignment) is to educational aspirations and occupational goals, beginning with the assumption that no curriculum is inappropriate to an educational goal of up to two years of college. A college preparatory as well as a general program presumably assists students to meet admissions requirements for junior or community college. Because of the increasing number of non-degree credit programs at this level, which are, for the most part, occupational in nature, and because some "vocational" offerings are doubtless prevocational, we also feel that an occupational curriculum can sustain a goal of two years of college. We accept, on the other hand, the argument that a college preparatory curriculum may be inappropriate for a youngster who wants no more than a high school diploma. When it comes to aspirations for four or more years of college, we believe a college preparatory program to be appropriate, but a general or an occupational one to be inappropriate, the latter especially so.

Judgments regarding the appropriateness of curriculum to occupational goals are more difficult, because assumptions are needed as to the *level* and *types* of education and training implied by occupations. Using counseling and guidance materials published by the U.S. Bureau of Labor Statistics,[9] we have assigned each three-digit Census occupation to one of the following categories: (1) occupations that typically call for four or more years of college; (2) occupations not typically requiring a baccalaureate, but for which other pre-employment training is often available[10]; and (3) a residual category, "no special requirements," in the sense that pre-employment or multi-employer appreticeship is relatively uncommon. In the first category are such jobs as professor or teacher, physician, engineer, and the like. The second includes actors, nurses, technicians, a variety of clerical, sales, managerial, and skilled manual work, some service jobs (e.g., hairdresser), and so forth. The third embraces a number of occupations requiring little specialized preparation (e.g., file clerk), as well as a number of occupations by and large restricted to a single industry sector where training is often in-house (e.g., postal clerk, locomotive fireman).

Several of our designations are somewhat arbitrary in nature, and we hope that other researchers will refine and extend the classifications and the exploratory analysis to which we will turn in a moment. First, however, Table 2.5 presents the

[9]Precise references may be found in the source note, Appendix C.

[10] Such training may be provided in secondary schools (e.g., practical nurse); in various community college, proprietary school, or other settings (e.g., apprenticeships); or in both.

Table 2.5. Employment in major occupation groups and by sex, according to level and type of pre-employment occupational preparation offered, 1970 (N in thousands)

Major occupation group, sex	N	A baccalaureate degree + is normally required	Percent employed in occupations for which:[a] Some other pre-employment preparation is available	No pre-employment training is necessary
Total, all occupations, both sexes	76,931	19%	42%	38%
Professional, technical	11,699	77	22	b
Managers (nonfarm)	6,315	88	8	4
Sales	5,432	3	93	4
Clerical	13,994	—	47	53
Craftworkers	10,594	—	54	46
Operatives	13,493	—	55	45
Private household	1,168	—	—	100
Other services	8,447	—	40	60
Farm laborers, foremen	962	—	—	100
Farmers, farm managers	1,426	—	100	—
Laborers (nonfarm)	3,431	—	—	100
Total				
Men, all occupations	47,915	22	39	39
Women, all occupations	29,016	15	48	38

[a]Detail may not add to total due to rounding.

bLess than 0.5 percent

Source: U.S. Bureau of the Census (1973), and authors' judgments, described in Appendix C.

distribution of *all* employed persons in the 1970 Census of Population, cross-classified by major occupation group and by our measure of "pre-employment preparation opportunities." At a glance, it can be seen that a large proportion of the work force in professional and managerial categories is in specific occupations for which a college education is often required or preferred, at least for new entrants to the labor market. Overall, we judge that only about one-fifth of all jobs necessarily imply four or more years of college; two-fifths are such that other off-the-job or apprenticeship training is available; and the remaining two-fifths or so can be entered without skills peculiar to the occupation.

The training requirements and opportunities associated with the occupational goals of students in the NLS are presented in Table 2.6. Several observations are of particular interest. First, the occupational goals of blacks (especially the boys) call for lower levels of education and training than might be assumed on the basis of educational aspirations. Second, the occupational goals of young black men in occupational programs are no higher than those of whites, despite the fact that blacks held considerably higher educational goals. Third, young black men in college preparatory programs often aspire to occupations requiring less than four years of college. Perhaps they are more cautious, or less certain of their ability to go to college. Finally, as expected, students in occupational programs more often than their peers aspire to occupations offering some pre-employment training opportunities below the baccalaureate. This is especially true of white girls in business and office programs. In judging the appropriateness of high school curriculum for occupational goals, we encountered a problem similar to the one regarding educational aspirations. For occupations typically requiring a college education, we judge a nonacademic program to be inappropriate, while for occupations with no special requirements, we feel that a college preparatory program is inappropriate. In several instances, a student's curriculum may be considered inappropriate to both educational and occupational goals. For example: (1) a nonacademic program of studies

Table 2.6. Pre-employment educational requirements and opportunities
for occupation desired at age 30 (age 35, for women),
by curriculum and race: men (1966) and women
(1968) enrolled in grades 10–12, base year
(N in thousands)

	N^b	Percent[a]		
		Occupation requires college 4 +	Other pre-employment training available	No special requirements
		Men		
Whites				
Vocational	404	25	63	12
Commercial	79	c	c	c
General	1,421	39	49	13
College preparatory	1,528	77	16	7
Total (or average)	3,540	54	36	11
Blacks				
Vocational	74	25	54	21
Commercial	20	c	c	c
General	239	39	40	21
College preparatory	127	56	28	16
Total (or average)	473	41	41	18
		Women		
Whites				
Vocational	96	c	c	c
Business and office	751	6	74	20
General	1,663	26	56	18
College preparatory	1,830	58	35	7
Total (or average)	4,364	36	51	14
Blacks				
Vocational	22	c	c	c
Business and office	100	20	55	25
General	312	22	61	17
College preparatory	149	60	39	1
Total (or average)	584	32	54	15

Detail may not add to 100 percent due to rounding.

Excludes those who said "don't know," who plan not to work, and those for whom a goal was not
ascertained.

Percent not shown; base less than 25 sample cases.

for a student who aspires to four or more years of college and to an occupation typically requiring such attainment; and (2) a college preparatory curriculum for a student who aspires to less than two years of college and an occupation for which four years of college is not typical. In Table A2.8, the reader may see at a glance the combinations considered either appropriate or inappropriate.

Looking at the NLS sample of young men, curricular choice (or assignment) is not congruent with a student's educational or occupational aspiration in a substantial minority of cases (Table 2.7). Those in a college preparatory program are the most likely to be "on track": only 8 percent of the white and 21 percent of the black males hold aspirations that are not congruent. Consistent with what has already been said, many young black men in academic programs may be hedging their bets—hoping for college, but considering occupations requiring less education. Alternatively, many black youths may not know as much about the kinds of occupations open to those with a college education. Certainly, in line with lower socioeconomic origins, fewer have direct access to such information through families and neighbors. As noted earlier, young black men in occupational programs are considerably more likely than white to aspire to college. Some of these youngsters may be attending well-established vocational schools in places like Chicago, from which it has been possible to go on to college. It is probable, however, that this is the case for only a few of these students.

Change in Curriculum Assignment

What factors prompt movement from one program to another, and what are the consequences of a shift? Before turning to these questions, we note that, once they've reached high school, relatively few boys and girls report changing their major program of studies, from one of our four categories to another, from one year to the next (Table 2.8). Fewer than one in ten students made such a move. The most mobile were black males in a college preparatory program in 1966: 10 percent shifted to an occupational curriculum and 7 percent moved to the general track. However, no black male in the NLS sample shifted to a

Table 2.7. Appropriateness of high school curriculum to occupational and educational aspirations: men enrolled in grades 10–12, 1966
(N in thousands)

| | | | Percent | | | |
| | | | Curriculum inappropriate to | | | |
	N^a	Curriculum fully appropriate	Occupational and/or educational goal, total	Occupational goal, only	Educational goal, only	Both goals
Whites						
Vocational	429	65	35	13	12	11
Commercial	126	64	36	9	19	7
General	1,842	48	52	8	22	22
College preparatory	1,905	92	8	5	1	2
Blacks						
Vocational	89	54	46	6	25	15
Commercial	27	41	59	4	48	7
General	304	45	55	9	25	21
College preparatory	136	79	21	13	3	5

^{a}Excludes those for whom occupational or educational aspirations were not ascertained.

Table 2.8. Comparison of high school curriculum group by sex and race: men (1966–67) and women (1968–69) enrolled in grades 9–11 in the base year and in grades 9–12 at the first reinterview (N in thousands)

Curriculum, 1966	N	Percent	Curriculum, 1967 (Percent)[a]			
			Voc	Com (or B&O)	Gen	Coll prep
			Men			
Whites						
Vocational	299	(8)	98	0	2	0
Commercial	97	(3)	b	b	b	b
General	1,603	(46)	2	2	94	1
College preparatory	1,519	(43)	1	1	2	96
Total (or average)	3,519[c]	(100)	(10)	(4)	(44)	(42)
Blacks						
Vocational	55	(11)	92	2	6	0
Commercial	21	(4)	b	b	b	b
General	307	(63)	3	4	93	0
College preparatory	108	(22)	8	2	7	84
Total (or average)	491[c]	(100)	(14)	(7)	(60)	(19)
			Women			
Whites						
Vocational	61	(1)	b	b	b	b
Bus and office	596	(14)	0	98	1	1
General	1,920	(46)	1	6	92	1
College preparatory	1,604	(38)	1	4	0	95
Total (or average)	4,181[c]	(100)	(2)	(18)	(43)	(37)
Blacks						
Vocational	24	(5)	b	b	b	b
Bus and office	70	(13)	0	93	3	4
General	314	(60)	0	1	98	0
College preparatory	112	(22)	0	3	1	96
Total (or average)	520[c]	(100)	(5)	(14)	(60)	(22)

[a]Detail may not add to 100 percent due to rounding.

[b]Percent not shown; base less than 25 sample cases.

[c]Excludes those for whom curriculum in either year was not ascertained.

college preparatory program between the two survey dates (1966–1967). The *gross* movement within all sex-race categories resulted in a *net* gain to occupational curricula.

Curriculum change seems to be congruent, in general, with the aspirations, likes, and dislikes of those who switched (Table

2.9). Youngsters who shifted to an occupational curriculum held lower educational aspirations in the base years than those who stayed in a general or college preparatory program. By the same token, those who moved into an occupational program possessed somewhat higher base-year goals than those who remained in an occupational area two years in a row.

Men who shifted to a vocational or commercial program more often raised than lowered their aspirations: 22 versus 17 percent. Among those who stayed in a curricular category from one year to the next, the pattern of change reveals a definite *sorting out process.* College preparatory men—85 percent of whom aspired to at least four years of college in the base year—were more likely to raise than to lower their already high aspirations. Just the opposite was true of men who stayed in occupational programs. On the other hand, among the young women, "movers" to an occupational curriculum were more likely to lower than to raise their educational goals, and only among "stayers" in the occupational area did more girls raise than lower their goals.

Among both men and women, those who shifted to an occupational curriculum were less likely than stayers (except for boys who remained in a general program) to say that they liked school "very much" at the time of the initial interview. Associated with the change in curriculum was a greater-than-average likelihood of reporting a change in attitude toward school, and most of the difference occurred because a large proportion of the "movers"—57 percent of the men and 44 percent of the women—said they liked school more.

Summary

Black youngsters in high school rank far lower than whites in socioeconomic origins (SEO) and scholastic aptitude (SA). When a group of high school students is divided by thirds simultaneously along the dimensions of SA and SEO, blacks in each third are more likely than are whites to report being in a college preparatory program. No systematic difference emerges between background measures and assignment to an occupational, as compared to a general, program.

Table 2.9. Comparison of educational aspirations and of attitude toward school, by sex: men (1966–67) and women (1968–69) enrolled in grades 9 to 12 in base year and at first reinterview (N in thousands)[a]

	Total or average[b]	Changed to occupational curriculum	Same curriculum both years		
			Occupational	General	College preparatory
Men (N)	4,273	128	454	1,838	1,567
Educational aspirations, 1966					
Coll 4+, 66	60%	44%	28%	49%	85%
Coll 2, 66	16	16	32	18	9
HS 12 or less, 66	24	40	41	33	6
Comparison of aspirations, 1966 & 1967					
Higher in 1967	11	22	8	12	9
Lower in 1967	10	17	19	13	3
Attitude toward school, 1966					
Liked school "very much," 66	40	30	39	20	44
Comparison of attitude toward school, 1966 & 1967					
Liked school more, 67	37	57	35	35	38
Liked school less, 67	7	4	8	7	7

Women (N)	4,949	239	642[c]	2,070	1,619
Educational aspirations, 1968					
Coll 4+, 68	50%	24%	11%	40%	81%
Coll 2, 68	21	20	36	23	14
HS 12 or less, 68	29	57	53	37	6
Comparison of aspirations, 1968 & 1969					
Higher in 1969	12	12	16	11	13
Lower in 1969	17	20	12	16	19
Attitude toward school, 1968					
Liked school "very much," 68	55	45	50	52	61
Comparison of attitude toward school, 1968 & 1969					
Liked school more, 69	36	44	31	36	36
Liked school less, 69	14	15	10	13	18

[a]Detail may not add to 100 percent due to rounding.

[b]Includes those who made other changes, not shown separately.

[c]Business and office only; excluded other vocational.

Blacks report greater satisfaction than whites with school, and less dissatisfaction. Among the boys, occupational students are the least satisfied, but this fact is probably unrelated to their program of studies, since large numbers name a vocational subject as their favorite. Among girls, curricular differences in satisfaction are small.

Asked to name the subject they "enjoy the most" and "dislike the most," almost no one places an occupational subject in the latter category. Indeed, while the common subjects of mathematics, humanities, and science are mentioned most frequently in both categories, the ratio of "enjoy" to "dislike" is especially high for vocational subjects, especially among white males in occupational programs. The ratio is somewhat lower (but still high) for black males. However, black youngsters, unlike white, often name a subject in the humanities as their favorite. Students in the low aptitude third are somewhat more inclined than are their peers to most enjoy a vocational subject.

Although choice of an occupational program might seem to imply having settled on an occupational goal, occupational students are about as likely as are their peers not to name an occupation (that is, to respond "don't know") when asked what kind of work they would like to be doing at age 30 (or 35). A high (and, for the group, unrealistic) proportion of boys and girls aspire to an occupation in the professional-technical category. Occupational goals are higher for men than for women, and for whites than for blacks. Business and office students, especially whites, aspire predominantly to clerical jobs, which tend to be sex-stereotypic and to command lower full-year earnings, as judged by 1970 Census data for all full-year workers. The evidence for sex segregation and occupational "crowding" is strong, since 69 percent of high school girls aspire to only nine three-digit occupations out of 297. Those occupations include secretarial work, teaching, nursing, and so forth.

Asked for information about a set of occupations, black youngsters demonstrate less "knowledge of the world of work" than do whites. Among the boys, vocational students (especially whites) display less information than do their counterparts in a general program of study. College preparatory students possess greater information than any other group, especially regarding occupations calling for college-level training. Young women in the business and office curriculum have greater knowledge of occupations than do their general counterparts; "other vocational" students have less. Academic women demonstrate more information than do those in other groups.

With respect to educational aspirations, boys set higher goals in the mid-1960s than did girls. Among the former, white lads more often than black planned a college education. The reverse was true for women; that is, black girls set higher educational goals than white. As would be expected, students in college preparatory programs held dramatically higher goals than did their peers. Between occupational and general students, the latter more often aspired to four or more years of college. The only exception was in the case of black men, where comparable proportions in the two categories wanted a baccalaureate or higher degree. The pattern of preceived encouragement and support from parents, teachers, and peers basically accords with differences among the curriculum groups in personal goals. Expectations were somewhat lower than aspirations, and black youngsters were more likely than white to offer "lack of money" as an explanation for the discrepancy.

In general, college preparatory students are more likely than others to be in the curriculum consistent with both their educational goals and the educational requirements typical of the occupations to which they aspire. Judged by the latter yardstick, young black men in occupational programs, while more frequently than their white peers wanting four or more years of college, are about as likely to have occupational objectives consistent with their high school program of studies. Such students, as well as many young black men in college preparatory studies, may be "hedging their bets" against not being able to attend college. Some such students may also lack information about careers related to a college education. Few students aspire to occupations for which pre-employment training of any kind is uncommon. Except for young black women, occupational students are more likely than are their general program peers to aspire to jobs offering pre-employment training below the baccalaureate.

Presumably, the resolution of discrepancies between goals

and curriculum can take place either through movement from one curriculum to another, or through a reassessment and modification of goals and preferences. Between the base year surveys and the first reinterviews, fewer than ten in every hundred students shifted from one major curricular group to another. The greatest movement was among young black men from a college preparatory to an occupational or, less frequently, to a general program. The net flow was clearly toward occupational studies, a matter discussed further in Chapter 3, where we investigate whether or not occupational programs enhance the holding power of schools.

The psychological correlates of moving from one curriculum category to another, or of staying in the same one for two years in a row, present a mixed picture regarding the apparent implication of curricular assignment for completing high school, a topic considered in greater detail in Chapter 3. The young men who moved to the vocational category in 1967 were among the least satisfied with school in 1966. Movement often prompted a change in attitude, heavily in favor of liking school more than in the base year. Boys who moved to an occupational program had lower base-year educational goals than did those who stayed in a general or college preparatory program. Yet respondents who remained in an occupational program two years in a row had the lowest goals of all in the base year, and their goals moved even lower by 1967. However, those who moved to an occupational program more often raised than lowered their aspirations from 1966 to 1967. Interestingly, young men who stayed in a college preparatory program from one year to the next also tended to raise their goals, which were already very high in 1966. Counter to the pattern for men, women who shifted to occupational curricula more often lowered than raised their educational aspirations. Somewhat unexpectedly, those girls who remained in an occupational program between 1968 and 1969 tended to raise their educational aspirations. This pattern may reflect the *relatively* low aspirations of business and office students in the base year.

3

Educational Attainment
and Postschool Training

What effect does high school curriculum have on educational attainment? As shown in Chapter 2, occupational subject matter is psychologically congenial for many students, even for those in college preparatory programs. Shifts in curriculum from one year to the next, which tend in the direction of occupational studies, often result in greater satisfaction with school. On the whole, however, students in occupational programs have relatively low aspirations, which among young men become even lower as they progress through high school. In this chapter, controlling for antecedent circumstances, we explore in greater depth whether occupational studies: (1) encourage completion of high school; (2) affect the probability of going on to college or of receiving other post school training; and (3) influence highest year of school completed.[1]

We begin with a description of rates of dropping out and of transition to college, and of the reasons students give for ending their formal education. This is followed by regression

---

[1] Ultimate educational attainment (even approximate) cannot be known for several years. Data for 1973 (boys) and 1972 (girls) refer to persons who at that time were 21 to 31 and 18 to 28 years old, respectively. Many respondents were still in school. Restricting attention to the out-of-school groups understates attainment. The "topping off" of the samples surely understates, as well, the influence of having pursued a college preparatory program.

analyses, within which we seek to ascertain whether "curriculum effects" exist apart from differences in family background, mental ability, and residence. It is conceivable (indeed, we would hypothesize) that an occupational program experience would increase the chances of finishing high school, but reduce the likelihood of going on to college. We make no a priori judgments of the *net* effect on highest year of school completed. The next section of this chapter seeks to answer the question of whether apparent curriculum differences in attainment still exist, when one controls statistically for educational goals. This investigation is followed by a testing of alternative path models of the attainment process, in order to detect direct and indirect effects of factors antecedent to school attainment. Finally, we examine the nature and extent of post school training outside regular school—training which may be substitutable or complementary to skills acquired in high school programs.

Dropout and Transition Rates[2]

Published dropout statistics are typically annual reports based on school district data, and are thus plagued by the problem of differentiating between the student who leaves the school system entirely, and the one who transfers to another school outside the district or outside the state. This difficulty is minimized in a longitudinal design, in which efforts are made to reinterview respondents whether or not they change place of residence. However, this approach contains an analogous problem—namely, what assumption should be made regarding the school enrollment of respondents who were *not* reinterviewed? Since we do not know whether they left the system or completed the twelfth grade, the number of dropouts among those reinterviewed plus the number not reinterviewed provides an outside estimate of the dropout rate. The low estimate, of course,

---

[2] We use the term "dropout" to refer to anyone who left school without completing 12 or more years of school, fully realizing that some youngsters are "pushed out." We do not wish to imply that having left school is necessarily a good or a bad thing. We use the term dropout only because it is conventional to do so. Occasionally we substitute the term "early school leaver."

would simply be the number of those reinterviewed who had left school early. Both figures, which represent the range within which the true annual rate from the initial survey to the first follow-up doubtless fell, are presented in Table 3.1

Table 3.1. Estimated high school dropout rates by curriculum, sex, and race: men (1966 to 67) and women (1968 to 69) enrolled in grades 10 to 12 in the base years
(N in thousands)

Curriculum, base year		Whites			Blacks	
	N	Low estimate[a]	High estimate[b]	N	Low estimate[a]	High estimate[b]
Men						
Vocational	429	10%	16%	89	12%	27%
Commercial	126	3	15	27	4	10
General	1,842	6	16	304	7	13
College preparatory	1,906	1	5	136	1	5
Total (or average)	4,439	4	11	574	6	13
Women						
Vocational	96	c	c	22	c	c
Business and office	751	3%	7%	100	1%	4%
General	1,663	4	7	312	6	6
College preparatory	1,830	1	4	149	3	9
Total (or average)	4,364	2	6	584	4	6

[a]Number reinterviewed who were not enrolled at first follow-up and had completed fewer than 12 years of schooling.

[b]Number reinterviewed who were not enrolled at first follow-up and had completed fewer than 12 years of schooling, plus number not reinterviewed at first follow-up.

[c]Percent not shown; base less than 25 sample cases.

These estimates reveal the following facts. First, over a one-year period, young men were more likely to leave school early than were women, and blacks more likely than whites. Second, compared to those from a general program in the same sex-race groups, the dropout rate for vocational men was *higher*; for commercial men, *lower*; for business and office women, *lower*; for college preparatory men and white women, *lower.*

(For black women, the data are inconclusive.) The generalizations from these data seem to be that, in contrast to a *general* curriculum:

• occupational programs for men, on balance, are associated with early withdrawal from high school; and

• business and office programs (at least for black women) encourage students to stay in school.

Most, if not all, studies show that transition from high school to college is strongly related to high school program. The NLS data for boys who were twelfth graders in 1966 and reinterviewed a year later show that 56 percent of the whites and 32 percent of the blacks were enrolled in college. Among whites, the proportions by curriculum were 16, 27, and 87 percent for vocational/commercial, general, and college preparatory students, respectively. Among blacks, the comparable figures were 22, 14, and 71 percent, respectively.

Such dramatic differences between the college preparatory and other tracks may have had the consequence of diverting research attention from differences between the general and occupational curricula. Much of the work that has been done with national surveys and other major studies does not investigate the full range of curriculum differences.

Why do young men leave school before high school graduation? Respondents who were no longer attending school at the 1966 survey were asked, "Why would you say you decided to end your education?" Differences by curriculum were minor. Two-fifths of all responses were categorized under a residual, "other" category. Compared to those from the general track, dropouts from an occupational program more often gave a response of "Had to work" (25 vs. 20 percent), "Lack of ability" (8 vs. 2 percent), or "Disliked school" (16 vs. 14 percent). The latter difference is solely attributable to the reasons given by black youth, where the occupational-general comparison is 15 vs. 5 percent.

What reason do young men with exactly 12 years of schooling give for not going on to college? Of those who were out of school in 1966, differences by high school curriculum were again minor. The fact that only 13 percent of the occupational graduates cited "couldn't afford college," compared with

18 percent from college preparatory and general programs, suggests the importance of underlying differences in aspirations.

Among girls, pregnancy and marriage rank as significant reasons for ending (or at least interrupting) schooling. Using data for young women out of school in 1968, we constructed a measure of the coincidence of the birth of a first child and termination of schooling. About one-third of female high school dropouts are accounted for by this measure (Table A3.1). Almost one-half of college preparatory high school dropouts left school for marriage and/or pregnancy, presumably because they are less likely to leave for other reasons. At each attainment level, the percentage of black women who bore a child within one year of leaving school is higher than for whites.

Curriculum and Educational Attainment

In an attempt to ascertain at what stage curriculum influences highest year of school completed, we regressed, in turn, four attainment variables on a common set of independent variables. The latter include scholastic aptitude (SA), socioeconomic origin (SEO), and a set of dummy variables for both area of residence at age 14 and most recent high school curriculum. The age 14 residence variables are: (1) A14R, lived on a farm or ranch or elsewhere in the country; (2) A14T, lived in a town or small city under 25,000 population; and (3) A14CTY, lived in a large city of 100,000 or more. The reference category is A14S: having lived in a suburb of a large city or in a city of 25,000 to 100,000 population. The curriculum variables are: (1) VOC, vocational; (2) COM, commercial; and (3) CP, college preparatory. The reference category is GEN, or general. The coefficient for each categorical (1,0) variable, if statistically significant, can be interpreted as a deviation (plus or minus) from the value for the excluded category. In effect, each curriculum coefficient addresses the question, Compared to those in a general program of studies, does having been in a vocational (or commercial, or college preparatory) program add to or subtract from attainment?

We used three dummy (1,0) dependent variables: (1) 12+, whether the respondent completed 12 or more years of school; (2) 13+, whether the respondent completed 13 or more years;

and (3) 13+/TNG, whether the respondent completed 13+ years *or* had some post school training. The final dependent variable, HSC, highest year of school completed, is in continuous form. Because the sample is restricted to respondents who had at least 10 years of education, HSC ranges from 10 to 20. In the first three equations, coefficients may be interpreted either as proportions or as contingent probabilities, depending on the set of characteristics a person possesses. In the HSC equation, coefficients are expressed, of course, in years.

Ordinary least squares regression results are presented in Table 3.2 for men (1973). Three variables dominate the results: SA, SEO, and whether enrolled in a college preparatory program in high school. Each of these variables positively influences attainment. Regarding completion of high school, the coefficient for VOC is positive but not significant for both color groups. Among white boys, COM is associated with a positive difference of about six percentage points in the probability of finishing high school.

We had contemplated a logit analysis of high school completion, since the probability of completing high school—given that the student has finished at least 10 years—is so high: .93 for white males and .78 for black. But the problem is not simply one of heteroscedasticity and unnecessarily large standard errors for regression coefficients. (The coefficients themselves are unbiased either way.) The more serious matter is what to make of the positive correlation between having been in a vocational program and highest year of school completed over the range from 10 to 12 or more years. As indicated in Chapter 2, as students (especially men) move through high school, *net* movement occurs from year to year *toward* occupational curricula. Thus the cross-sectional regression results seem to lead to a different conclusion than do the longitudinal results, which are admittedly limited to two one-year intervals (1966-67 for males and 1968-69 for females). (See Table 3.1 above.) A more refined statistical routine (i.e., logit) might well show more of the occupational coefficients to be statistically significant, but the implications of *net* flows of students toward occupational programs as they proceed through high school (as opposed to "curriculum holding power") would, of course, remain as a plausible explanation for the relationship. For this reason, we felt it unnecessary to go beyond ordinary least squares (OLS) regression analysis.

What about the transition to college? For both white and black males, the coefficients for VOC are negative, significant, and relatively large: -.10 in both instances. In other words, taking account of SA, SEO, and area of residence at age 14, having completed at least 10 years of school and having been in a vocational program reduces the probability of completing one or more years of college by at least 10 percentage points. We say "at least" because our sample is restricted to those not in school. If general students going to college attend a greater number of years than do vocational students, the ultimate difference will widen with the passage of time.

The effect of curriculum on highest year of school completed by young men is shown in columns 4 and 8 of Table 3.2. (This effect too is probably understated.) The coefficients for occupational curricula are uniformly negative, although only one (VOC for white youth) is statistically significant. For them, other things the same, having taken a vocational program reduces highest year of school completed by about half a year (-.52) as compared with the general program. The coefficient for black youngsters (-.26) is about half that size, and barely exceeds its standard error.

For the young women, SA, SEO, and CP (college preparatory) are again positive and in nearly every case statistically significant (Table 3.3). Compared to a general program, evidence for a positive effect of occupational studies on completion of high school is more compelling for women than for men. For young white women, the coefficients for VOC and B&O (business and office) are positive and significant. And, as shown in Chapter 2, the *net* flow toward occupational programs across the high school years is much less for women than men. Among the women, VOC adds 8 percentage points to the probability of completing high school; B&O adds 9 points. The coefficients for blacks are also positive, but are not significant. Concerning women completing one or more years of college, three of the

Table 3.2. Educational attainment and post school training: regression results for men (1973) (Standard errors in parentheses)

Explanatory variables and statistics	Whites				Blacks			
	$Y = 12+$ $(1,0)$	$Y = 13+$ $(1,0)^a$	$Y = 13+/$ TNG $(1,0)^a$	$Y = HSC$ $(yrs)^a$	$Y = 12+$ $(1,0)$	$Y = 13+$ $(1,0)^a$	$Y = 13+/$ TNG $(1,0)^a$	$Y = HSC$ $(yrs)^a$
SA	0.004** (0.0004)	0.01** (0.001)	0.004** (0.001)	0.05** (0.004)	0.005** (0.002)	0.01** (0.002)	0.01** (0.002)	0.03** (0.006)
SEO	0.02** (0.003)	0.07** (0.01)	0.04** (0.006)	0.32** (0.03)	0.03** (0.01)	0.05** (0.01)	0.05** (0.02)	0.36** (0.05)
VOC_{73}[b]	0.01 (0.02)	-0.10** (0.03)	-0.03 (0.03)	-0.52** (0.16)	0.07 (0.06)	-0.10** (0.06)	-0.04 (0.08)	-0.26 (0.24)
COM_{73}[b]	0.06** (0.03)	-0.05 (0.05)	-0.03 (0.05)	-0.25 (0.26)	-0.07 (0.12)	-0.01 (0.11)	0.02 (0.15)	-0.08 (0.45)
CP_{73}[b]	0.03** (0.01)	0.28** (0.02)	0.10** (0.02)	1.44** (0.12)	0.13** (0.06)	0.21** (0.06)	0.03 (0.08)	1.04** (0.25)
A14R[c]	-0.004 (0.02)	-0.01 (0.03)	-0.06** (0.03)	-0.11 (0.14)	0.03 (0.07)	0.03 (0.07)	-0.02 (0.09)	0.48** (0.27)

A14T[c]	-0.005	0.03	-0.04	0.07	0.06	0.02	-0.01	0.35
	(0.01)	(0.03)	(0.03)	(0.13)	(0.07)	(0.07)	(0.09)	(0.28)
A14CTY[c]	-0.02	0.03	-0.03	0.17	-0.03	-0.07	-0.01	-0.45*
	(0.02)	(0.03)	(0.03)	(0.14)	(0.06)	(0.06)	(0.08)	(0.26)
Constant	0.32	-1.30	-0.14	4.36	0.05	-0.88	-0.39	6.52
R^2	0.10	0.39	0.13	0.40	0.10	0.25	0.10	0.35
F	27.49**	135.97**	33.17**	144.75**	5.35**	13.67**	4.95**	21.09**
N	1,971	1,719	1,719	1,719	377	329	329	329
Mean (Y)	0.93	0.49	0.78	13.7	0.78	0.25	0.55	12.4
SD (Y)	0.25	0.50	0.41	2.5	0.41	0.43	0.50	1.8

[a]Restricted to those out of school who had completed 10 or more years of school.

[b]Reference group: *general* curriculum.

[c]Reference group: respondents living in small city or suburb at age 14.

*Significant at 0.10 level (2-tailed t test except for SA and SEO).

**Significant at 0.05 level.

Table 3.3. Educational attainment and post school training: regression results for women (1972) (Standard errors in parentheses)

Explanatory variables and statistics	Whites				Blacks			
	$Y = 12+$ (1,0)	$Y = 13+$ (1,0)	$Y = 13+/$ TNG (1,0)[a]	$Y = HSC$ (yrs)[a]	$Y = 12+$ (1,0)	$Y = 13+$ (1,0)[a]	$Y = 13+/$ TNG (1,0)[a]	$Y = HSC$ (yrs)[a]
SA	0.002** (0.0005)	0.006** (0.001)	0.004** (0.001)	0.03** (0.00)	0.0015 (0.0012)	0.007** (0.001)	0.003 (0.002)	0.02** (0.00)
SEO	0.02** (0.003)	0.06** (0.005)	0.04** (0.006)	0.21** (0.02)	0.03** (0.009)	0.06** (0.01)	0.05** (0.01)	0.17** (0.03)
VOC$_{72}$[b]	0.08* (0.045)	0.03 (0.06)	0.03 (0.08)	0.30 (0.26)	0.04 (0.09)	-0.19** (0.09)	-0.008 (0.12)	-0.30 (0.30)
B&O$_{72}$[b]	0.09** (0.02)	-0.12** (0.02)	0.02 (0.03)	-0.09 (0.08)	0.03 (0.04)	-0.14** (0.04)	0.02 (0.06)	-0.24 (0.15)
CP$_{72}$[b]	0.10** (0.02)	0.33** (0.02)	0.24** (0.03)	1.27** (0.09)	0.11** (0.04)	0.26** (0.05)	0.18** (0.06)	0.85** (0.17)
A14R[c]	0.05** (0.02)	0.08** (0.02)	-0.02 (0.03)	0.35** (0.10)	0.06 (0.05)	0.09* (0.05)	-0.14** (0.06)	0.32* (0.17)
A14T[c]	0.04** (0.01)	0.04* (0.02)	-0.05* (0.03)	-0.15* (0.09)	0.01 (0.05)	-0.02 (0.05)	-0.12* (0.07)	-0.11 (0.18)

A14CTY[c]	0.02	0.06**	0.04	0.25**	-0.05	-0.05	-0.06	-0.32**
	(0.02)	(0.02)	(0.03)	(0.10)	(0.04)	(0.05)	(0.06)	(0.16)
Constant	0.40	-1.11	-0.21	7.17	0.45	-0.92	-0.03	9.24
R^2	0.09	0.41	0.16	0.36	0.04	0.29	0.10	0.20
F	27.91**	200.48**	45.51**	134.75**	3.94**	29.47**	6.91**	15.23**
N	2,289	2,289	1,927	1,927	546	546	447	447
Mean (Y)	0.91	0.40	0.67	12.77	0.85	0.30	0.60	12.26
SD (Y)	0.28	0.49	0.47	1.76	0.36	0.46	0.49	1.35

[a]Restricted to those out of school who had completed 10 or more years of school.

[b]Reference group: *general* curriculum.

[c]Reference group: respondents living in small city or suburb at age 14.

*Significant at 0.10 level (2-tailed t test except for SA and SEO).

**Significant at 0.05 level.

four occupational coefficients are negative and significant: $-.12$ and $-.14$ for B&O among whites and blacks, respectively; and $-.19$ for VOC among black women. None of the occupational curriculum coefficients is significant in the HSC regressions.

These results suggest that occupational programs may have an independent net negative impact on attainment of formal schooling (at least for men), but two other factors should be kept in mind as well. First, a reduction in educational attainment should not necessarily be regarded with reproach. Indeed, it is possible to argue that in many cases it should be applauded. Second, results from use of the dependent variable 13+/TNG (i.e., some college *or* postschool training) should not be overlooked. In comparison with the earlier results, the occupational coefficients here are smaller in size, and are in no case statistically significant. In these results the effects of SA, SEO, and CP are also less strong, suggesting that opportunities afforded by noncollegiate forms of postsecondary training lessen the otherwise inhibiting effects on attainment of low SA, low SEO, and nonacademic studies. The coefficients of determination (R^2) are also noticeably smaller, and the mean values for the dependend variables also point to this conclusion. For example, 49 percent of the out-of-school white men, but only 25 percent of the black, completed 13 or more years of school. The comparable mean values for completion of college *or* some postschool training are 78 and 55 percent—about the same *absolute* gap, but a smaller *relative* one.

All of these results suggest that, first, postsecondary activities other than formal schooling constitute avenues for attainment that do not rely so heavily on origins and scholastic aptitude; and that, second, accounting for these forms of attainment leads to results showing no disadvantage among occupational program graduates.

A third observation concerns residence at age 14. The uniformly negative coefficient in the 13+/TNG equation for A14R is consistent with the lesser availability of postschool training opportunities in rural areas. However, compared to the experience of the excluded category—persons who live in the suburbs or in a city of 25,000 to 100,000 population—having grown up in a rural area is associated with additional years of *regular* school completed. The only exception is white men; and even in this category the coefficient is not significant. For black men and women, on the other hand, having lived in a large city (A14CTY) has a depressing effect on attainment. This may be attributable to chaotic conditions in many inner city schools, or perhaps to the attraction of economic opportunities in urban areas. These observations are, of course, speculative.

Are occupational program experiences especially beneficial to the attainments of students in the lowest third of the scholastic aptitude distribution? Tables A3.2 and A3.3 present analogous regression results for these groups. Results with this subset show that commercial programs for white males, and business and office programs for white females, influence educational attainment in a positive way, by enhancing completion of high school. All of the statistically significant coefficients for occupational curricula in the 13+ equation are negative. Interestingly, the VOC coefficient for black men is positive (+.08), although not significant. In terms of *net* effects on highest year of school completed, only two coefficients (COM for white boys, and B&O for white girls) are significant, and both are positive. Once again, except for white boys, having grown up in a rural area is positively associated with highest year of school completed, and the coefficient is especially large (.57) for young black men. Access to historically black colleges in the South may be the explanation, although this is speculation. In any event, a comparison of coefficients in Tables 3.2 and 3.3 with those in A3.2 and A3.3 suggests that, among those who completed at least 10 years of schooling, occupational programs may add more to (or subtract less from) the educational attainment of the lowest SA third than for students of higher ability levels.

Curriculum, Aspirations, and Attainment

One would expect occupational students to hold lower aspirations than their more academic peers, since programs for the former are intended to prepare a person for entry to the labor market, while college preparatory programs are designed to facilitate later work in college. The question arises whether, controlling for aspirations, curriculum still bears a systematic relationship to educational attainment. To examine this question, we restricted attention to boys and girls who, in the base year surveys, were enrolled in grades 10 to 12, and who aspired to at least two years of college.

Nearly all of the members of this group (97 percent of the men and 94 percent of the women) completed high school (Table 3.4). Using the same set of explanatory variables as before, it appears that, for boys, having been in a vocational program reduces by 5 percentage points the probability of finishing high school. Among young women who aspired to college, the coefficients for occupational curricula are uniformly negative for completion of at least one year of college. Only in the case of business and office, however, is the relationship statistically significant (-.14). Consistent with data shown earlier, SA and SEO are more strongly related to college attendance than to high school completion.

For the young men, we constructed three additional variants of the attainment model. The results of one of these models are presented in Table A3.4,[3] which shows the interaction of the curriculum dummies with educational aspirations, drawing a distinction between respondents who wanted four or more years of college and those who wanted less. The excluded category is general track students who wanted less than four years of college. The dependent variable is HSC$_{73}$ (highest year of school completed). Only for white males are there sufficient sample cases for any statements to be made about VOC/COM students. Neither coefficient is statistically significant. A second regression, not given here, showed the interaction of the curriculum dummies with having specified (or not specified) an occupational aspiration in 1966. There were simply too few cases of

---

[3] Alternative models were not possible for young women, because we had data for fewer years, and because they were two years younger than the boys when first interviewed in 1968.

Table 3.4. Completion of high school and transition to college
by 1972 or 1973: regression results for men and women,
all races, enrolled in grades 10 to 12 (1966, 1968),
who aspired to two or more years of college
(Standard errors in parentheses)

Explanatory variables and statistics	Men		Women	
	$Y = 12+$ $(1,0)$	$Y = 13+$ $(1,0)$	$Y = 12+$ $(1,0)$	$Y = 13+$ $(1,0)$
SA	0.002** (0.0005)	0.01** (0.001)	0.001** (0.0007)	0.01** (0.001)
SEO	0.01** (0.004)	0.05** (0.01)	0.02** (0.005)	0.06** (0.01)
$VOC_{72(73)}$[a]	−0.05** (0.025)	−0.09 (0.06)	0.09 (0.06)	−0.01 (0.12)
COM_{73}[a]	−0.04 (0.04)	−0.07 (0.09)	— —	— —
$B\&O_{72}$[a]	— —	— —	−0.002 (0.03)	−0.14** (0.05)
$CP_{72(73)}$[a]	−0.01 (0.02)	0.17** (0.04)	0.04** (0.02)	0.18** (0.04)
A14R[b]	0.01 (0.02)	0.10** (0.05)	0.04 (0.03)	0.02 (0.05)
A14T[b]	−0.01 (0.02)	0.01 (0.04)	0.03 (0.02)	−0.05 (0.04)
A14CTY[b]	−0.005 (0.02)	0.05 (0.05)	−0.001 (0.03)	−0.02 (0.05)
Constant	0.63		0.60	−0.97
R^2	0.07	0.25	0.04	0.23
F	5.89**	27.23**	4.70**	28.83**
N	668	668	735	735
Mean (Y)	0.97	0.64	0.94	0.48
SD (Y)	0.17	0.48	0.23	0.50

[a]Reference group: *general* curriculum.

[b]Reference group: respondents living in small city or suburb at age 14.

*Significant at 0.10 level (2-tailed t test except for SA and SEO).

**Significant at 0.05 level.

"not specified" to warrant a statement about the implications of having been able to express an occupational goal. With respect to the third variant, we note that when former college preparatory students are excluded from the universe, among high school male students in 1966 who wanted four or more years of college and were out of school in 1973, having been in the vocational curriculum is associated with a reduction of - .54 in highest year of school completed (Table A3.5).

Path Models of Attainment

Using Project Talent data, Jencks and his associates (1972) designed path models to estimate the effects of the college preparatory curriculum on chances of going to college for males and females combined. Using the hypothesis that aspirations are "causally prior" to choice of curriculum produced a 25 percent reduction in the measured effect of curriculum (Jencks et al., 1972, p. 168, fn. 35). Using the NLS data for males only, and *excluding* young men in the academic track, we formulated two versions of an educational attainment path analysis. In the first, aspirations were treated as by Jencks; this is the "goal directed" model. In the second, choice of an occupational curriculum (vs. the general curriculum) is hypothesized to influence aspirations; this is the curriculum "tracking" model, and is consistent with the one used by Creech and others (1977, p. 359) with the Longitudinal Study of the High School Seniors of 1972.

In the present study, three models were tested: the basic, goal directed, and tracking models (Figure 3.1). In the *basic model,* we ignore educational aspirations entirely, and consider: (1) scholastic aptitude (SA), measured in the high school, to be a function of socioeconomic origins (SEO) and place of residence at age 14; (2) curriculum (1 if VOC/COM; 0 otherwise) to be a function of SA, SEO, and residence at age 14; and (3) HSC_{73}, highest year of school completed, to be a function of all of the preceding variables. This three-equation model is similar to our earlier regression analysis in that it contains the same variables, except that it excludes college preparatory students from the universe. By hypothesizing a recursive system,

Figure 3.1. Models of the educational attainment process

A. *Basic model* (Equations 1, 4, and 6)[a]

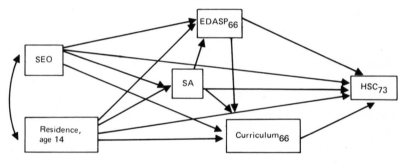

B. *Goal-directed model* (Equations 1, 2, 5, and 7)[a]

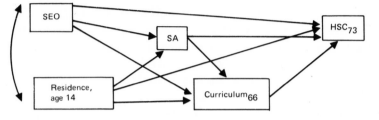

C. *Tracking model* (Equations 1, 4, 3, and 7)[a]

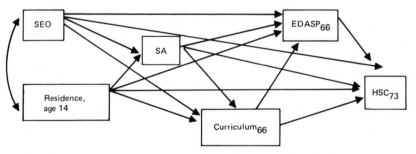

[a]See Tables 3.5 and A3.6 for parameters, based on NLS data.

which accords with the temporal ordering of the variables, we are able to measure the *direct* effects of each variable, as well as the *indirect* effects of SEO, residence at age 14, and SA.

The *goal-directed* and *tracking* models include educational aspirations (EDASP) as expressed in 1966. In the first variant, $EDASP_{66}$ is considered a function of SEO, residence at age 14, and SA; and, in turn, educational goals along with the antecedent variables are conceived to influence curriculum "choice." In the second variant, the *tracking model,* $EDASP_{66}$ is conceived to be a function of SEO, residence at age 14, SA, and curriculum assignment. Since the temporal ordering of curriculum choice (or assignment) and $EDASP_{66}$ in the lives of young men is not clear—and, indeed, no doubt differs among individuals—a comparison of the results of the *goal-directed* and *tracking* models provides a test of the relative importance of each as a function of the other.

We present the results for men of all races first, and then discuss differences in the experience of whites and blacks. Following Hill (1977), we use partial regression coefficients throughout, and solve the system of equations for *direct* and *indirect* effects, using the chain-rule formula. The regression results for *all* men who were enrolled in grades 10 to 12 in 1966 are shown in Table A3.6. In Table 3.5 the results are summarized, showing partial regression coefficients on HSC_{73} (in years) only when a coefficient is statistically significant at or below the .10 level.

First, consider the basic model. One point on the index of socioeconomic origins (SEO) adds about two-tenths of a year to HSC_{73}. Most of the effect (71 percent) is direct; and *indirect* effect through scholastic aptitude (SA) accounts for the remainder. Having lived in a large city at age 14, in comparison with the suburbs or a small city, reduces HSC_{73} by - .14 years, with the entire effect being *indirect* through SA. Each point on the scholastic aptitude scale adds .03 years to HSC_{73}. In other words, abstracting from the ramifications of SA for the probability of being in a college preparatory program, 15 points for nonacademic students adds nearly half a year to attainment

(.03 × 15 = .45 years). In comparison with students from a general program, having enrolled in an occupational curriculum lowers HSC_{73} by −.32 years. Finally, we note the *absence* of a relationship between the three antecedent variables (SEO, residence at age 14, and SA) and VOC/COM_{66}. None of the effects of these variables in the three models is *indirectly* felt though curriculum choice (or assignment).[4]

The factors influencing educational attainment are more complex in the *goal-directed* model. Several variables antecedent to either $EDASP_{66}$ or VOC/COM_{66} have *indirect* effects through SA and $EDASP_{66}$. The most salient finding is that educational aspirations have a very slight effect (.01 years) on HSC_{73} through choice of an occupational curriculum. The influence is *positive,* because high aspirations lower the probability of choosing an occupational curriculum, and thereby add to attainment. The addition of aspirations to the model reduces the *direct* effect of occupational curriculum from −.32 to −.23, or by nearly one-third. The importance of curriculum for $EDASP_{66}$ is confirmed by the *tracking* model. Having been in an occupational program reduces HSC_{73} by −.32, of which −.23 is the direct effect and −.09 the *indirect* effect of VOC/COM through a reduction in $EDASP_{66}$.

The data for young white men yield comparable results (Tables A3.7 and A3.8). The coefficients for VOC/COM_{66} are somewhat smaller, and its direct effect on highest year of school completed is not quite statistically significant. Other differences are minor. However, testing the model with the sample of young black men yields results of considerable interest. (See Tables A3.9 and A3.10.) First of all, having lived in a rural area at age 14 has a significant *indirect* effect on attainment, because rural origin is associated with lower measured ability (SA), which in the two variants of the basic model depresses

---

[4] Once again, we note that the universe excludes young men in a college preparatory program. The correlation coefficients between SA and SEO, on the one hand, and CP on the other, imply strong indirect effects of background variables on HSC through CP—a matter, however, that is beyond our interest here.

Table 3.5. Marginal contribution of explanatory variables to highest year of school completed: men, all races, enrolled in grades 10 to 12 (except in college preparatory curriculum) in 1966, *not* enrolled but interviewed 1973

| | Indirect effect | | | | | Direct effect | Total effect in years (=100%) |
| | Via SA through $EDASP_{66}$ | Via SA or $EDASP_{66}$ through VOC/COM_{66} | Through | | | | |
			SA	$EDASP_{66}$	VOC/COM_{66}		
Basic model							
SEO	—	—	0.06(29%)	—	—	0.15(71%)	0.21
A14CTY	—	—	-0.14(100%)	—	—		-0.14
SA	—	—	—	—	—	0.03(100%)	0.03
VOC/COM_{66}	—	—	—	—	—	-0.32(100%)	-0.32
Goal-directed model							
SEO	0.02(7%)	a(1%)	0.04(21%)	0.04(20%)		0.11(52%)	0.21
A14R	—	-a(3%)	-0.10(74%)	-0.12(97%)			-0.12
A14CTY	-0.04(26%)	a					-0.14

SA	—	—	a(1%)	0.01(26%)	0.01(3%)	0.02(74%)	0.03
EDASP$_{66}$	—	—	—	—	—	0.20(97%)	0.21
VOC/ COM$_{66}$	—	—	—	—	—	-0.23(100%)	-0.23
Tracking model							
SEO	0.02(7%)	0.04(21%)	a(1%)	0.04(20%)		0.11(52%)	0.21
A14R				-0.12(100%)			-0.12
A14CTY	-0.04(26%)	-0.10(74%)					-0.14
SA	—	—	—	0.01(26%)		0.02(74%)	0.03
VOC/ COM66	—	—	—	-0.09(28%)	—	-0.23(72%)	-0.32
EDASP$_{66}$	—	—	—	—	—	0.20(100%)	0.20

[a]Less than 0.01 year.

Note: Dashes (—) designate causal linkages ruled out by the model.

EDASP$_{66}$.[5] Second, the coefficient for VOC/COM$_{66}$ is large, negative, and statistically significant in all three models. Adding EDASP$_{66}$ to the set of equations reduces the VOC/COM coefficient very slightly, from $-.53$ to $-.51$. The reason for this small difference is that among young black men not enrolled in a college preparatory program, educational aspirations are essentially unrelated to choice of (or assignment to) an occupational rather than a general curriculum. An intriguing relationship is the positive association of SA with having been in an occupational program. This finding may simply reflect the fact that larger schools were more likely to report mental ability scores than were smaller ones, and vocational program opportunities are likely to be greater in larger schools.

Finally, a comment is warranted on the sample of young women who were enrolled in grades 10 to 12 in 1968. Restricting attention to nonacademic program participants, having been in an occupational program in 1968 (VOC/B&O$_{68}$) makes essentially no difference for highest year of school completed (Table A3.11). The absence of even a *direct* effect indicates that nonacademic program distinctions make little or no difference for early educational attainment. In earlier results, we found a positive effect of a business and office curriculum for completion of high school, and a negative effect for college. These two effects may counterbalance each other. (The absence of a "curriculum effect" may, of course, be a consequence of the brief period of time between 1968, the base year, and 1972, the most recent year for which follow-up data are available.)

Postschool Training: Nature and Extent

The nature and extent of postschool training is not only of interest in its own right, but also needs to be understood in order to interpret "curriculum effects" on earnings and the like. In the base year survey for men, those out of school were asked

[5]The small *positive* effect (0.3) of A14R through SA stems from: (1) the *positive* relationship between SA and VOC/COM$_{66}$; and (2) the negative coefficient for VOC/COM$_{66}$ in the final equation. To be specific, A14R *lowers* SA, which *reduces* the likelihood of being in a VOC/COM program, and thereby *raises* HSC$_{73}$ by .03 of a year.

a series of questions concerning occupational training and part-time, adult education.[6] In each subsequent survey, a single set of questions was asked. Besides source, the interviewer asked about length of training (months); intensity (hours per week); whether the course or program was completed and, if not, the reason; and whether the education or training was used on present (or last) job.

Approximately two of every three men out of school in 1971 who had completed 10 to 15 years of school reported having received some postschool training (Table 3.6). This proportion would be even higher if training in the military service were included. Nearly half of the out-of-school women 18 to 28 years old in 1972 reported some training. High school dropouts reported training less frequently than did graduates. However, only among blacks is having attended college associated with a higher probability of training as compared with high school graduation.

Differences in receipt of training are slight between former occupational and general students with exactly 12 years of school, at least among the men. Among women graduates, however, former business and office students are somewhat more likely than are their general-curriculum peers to report some training. Source of training varies by curriculum (Table A3.12). Men from occupational programs, for example, are somewhat more likely than are former general (and especially college preparatory) students to report company training, or apprenticeship and other vocational training. On the other hand, they are less likely to have attended business colleges or technical institutes, or to have taken part-time adult courses.

---

[6] The sources measured in the first survey were "business college or technical institutes such as drafting, electronics training, etc."; "a full-time program lasting six weeks or more at a company training school"; "apprenticeship training or any other vocational or technical training (*not* counting on-the-job training given informally);" "additional general courses in a regular school, such as English, math or science;" and (for military veterans), training other than basic training. The next-to-last question was prefaced: "Since you stopped going to school full time, . . ." A common lead-in was used for the first three sources: "Aside from regular school . . . ." The 1968 questions asked of women were less precise as to source.

Table 3.6. **Percentage of respondents reporting postschool training, by highest year of school completed, high school curriculum (most recent), sex, and race: men (1971) and women (1972) *not* enrolled in school (N in thousands)**

	Whites		Blacks	
	N	Percent some training	N	Percent some training
	Men[a]			
10 to 11, total (or average)	852	58%	228	37%
12, total (or average)	2,514	68	324	59
Vocational	401	65	54	51
Commercial	136	67	9	b
General	1,487	66	227	56
College preparatory	489	78	34	71
13 to 15, total (or average)	596	67	45	78
10 to 15, total (or average)	4,040	67	621	51
	Women			
10 to 11, total (or average)	2,303	33%	661	38%
12, total (or average)	6,501	52	771	51
Vocational	129	42	39	46
Business and office	2,061	54	160	60
General	2,844	46	454	46
College preparatory	1,354	64	112	66
13 to 15, total (or average)	1,643	51	141	66
10 to 15, total (or average)	10,447	48	1,573	47

[a]Excludes non-basic training received in the military service.

[b]Percent not reported; base less than 25 sample cases.

The intercolor difference in training between young black and white men is sizable, although smaller in 1971 than in 1966. In 1966, 48 percent of the whites with 10 to 15 years of schooling reported some training, compared with only 29 percent of the blacks (table not shown). Both duration and intensity of training differed as well. Among out-of-school whites in

1966 who reported some training, median hours of training totaled 520; among comparable blacks, only 398 hours.[7]

Between 1966 and 1973, data from the NLS suggest that the nation progressed toward its goal of greater equality between blacks and whites. The proportion of black men reporting at least one year of college *or* some postschool training rose relative to their white counterparts (Table A3.13).[8] To illustrate, among male respondents who were no longer enrolled in school in 1966, 61 percent of the whites but only 36 percent of the blacks had completed one or more years of college or had received postschool training, including non-basic military training. By 1973, the comparable proportions were 78 and 55 percent. Thus, while blacks were only 60 percent as likely as whites to have had some postsecondary training in 1966, by 1973 they were 70 percent as likely.

The improvement was especially great among blacks in the lowest third of the mental ability distribution. In 1966, 46 percent of young white men in the lowest third of the SA distribution reported some postsecondary education or training; this fraction rose to 47 percent in 1973. Among comparable black men, the proportion rose from 33 to 56 percent. As indicated in Table 3.7, black men with 12 to 15 years of education made especially rapid gains in terms of postschool training, even ignoring training in the military. Indeed, among men with 13 to 15 years of schooling, by 1971 the percentage of blacks reporting some postschool training (exclusive of military) exceeded that for whites. Moreover, by 1971, the average duration of such training favored blacks (table not shown). In 1966, median hours of training (excluding military) for blacks with some training was only 71 percent of the figure for whites; by 1971, this percentage was 107. Exclusive of military training, in 1971 the median number of hours for blacks with 10 to 15 years of

[7]Median hours among blacks exceeded those for whites in the case of military, regular courses, and "other vocational." Figures for whites exceeded those for blacks for business colleges and technical institutes, and for company training programs.

[8]The attainments of white and black women—roughly equal to begin with—increased at approximately identical rates.

schooling was 392; for whites, 365. Almost surely, much of the improvement reflects both economic expansion over much of the period, and manpower training efforts of both the public and private sectors.

As was true of the young men, young women received training after high school from such sources as business and technical schools, adult education, and company-sponsored training programs. By 1972, nearly half of both white and black women (48 and 47 percent, respectively) with 10 to 15 years of school had received such training.

Participation in postschool training varied with the level of formal schooling. Among white women, for example, only 33 percent of high school dropouts had some training, while over 50 percent of high school graduates did; and the same pattern obtains for blacks. Furthermore, the type of training received varied by level of schooling. Among women of either race, those who had gone to college tended to gain training outside college of a "professional or technical" nature, while those with high

Table 3.7. Percentage of respondents reporting training outside regular school (excluding military) as of 1966 and 1971, by highest year of school completed 1966, high school curriculum and race: men *not* enrolled in the base year (N in thousands)

| | Whites | | | Blacks | | |
| | | Percent with some training | | | Percent with some training | |
	N	*1966*	*1971*	*N*	*1966*	*1971*
10 to 11, total (or average)	852	27%	58%	228	20%	37%
12, total (or average)	2,514	40	68	315	21	59
Vocational	401	36	65	54	23	51
Commercial	136	30	67	9	a	a
General	1,487	40	66	227	21	56
College preparatory	489	47	78	34	18	71
13 to 15, total (or average)	596	42	67	45	39	78
10 to 15, total (or average)	4,040	38	67	621	22	51

aNot calculated; base less than 25 sample cases.

school diplomas tended to gain clerical or secretarial types of training.

Among the high school graduates who did not go to college, several differences are related to curriculum. Women from college preparatory programs were more likely than were their classmates to receive some training and, among whites at least, were more likely to receive "professional or technical" or "clerical" training. Women from business and office high school programs tended to get clerical or secretarial training, presumably to supplement the skills gained in school. Among women from the general curriculum, there were no extraordinary differences in the amount or type of training received.

Summary

Cross-sectional and longitudinal data are inconsistent as to the relationship between high school curriculum and the probability of completing high school, once the student has reached the tenth grade. Following boys and girls from one year to the next indicates that, compared to peers in a general program, occupational programs may encourage boys to leave school before graduation, while business and office studies may enhance retention in school for girls, especially blacks. Controlling for scholastic aptitude (SA), socioeconomic origins (SEO), and residence at age 14, multiple linear regression analysis indicates that for those who completed at least 10 years of school, occupational studies may raise the probability of completing grade 12.[9] However, at least for young men, this positive relationship over the years 10 to 12 or more may simply reflect the *net* flow of students toward occupational studies as they near the twelfth grade.

Evidence on the transition to college is clearer. A very high proportion of college preparatory students, of course, go on to college. General students are much less likely, and occupational students are least likely to do so. One exception is that between

[9]Although the coefficients are all positive, they are not statistically significant for white men in a vocational program, or for any black group.

1966 and 1967, in comparison with their general counterparts, proportionately more young black men in the twelfth grade from occupational programs were enrolled in college in 1967. In any event, in regression analyses, with the possible exception of white women from "other vocational" programs, having been an occupational student reduced the probability of completing at least one year of college.

Given the young age of the two cohorts, the overall effect of curriculum on attainment, as measured by highest year of school completed, will not be known with precision for several years. Nevertheless, data on youth out of school at the most recent survey (boys, 1973; girls, 1972) suggest that, compared to the former general students, those from occupational programs have acquired less education, controlling for background variables. Except for white women from "other vocational" areas, the signs of the occupational coefficients are uniformly negative. The effect for white men (-.52 years) is twice as large as that for blacks, and is statistically significant.

The reasons offered by male respondents for dropping out or terminating their education after grade 12 are of interest. Blacks more often than whites said they "had to work." Occupational male students who left school before graduation were slightly more likely than those in the general curriculum to say they "had to work," "lacked ability," or "disliked school." However, compared to the college preparatory student who did not go on to college, occupational males were no more likely (indeed, slightly less so) to say they "couldn't afford college," suggesting that underlying differences in aspirations may be important in explaining differences in college attendance. Women, as might be expected, often left school because of marriage or pregnancy.

Since noncollegiate forms of education and training are viable alternatives to college for some individuals, we examined factors associated with completion of either one or more years of college *or* some postschool training. As would be expected, having been in a college preparatory program becomes less salient in this variant of the model. The same is true for scholastic aptitude and socioeconomic origins.

Since the educational goals of students are related systematically to both curriculum and attainment, we repeated our regression analysis for youths who in the base years aspired to at least two years of college. Among the boys, having been a vocational student reduced the probability of completing high school. Among the girls, having been a business and office student made no difference, as compared to their general program peers. Only in the case of business and office studies was there a statistically significant effect on completion of a year or more of college. For other groups, the coefficients for the occupational curriculum variables were negative but not significant. A related analysis using a set of curriculum-aspiration interaction terms points to the importance of both variables. We conclude that while curriculum and aspirations are moderately intercorrelated, they have separate as well as joint effects.

Path analysis of the men's experience tends to confirm this last observation. We excluded college preparatory students entirely in order to see whether (and how) antecedent variables influence choice of (or assignment to) an occupational program, and how curriculum choice (or assignment) interacts with aspirations in the educational attainment process. Confirming an observation made in Chapter 2, choice of an occupational program over a general one is essentially unrelated to SA and SEO. These variables, together with residence at age 14, do of course have direct effects on attainment, but they do not appear to operate through choice of curriculum. Ignoring educational aspirations, having been an occupational program student in 1966 reduces highest year of school completed by about one-third of a school year. Adding aspirations to the model reduces the curriculum effect by about one-third, and adds to the explanatory power of the model. For some, educational goals doubtless influence curriculum choice; for others, being in a particular curriculum leads to revision of aspirations. We tested two models with these differing assumptions as to the direction of causal influence. If anything, the *tracking model* (curriculum influences $EDASP_{66}$) seems to fit the experience of young men better than does the *goal-directed* model, wherein $EDASP_{66}$ is conceived to influence curriculum choice.

Among young black men, the addition of $EDASP_{66}$ to the *basic* model subtracts very little from the direct, negative effect of an occupational program on attainment. Having been an occupational student reduces attainment by about half a year. This is an especially important finding, since the more able black lad (as measured by SA) who is *not* a college preparatory student, often finds himself in an occupational program. Indeed, part of the positive impact on attainment of having grown up in a rural area results from a reduced probability of choosing (or being assigned to) an occupational program.

Nearly two-thirds of the out-of-school young men and one-half of the women with 10 to 15 years of schooling report having had some postschool training. Dropouts report considerably less training than do graduates; and except for blacks, those with some college are no more likely to have received training than are high school graduates. Black and white women are about equally likely to have received training. Black men are less likely to have had training than whites; and duration of training (in hours) is lower for black men than for white. This black-white gap did narrow in *relative* terms, however, between 1966 and 1973.

4

Labor Market Outcomes

We turn now to the relationship between high school curriculum and labor market experience. An assumption underlying federal policy on vocational education is that acquisition of marketable skills in the form of occupational competencies should reduce youth unemployment. The first section of this chapter examines this matter, along with differences in labor force participation and in job changing associated with curricular experiences in high school. The next section examines occupational assignments, industry attachment, and self-employment status. This is followed by the presentation of multiple linear regression results, testing to see whether occupational students, on the average, fare better than do their general counterparts in terms of rate of pay, earnings, and occupational status. Finally, we examine early career mobility patterns, to aid in the interpretation of the regression results.

Labor Force Participation, Unemployment, and Employment Stability

Approximately 19 of every 20 male respondents who were no longer in school were either working, or not working but seeking work (unemployed) at each survey. Women, of course, present a different pattern. Many do not participate in or seek paid employment because of family responsibilities. Others work part-time, usually by choice, but sometimes because of the work opportunities available to them. Such patterns, by level of education and most recent high school curriculum, are of interest in their own right. In addition, they must be understood in order to interpret differences in economic outcomes discussed later in this chapter.

Approximately two of every three out-of-school female respondents in the National Longitudinal Survey (NLS) were in the labor force at the time of the base year survey (Table A4.1). A slightly smaller fraction participated in the labor force at the most recent follow-up for which data are available (1972), no doubt because of increased family responsibilities in early adulthood. By and large, the more education, the higher the participation rate, and the larger the proportion of employed women working full time. Several factors underlie these relationships. First, marriage and pregnancy are important reasons for leaving school. Second, by 1972, women with fewer years of education had been out of school longer and, therefore, were more likely to be married or to have children. Finally, women with more education generally command a higher rate of pay. If what economists call the "substitution effect" (of paid work for work at home) exceeds the "income effect" (the propensity to "purchase" more leisure), greater participation would be expected.

In 1972, participation rates of high school graduates with different curriculum backgrounds were quite similar. However, the percentage of employed women working full time (35 or more hours per week) was higher among former occupational students. The full-time rate was especially high for white women from "other vocational" programs and for blacks from business and office curricula.[1]

In an earlier report, one of the authors (Grasso, 1975, pp. 148-150) reported no perceptible relationship between several

---

[1] White women from business and office programs were more likely than were their peers to be "married with children," and less likely to be "not married with no children," i.e., single, divorced, separated, or widowed, and without children. Black women from occupational programs were more likely than were their peers to be "not married with children." Overall, the major racial difference is that blacks are more likely to have children, especially among those who are single, divorced, separated, or widowed.

measures of unemployment and high school curriculum. His findings, based on multiple linear regression analysis of data provided by male high school graduates up to 1969, controlled for several background variables, including scholastic aptitude, residence in 1969, and years of work experience. We present here, in tabular form, repeated cross-sectional measures of unemployment for both sexes, by high school curriculum (Figure 4.1 and Table A4.2).

Across the four sex-race groups, there are 24 observations (yearly interviews) in which it is possible to compare the unemployment rates of former vocational students (i.e., vocational men and "other vocational" women) with those of their general curriculum peers. The unemployment rate among the former was lower than among the latter in 15 of the comparisons (62 percent). Unemployment rates among commercial men, and among business and office women, were lower than those of their general curriculum peers in 11 comparisons out of 17 (65 percent). The entire difference is attributable to the generally lower unemployment rates for the occupational curriculum women. (An inadequate number of cases prevents a statement about black men from the commercial curriculum.) We are not sure how to explain the divergent pattern for black women from the college preparatory curriculum, except that it may be that clerical skills are especially important for those women who do not go on to college. We note that general economic conditions, such as the 1971 recession, clearly dominate the unemployment experience of this cohort. Research points to a strong inverse relationship between a person's age and the probability of being unemployed. Changing economic conditions clearly offset the reduction that would be expected from year to year as the cohorts mature.

Survey week unemployment rates say nothing about the severity of unemployment, as measured, for example, by its duration. Because of the size of the NLS samples, and the fact that relatively few of those in the labor force at each survey date were unemployed, it is necessary to cumulate observations over the years to examine differences in duration. Up to the

Figure 4.1 Unemployment rates, by high school curriculum (most recent), race and sex: men and women *not* enrolled who had completed exactly 12 years of education as of the year in question

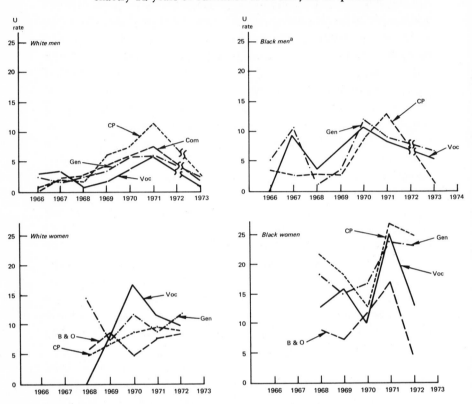

^aCommercial graduates not shown; inadequate sample cases.

Note: ∫∫ signifies the fact that male respondents were *not* interviewed in 1972. Since the overall unemployment rate in 1972 was lower than in 1971 but higher than in 1973, the 1972 values implied from the lines above may not be far off target.

survey week, we can say that white male graduates of occupational programs report shorter spells of unemployment than do their general peers (Table A4.3).[2] For example, among the former, over the period 1966 to 1971, in 63 percent of the observations the current period of unemployment had lasted one to

[2] Our discussion involves "duration-to-date" of the period of unemployment for respondents who were unemployed during one of the NLS survey weeks.

four weeks. The same was true for 51 percent of the observations on unemployed white graduates from the general track. Among black male graduates, proportionately more current periods of unemployment of former occupational students were either short (one to four weeks) or long (15 or more weeks), compared to periods reported by their general curriculum counterparts. Over the years 1968 to 1972, the current spells of joblessness of former occupational women students were on the average shorter than those of their general counterparts: 6.5 versus 7.6 weeks for white students, and 7.2 versus 8.4 weeks for black (table not shown).[3]

Another measure of joblessness for men is the total number of periods of unemployment between 1966 and 1970. Interestingly, graduates from occupational programs (especially whites) are more likely than are their general peers to have had at least one spell of unemployment during that time (Table A4.4). Yet essentially all of the difference is attributable to the greater number of former vocational students who had a single spell. In other words, while the incidence of unemployment among general program graduates was lower, those who had some unemployment were more likely than were their vocational (although not commercial) counterparts to have had more than one bout of joblessness.

Except in 1966, respondents who were unemployed at the time of the survey were asked why they had decided to look for work. The number of observations among the men is barely sufficient for a statement as to the relationship between this measure and most recent high school curriculum. Over the period 1967 to 1971, unemployed former occupational students were slightly more likely than were their general peers (32 versus 29 percent) to say that losing a job (layoff or discharge) was their reason for being unemployed (Table A4.5). On the whole, however, differences by curriculum were minor.

It may well be that male vocational graduates are somewhat more likely than are their general peers to be laid off in an

---

[3] Consistent with the prevalence figures, black women from a college preparatory program also report higher-than-average duration of current period of unemployment.

economic recession. As shown later in this chapter, there is an enormous amount of job changing in the first few years out of school. In 1966, those who had had a "first job" different from their current job were asked why they left their initial employer. In 1971 and again in 1973, those who had left their 1970 and 1971 employers, respectively, were asked the reason for the separation. We computed the ratio of "involuntary" to all other separations for each of these three sets of data (1966, 1971, and 1973), and found it highest in 1971 (Table A4.6). At that time, proportionately more of the graduates from vocational programs, compared to their general peers, reported having separated involuntarily from their 1970 jobs. Between first job and 1966 job on one hand, and between jobs in 1971 and 1973 on the other hand, former vocational students were less likely than were their peers to have made involuntary changes.

There is essentially no difference among the graduates of general and occupational programs in the percentage of respondents who changed employers one or more times between 1966 and 1970 (Table A4.7). Nor is there any apparent difference in the number of changes among those who made at least one change (table not shown). Indeed, there is relatively little difference between blacks and whites: 79 percent of the former and 77 percent of the latter changed employers at least once. This means that at least one-fifth of the respondents out of school in 1970 changed jobs each year. (This number doubtless understates the extent of movement, since it ignores multiple moves over the period, as well as moves within the year.)

Of the young men interviewed in both 1970 and 1971, approximately three in ten had a different current (or last) employer in the two year period. This very high rate reflects the impact of the recession of 1971. Nearly half the respondents who moved also reported a change in their occupation: 53 percent of the blacks and 46 percent of the whites were in different three-digit occupational categories (table not shown).

Occupation, Industry, and Class of Worker

In 1973, male graduates who were out of school were distributed across major occupational categories (1-digit level) as shown in Table 4.1. Over half the young graduates were in craftworker or operative jobs, except for former college preparatory students who had not gone on to college. The proportion is highest for those from vocational programs: 67 percent of the whites and 73 percent of the blacks. At the same time, former vocational graduates were least likely to be assigned to white-collar positions. Among the women graduates, differences by curriculum are quite striking. As expected, a very high proportion of women from business and office programs hold clerical jobs. Perhaps reflecting the language and mathematics skills expected of workers in many clerical jobs, former college preparatory students are also more likely than are their general peers to hold clerical positions. The difference is especially great for black women.

The occupations held by young men with differing levels of education vary in several respects, yet perhaps the most striking fact is that male dropouts (especially whites) with 10 to 11 years of school are distributed across the occupational spectrum in nearly the same way as are those with exactly 12 years (Table A4.8). Nearly equivalent fractions of the two groups are in craftworker and operative categories. Those with 12 years of schooling are somewhat more likely than are those with 10 or 11 years to be in white-collar positions. Early school leavers are more likely than are graduates to be nonfarm (and for blacks, farm) laborers. The biggest difference between graduates and men with "some college" is the likelihood of working in white-collar jobs. Two other important findings in these relationships by level of education are evident. First, at each level of education, blacks, on the average, hold lower-level jobs than do whites. Second, additional years of education (some college for whites, and high school graduation *and* some college for blacks) makes a difference for many young men in gaining access to better jobs.

The occupations held by women also vary by level of schooling. Women with 10 or 11 years of school are more likely to be employed in blue collar or service jobs, while those with 13 to 15 years of school occupy a larger percentage of professional or technical jobs. Much of the variation reflects improved

Table 4.1 Occupation (major group) on current (or last) job (1972, 1973), by high school curriculum (most recent, 1972, 1973): men and women *not* enrolled, but interviewed (1972, 1973), who had completed exactly 12 years of school (N in thousands)

	Vocational	Commercial (or B&O)	General	College prep
		Men		
Whites (N)	564	194	2,085	597
Prof, tech[a]	4%	0%	3%	8%
Managerial	5	9	11	16
Clerical	3	12	7	9
Sales	3	8	4	5
Craftsmen	36	22	31	29
Operatives	31	32	28	15
Service	4	7	6	12
Farm	6	2	4	2
Laborer, nonfarm	7	6	6	5
Armed forces	0	0	0	0
Blacks (N)	77	13	252	53
Prof, tech[a]	2%	b	4%	6%
Managerial	3	b	4	10
Clerical	3	b	6	6
Sales	0	b	4	2
Craftsmen	22	b	22	12
Operatives	51	b	44	36
Service	5	b	8	9
Farm	0	b	2	0
Laborers, nonfarm	15	b	7	19
Armed forces	0	b	0	0
		Women		
Whites (N)	106	1,180	1,384	854
Prof, tech[a]	5%	5%	5%	11%
Clerical	29	74	52	55
Sales	14	3	8	8
Service	12	11	16	15
Other	40	7	19	11
Blacks (N)	16	98	233	56
Prof, tech[a]	b	6%	2%	2%
Clerical	b	60	41	68
Sales	b	1	2	0
Service	b	18	24	5
Other	b	15	31	25

[a]Detail may not add to 100 percent due to rounding.

[b]Percentages not shown; base less than 25 sample cases.

opportunities for high school graduates over dropouts. In addition, the relationship between schooling and professional work is attributable primarily to former college preparatory students (table not shown). Over one-third of the women from college preparatory programs with some college held professional or technical jobs, and former college preparatory students constitute 67 percent of the subset of those with 13 to 15 years of school. Among those with less than high school graduation, the occupational distributions of the business and office and the college preparatory women differ very little. By contrast, fewer high school dropouts from the general track hold clerical jobs, and relatively more of them hold blue-collar and service jobs.

Controlling for level of education, differences among the men in industry attachment, by high school curriculum, are slight (Table A4.9). The distribution of employed young women by industry group is materially different than that of young men (Table A4.10). Very few of the women are employed in extractive industries or construction; a small proportion is employed by manufacturing firms. The vast majority of young women work in service-producing organizations. In general, differences among the women by race are small. The relationship is direct between level of education and the probability of being employed in the professional and related services sector. The lower the level of attainment, the more likely a young woman is to be employed in trade, personal services, or manufacturing.

Men and women in the NLS have been out of school for such a short time that it would be unrealistic to expect that any substantial fraction would be self-employed. Some vocational educators do argue that occupational studies enhance the chance of being able to work for oneself. There is no evidence in the NLS surveys that former occupational students are more likely than are their peers to be self-employed. In 1973, 8 percent of the white graduates from vocational programs and 9 percent from the general track worked for themselves. One percent of the black male graduates in each category were self-employed. Since only 3 percent of the women were self-employed in 1972, curriculum differences in their case were not examined.

As pointed out in Chapter 2, high school students in occupational programs were somewhat more likely than were their general curriculum peers to aspire to or prefer an occupation for which pre-employment preparation below the baccalaureate degree is sometimes available. (See Table 2.6.) Substantial fractions wanted an occupation for which a college education is often required or preferred. Fewer than one-fifth wanted an occupation by age 30 (or 35) for which there are "no special requirements." Among high school graduates no longer in school at the most recent follow-up, only some of whom are the same individuals as the tenth to twelfth graders in the base year surveys, there is practically no difference by curriculum in whether they held occupations for which pre-employment training opportunities below college are available (Table 4.2). The only significant exception is.black women, where the figures are 70 percent of those from business and office programs, and 61 and 44 percent for former general and college preparatory students, respectively.

Table 4.2 shows the percentage of young women in the NLS who held sex-stereotypic occupations. The sex composition of each occupation is based on data from the 1970 Census of Population as to the percentage of all workers in each detailed occupation who were women. In 1972, over half the employed young women in the NLS—60 percent of the whites and 51 percent of the blacks—were assigned to occupations in which women represent 80 percent or more of the total. Young white women from "other vocational" programs were less likely than the average to hold stereotypically female jobs. The same was true of women from general programs. The more likely groups to be in "female jobs" were business and office and college preparatory graduates.

Rate of Pay, Earnings, and Occupational Status

Research on the relationship between curriculum and labor market and other postschool outcomes may be conceived as constituting the major evidence on the effectiveness of vocational education programs. A large body of work has been completed since the passage of the Vocational Education Act of 1963;

however, it does not provide compelling evidence supporting the alleged labor market benefits of high school-level vocational education.

We now turn to the presentation of our multiple linear regression results, examining the experience of the young men first, followed by a comparable analysis of the young women. The explanatory variables in our single-equation models vary somewhat with the dependent variable in question. For men, we seek to ascertain whether occupational curricula have independent effects different from the general program on one or more of the following outcomes:

Hourly rate of pay, 1971 (in dollars)

Change in hourly rate of pay, 1966-1971 (in dollars)

Change in hourly rate of pay, 1966-1971 (percent)

Wage or salary earnings in past year, 1971 (in dollars)

Duncan index of current occupation, 1971 (index with approximate range from 0-100)

1969 full-year earnings of men in the experienced civilian labor force in 1970 for respondent's 1971 occupation (in dollars)

We use 1971 rather than 1973, because the telephone interview in the latter year elicited less information on other important variables. In the case of women, we limit the wage or salary earnings regressions to respondents out of school for two years in a row.

Our dependent variables in the regression for women are:

Hourly rate of pay, 1972 (in dollars)

Wage or salary earnings in past year, 1972 (in dollars)

Bose index of current occupation, 1972 (approximate range 0-100)

1969 full-year earnings of women in the experienced civilian labor force in 1970 for respondent's 1972 occupation (in dollars)

Our curriculum comparisons are always between vocational, commercial (business and office), or college preparatory, on one hand, and general (the excluded category) on the other. Included as explanatory variables in virtually all equations are: scholastic aptitude (SA); socioeconomic origins (SEO); years of work experience (WEXP); whether the respondent resides in a

Table 4.2. Pre-employment educational requirements and opportunities and (for women only) sex composition of occupation of current (or last) job, 1972 or 1973, by high school curriculum (most recent), sex, and race: men (1973) and women (1972) *not enrolled in school*[a] who had completed exactly 12 years of school (N in thousands)

| | | Curriculum (most recent) | | | |
	Total (or average)	Vocational	Commercial (or B&O)	General	College preparatory
			Men		
Whites (N)	3,441	564	194	2,085	597
Occupation requires college 4+	15%	11%	18%	16%	19%
Other pre-employment training available	48	49	34	48	48
No special requirements	37	40	48	36	33
Blacks (N)	394	77	13	251	53
Occupation requires college 4+	6%	4%	b	4%	14%
Other pre-employment training available	45	45	b	49	35
No special requirements	48	51	b	47	51

	3,597	106	Women		
			1,180	1,384	854
Whites (N)					
Occupation requires college 4+	6%	11%	4%	7%	8%
Other pre-employment training available	62	62	64	62	57
No special requirement	32	26	32	31	35
Occupation 0-59% female	17	35	13	20	19
Occupation 60-79% female	23	18	22	24	22
Occupation 80-100% female	60	47	65	56	59
Blacks (N)	408	16	98	233	56
Occupation requires college 4+	3%	b	3%	3%	0%
Other pre-employment training available	60	b	70	61	44
No special requirements	37	b	28	37	56
Occupation 0-59% female	22	b	25	25	17
Occupation 60-79% female	27	b	20	31	21
Occupation 80-100% female	51	b	55	44	62

[a] Further restricted, in the case of women, to wage or salary workers employed full-time.

[b] Percent not reported; base less than 25 sample cases.

Standard Metropolitan Statistical Area (SMSA) (SMSA = 1 if yes, 0 otherwise); and whether the respondent received some postschool training (TNG = 1 if yes, 0 otherwise). The regression coefficient for each of these variables is expected to have a positive sign. The SMSA variable is included not only to reflect cost of living (and wage level) differences, but also because job opportunities and curriculum assignment might be expected to be systematically related to the size of the area. For men, but not for women, we add a region-of-residence variable (1 if SOUTH, 0 otherwise), again to control for wage levels when examining the respondent's wage rate or earnings. Due to policy changes at the Census Bureau in protecting the confidentiality of respondents, the NLS tapes for the 1972 survey of women do not contain the region of residence. In any event, since Duncan and Bose scores, as well as 1969 earnings for *all* workers, are based on national averages, we do not use SOUTH when examining these proxies of long-term career possibilities.

In regressions for the young men, we also add military service (MLSVC) (1 if respondent has had military experience, 0 otherwise). For young women, whose attachment to the labor force is often less secure, we include tenure on current job (TNR, expressed in years) and whether the respondent works full-time (FT = 1 if 35+ hours per week, 0 otherwise). Occasionally, the respondent's occupation (%FM, OCC) is added to regressions for women in order to see whether it makes much difference whether NLS females held sex stereotypic jobs.[4] In selected regressions we include whether the respondent's job is covered by a collective bargaining agreement (CB = 1 if yes, 0 otherwise), to see whether the addition of this variable, which other research shows to bear a strong positive relationship to rate of pay (Andrisani and Kohen, 1975), changes the sign, size, or statistical significance of the coefficients of our curriculum variables.

[4]We intended to examine the implications for labor market success of women holding sex stereotypic occupational aspirations. However, this proved not to be possible for reasons of inadequate elapsed time from 1968 to 1972 and insufficient sample cases.

Men. Our regression results for young men with exactly 12 years of school are shown in Table 4.3. We show regression coefficients only for curriculum, work experience, and training variables, since these are the variables in which we are principally interested. Several observations are in order. First of all, vis-a-vis a general curriculum, in no case is the coefficient for VOC statistically significant. Indeed, the coefficients for black men are uniformly negative. For white men, two of the coefficients are positive; VOC adds $.10 to the hourly rate of pay and $487 to annual earnings. Even among whites, however, the VOC coefficient subtracts from predicted Duncan score and 1969 full-year earnings in current (most recent) occupation, our two measures of longer-term earnings. Second, the data suggest that while COM subtracts from rate of pay and earnings in the short run, longer-term possibilities appear brighter. The predicted Duncan score and 1969 earnings are related positively to COM. Having been in a college preparatory program makes little difference compared to a general program. Third, years of work experience is positive and statistically significant for rate of pay and annual earnings for both whites and blacks. The values for blacks, however, are between one-third and one-half of those for whites, suggesting that the age-earnings profile for black men is considerably more flat. However, as shown later in this chapter, there is a real question as to whether the cross-sectional age-earnings profile is descriptive of the trajectory of earnings from year to year that this cohort can expect as they grow older.

The two other variables in Table 4.3 are also of some interest. Military service seems to have made little difference, one way or the other, for later success in the civilian economy, at least in terms of direct impact. (It could have added to subsequent educational attainment, a topic outside of our concern here.)

The addition of our collective bargaining variable (CB) improves the "fit" of the models considerably, especially for young white men. For example, in the hourly-rate-of-pay equation for this group, the coefficient for CB is $1.03, a figure both

Table 4.3. Selected unstandarized regression coefficients: men, not enrolled 1971,
with exactly 12 years of schooling, by race[a]
(Standard errors in parentheses)

Dependent variables	Explanatory variables					
	VOC_{71} (1,0)	COM_{71} (1,0)	CP_{71} (1,0)	$WEXP_{71}$ (years)	$MLSVC_{71}$ (1,0)	$TNG(IM)_{71}$ (1,0)
Whites:						
$ per hour, 71	0.10 (0.16)	-0.28 (0.24)	-0.14 (0.16)	0.21** (0.02)	-0.04 (0.12)	0.40** (0.12)
W&S earnings, 71	487 (431)	-252 (639)	587 (440)	634** (67)	-188 (332)	588** (333)
Duncan score, 71	-1.82 (1.92)	4.96* (2.99)	2.54 (1.93)	1.17** (0.31)	-1.96* (1.43)	7.01** (1.45)
1969 full-year earnings, 71	-140 (330)	434 (514)	65 (333)	148** (53)	-227 (246)	346* (250)
Blacks:						
$ per hour, 71	-0.19 (0.25)	b	b	0.10** (0.04)	0.17 (0.12)	0.24* (0.18)
W&S earnings, 71	-376 (631)	b	b	217** (108)	385 (556)	417 (484)
Duncan score, 71	-1.15 (3.12	b	b	-0.69 (0.54)	-0.06 (2.52)	8.32** (2.34)
1969 full-year earnings, 71	-324 (421)	b	b	8 (73)	63 (340)	831** (315)

[a]Regressions control for SA, SEO, $SOUTH_{71}$, and $SMSA_{71}$. Collective bargaining variable *not* included. *General* curriculum is the excluded category. Wage and salary earnings regression further limited to respondents not enrolled in either 1970 or 1971.

[b]Coefficient *not* reported; inadequate sample cases.

*Significant at .10 level (1-tailed t test except for curriculum variables).

**Significant at .05 level.

Source: Tables A4.11, A4.13, A4.15, and A4.17.

large and statistically significant (see Table A4.11). The coefficient of determination (R^2) rises from .19 to .30. The regression coefficient of CB is also significant for young black men, but is considerable smaller in size at $.46. The R^2 rises from .22 to .25. Because collective bargaining coverage is negatively correlated with living in the South, the addition of CB reduces the negative coefficient for the $SOUTH_{71}$ variable from $-.61 to $-.37 among white men, and from $-.59 to $-.42 among blacks.

For young white men, but not for black, collective bargaining raises hourly rate of pay more than it does annual earnings (Table A4.13). To illustrate, evaluating the hourly wage-rate equation at the mean values for SA, SEO, and $WEXP_{71}$, and assuming that the respondent has had some postschool training, the calculated wage rate for a young white man covered by collective bargaining is $4.20, or $.60 (17 percent) higher than the calculated value ignoring CB.[5] In the annual earnings equation, the calculated value rises from $7,706 to $8,497, or by 10 percent, when CB is added. In other words, the higher wage rate seems to compensate for a calculated shortfall of 117 in annual hours (2,140 hours minus 2,023). Evaluating the equations for black men in the same way as for white yields predicted values of $3.44 without CB, and $3.54 with this variable included. Annual earnings change from $7,005 to $7,211. Dividing the latter by the former indicates essentially no change in estimated annual hours of work (2,036 hours vs. 2,037).

For our purposes, it is important to note that the curriculum coefficients change very little when CB is added. The biggest change is among whites, where the coefficient for VOC_{71} in the wage-rate equation moves from $.10 to $.04; but in neither instance is the variable statistically significant. In the annual earnings equation, although not statistically significant, for white men the coefficient of VOC_{71} changes from $487 to $363.

[5] In each case, the following additional assumptions are uniformly applied: (1) general curriculum; (2) no military service; (3) non-SMSA; and (4) non-South.

The basic pattern of relationships is much the same for high school and college dropouts as it is for high school graduates (Table 4.4). (Since CB makes little difference for the curriculum variables, we use the models without CB.) While not statistically significant, VOC is uniformly positive in its relationship to hourly rate of pay and earnings. It adds $.53 to the wage rate of those with "some college," a coefficient that is nearly significant at the .10 level. The MLSVC coefficients are uniformly negative for dropouts and high school graduates, but are positive for those with "some college," suggesting that perhaps military service is advantageous, on the average, only for youths who take advantage of educational benefits after leaving service. Finally, we wish to point out that some postschool training adds as much or more to the earning power of high school dropouts as it does for graduates and for men with 13 to 15 years of school.

In order to test·for "interaction effects" of curriculum with other variables, we regressed hourly rate of pay on the set of explanatory variables, exclusive of curriculum, used in our earnings equation. (The sample was segmented by high school curriculum.) The results are presented in Table 4.5. The first observation is that mean rate of pay is higher for vocational than for general curriculum whites ($3.80 vs. $3.69), but lower for vocational blacks ($3.00 vs. $3.16). Second, scholastic aptitude makes a much greater contribution to the pay of vocational than of general (or college preparatory) high school graduates. Third, years of work experience (WEXP) makes little or no difference for black vocational graduates, and among whites the coefficient, although significant, is considerably smaller than for general or college preparatory students ($.13 versus $.23 and $.30). Fourth, postschool training increases the hourly wage across the board. Consistent with Grasso (1975), postschool training may have a slightly greater effect on the hourly earnings of vocational than of former general students.

Our WEXP variable, in the case of men, is simply age, since we control for highest year of school completed.[6] In Table 4.5,

---

[6] For males, $WEXP_{71}$ is defined as "age minus highest year of school completed minus 5." For females WEXP is defined as the number of years since leaving school during which a woman worked at least half a year.

Table 4.4. Selected unstandardized regression coefficients: men, all races, *not* enrolled 1971, by highest year of school completed[a]
(Standard errors in parentheses)

Dependent variable	Explanatory variables					
	VOC_{71} (1,0)	COM_{71} (1,0)	CP_{71} (1,0)	$WEXP_{71}$ (years)	$MLSVC_{71}$ (1,0)	$TNG(IM)_{71}$ (1,0)
0-11 years completed:						
$ per hour, 71	0.13 (0.28)	b	b	0.10** (0.04)	−0.02 (0.22)	0.43** (0.20)
W&S earnings, 71	415 (706)	b	b	366** (95)	−315 (574)	637 (516)
Duncan score, 71	−2.69 (3.07)	b	b	0.64* (0.40)	−1.52 (2.39)	3.39* (2.18)
1969 full-year earnings, 71	−351 (574)	b	b	83 (75)	−88 (448)	91 (408)
12 years completed:						
$ per hour, 71	0.05 (0.13)	−0.30 (0.21)	−0.20 (0.14)	0.20** (0.02)	−0.02 (0.10)	0.39** (0.10)
W&S earnings, 71	324 (368)	−256 (565)	502 (382)	585** (58)	−122 (288)	603** (284)
Duncan score, 71	−1.84 (1.66)	4.88 (2.61)	2.08 (1.70)	0.98** (0.27)	−1.60 (1.25)	7.24** (1.25)
1969 full-year earnings, 71	−194 (279)	362 (439)	2 (286)	135** (45)	−185 (210)	427** (211)
13-15 years completed:						
$ per hour, 71	0.53 (0.34)	b	0.01 (0.20)	0.28** (0.05)	0.19 (0.20)	0.17 (0.19)
W&S earnings, 71	353 (1,069)	b	108 (625)	613** (155)	208 (655)	966* (623)
Duncan Score, 71	−2.06 (4.48)	b	−1.73 (2.54)	2.90** (0.62)	2.33 (2.46)	1.38 (2.41)
1969 full-year earnings, 71	−957 (768)	b	−267 (435)	374** (107)	340 (421)	336 (413)

Regressions control for SA, SEO, SOUTH71, and SMSA71; collective bargaining variable *not* included. *General* curriculum is the excluded category. Wage and salary earnings regression further limited to respondents not enrolled in either 1970 or 1971.

[a]Coefficient *not* reported; inadequate sample cases.
*Significant at .10 level (1-tailed t test except for curriculum variables).
*Significant at .05 level.
ource: Tables A4.12, A4.14, A4.16, and A4.18.

Table 4.5. Hourly rate of pay, 1971: regression results for
men who have completed exactly 12 years of schooling,
1971, not enrolled but interviewed 1971
(Standard errors in parentheses)

	Whites			Blacks	
	VOC_{71}	GEN_{71}	CP_{71}	VOC_{71}	GEN_{71}
SA	0.16*	−0.001	−0.05	0.12	0.06
	(0.10)	(0.04)	(0.09)	(0.11)	(0.08)
SEO	0.01	0.01*	0.01	−0.01	0.002
	(0.01)	(0.007)	(0.01)	(0.02)	(0.01)
$WEXP_{71}$	0.13**	0.23**	0.30**	0.02	0.11**
	(0.06)	(0.03)	(0.06)	(0.07)	(0.05)
$MLSVC_{71}$	−0.19	0.01	−0.28	0.40	0.08
	(0.27)	(0.15)	(0.29)	(0.41)	(0.26)
$SOUTH_{71}$	−0.59*	−0.61**	−0.70**	−0.28	−0.65**
	(0.34)	(0.16)	(0.31)	(0.35)	(0.28)
$SMSA_{71}$	0.37*	0.16	−0.02	0.48	0.29
	(0.29)	(0.17)	(0.33)	(0.42)	(0.28)
$TNG(IM)_{71}$	0.41*	0.35**	0.49**	0.43*	0.39*
	(0.31)	(0.16)	(0.29)	(0.32)	(0.25)
Constant	0.34	0.47	0.89	1.96	1.64
R^2	0.19	0.19	0.27	0.46	0.17
F	3.22**	12.30**	5.92	2.56**	2.99**
N	105	368	118	29	110
Mean (Y)	3.80	3.69	3.58	3.00	3.16
SD (Y)	1.39	1.52	1.59	0.91	1.31

*Significant at 0.10 level (1-tailed t test for all variables).
**Significant at 0.05 level.

therefore, the relatively small coefficient for $WEXP_{71}$ in the
VOC equation indicates that the age-earnings profile for vocational students is flatter than it is for their general peers. The
fact that VOC is positively related to current rate of pay but
negatively associated with Duncan score and with 1969 full-year
earnings is consistent with a flatter profile.

A better test of the implication of curriculum for the
growth in earnings over time is to relate curriculum to the ac-

tual change in pay from one survey to another. We did this in both arithmetic (dollars) and percentage terms for the period 1966 to 1971. The results are shown in Table 4.6. Over this five-year period, among men with 12 years of school employed at both survey dates, rates of pay increased by an average of $1.72, or 82 percent. The increase for blacks was somewhat less than for whites: $1.56 versus $1.74. In relative terms, blacks actually gained on whites. These longitudinal results point to the following effects of a year of labor market exposure: $.35 for whites and $.31 for blacks, numbers considerably higher than the implied influence of WEXP in the cross-sectional model. It may well be that improvements in the earnings of young black men entering the labor force have been rising so fast that the age-earnings profile has been compressed.

Several other relationships in Table 4.6 deserve comment. First, having been an occupational student has the effect, if anything, of reducing the growth of rate of pay over time. The coefficient—minus $.28 in rate of pay over the five years—is nearly significant at the 10 percent level. Second, some regression toward the mean is evident. The coefficient for beginning rate of pay ($/HR$_{66}$) is uniformly negative. Thus, gains (and possibly a few losses) over time compensate for initially high or low wage rates. Third, among whites (but not among blacks), measured mental ability correlates rather strongly with increase in rate of pay. A ten point difference in SA means $.20 over the five-year period. Finally, TNG(IM)67-71 is strongly related to growth in wage rate: $.44 for whites, and $.61 for blacks. This finding is very important, for it suggests that manpower training and similar programs have had beneficial effects on the earning power of young men.

Women. Unlike the results for men, evidence of a beneficial effect of occupational studies (at least, acquisition of business and office skills) is quite evident in the case of young women (Table 4.7). B&O adds $.27 to the predicted hourly wage of whites, and $.26 to the wage rate of blacks. And, since B&O graduates work more hours in the year, the impact on annual earnings is even greater: $665 for whites, and $683 for blacks.

Table 4.6. Change in hourly rate of pay, 1966 to 1971: regression results for men, *not* enrolled either year, who were employed for wages or salary both years, whose highest year of school completed was 12 in both 1966 and 1971
(Standard errors in parentheses)

Explanatory variables and statistics	Arithmetic change, 1966–71			Percentage change, 1966–71		
	Total	Whites	Blacks	Total	Whites	Blacks
SA	0.02** (0.006)	0.02** (0.009)	-0.02 (0.01)	0.7 (3.5)	0.7 (0.4)	-1.3 (1.0)
SEO	0.03 (0.05)	0.02 (0.06)	0.06 (0.10)	2.6 (2.6)	1.8 (2.9)	8.5 (8.4)
VOC_{71}[a]	-0.28 (0.21)	-0.22 (0.25)	b	-5.2 (10.8)	0.5 (11.9)	-34.3 (29.8)
COM_{71}[a]	-0.23 (0.33)	b	b	-20.0 (16.9)	-18.5 (17.5)	b
CP_{71}[a]	-0.05 (0.24)	-0.02 (0.27)	b	-4.7 (12.0)	-4.4 (12.7)	b
$SOUTH_{71}$	-0.67** (0.18)	-0.69** (0.21)	-0.27 (0.38)	-25.4** (9.1)	-29.2** (10.0)	-19.8 (30.9)
$SMSA_{71}$	0.52** (0.17)	0.63** (0.22)	0.41 (0.35)	21.3** (8.9)	23.8** (10.3)	20.2 (20.8)

		b				b
TNG(IM)$_{66}$	-0.03	-0.02		-8.3	-3.1	-48.3*
	(0.18)	(0.20)		(9.0)	(9.5)	(36.7)
TNG(IM)$_{67-71}$	0.44**	0.44*	0.61*	23.5**	15.6*	63.6**
	(0.20)	(0.24)	(0.34)	(10.1)	(11.2)	(28.1)
\$/HR$_{66}$	-0.52**	-0.53**	-0.35	-52.8	-49.6**	-73.7**
	(0.09)	(0.10)	(0.22)	(4.7)	(4.9)	(17.8)
Constant	0.89	0.83	3.27	110.7	107.4	248.9
R^2	0.13	0.14	0.18	0.26	0.26	0.34
F	6.24**	5.06**	1.61	14.67**	11.53**	3.90**
N	423	331	78	423	331	78
Mean (Y)	1.72	1.74	1.56	82.5	80.0	98.8
SD (Y)	1.65	1.70	1.30	91.1	86.3	118.8

[a]Reference group: *general* curriculum.

[b]Variable not included; inadequate sample case.

*Significant at 0.10 level (1-tailed t test except for curriculum variables).

*Significant at 0.10 level.

**Significant at 0.05 level.

Table 4.7. Selected unstandardized regression coefficients: women, *not* enrolled 1972, employed for wages or salary 1972, with exactly 12 years of schooling, by race[a]
(Standard errors in parentheses)

Dependent variable	Explanatory variables					
	$VOC72$ (1,0)	$B\&O72$ (1,0)	$CP72$ (1,0)	$WEXP72$ (years)	$TNR72$ (years)	$TNG72$ (1,0)
Whites						
$ per hour, 72	b	0.27** (0.08)	0.24** (0.10)	0.10** (0.02)	0.01** (0.002)	0.10* (0.07)
W&S earnings, 72	b	665*** (181)	225 (219)	222** (38)	25** (4)	189 (162)
Bose score, 72	b	3.34** (0.84)	-0.03 (0.99)	0.40** (0.17)	0.01 (0.02)	1.31** (0.74)
1969 full-year earnings, 72	b	262** (127)	198 (150)	32 (26)	1 (3)	-81 (112)
Blacks						
$ per hour, 72	b	0.26** (0.12)	b	-0.06** (0.03)	0.02** (0.003)	0.11 (0.11)
W&S earnings, 72	b	683* (365)	b	-54 (81)	54** (10)	64 (340)
Bose score, 72	b	-0.30 (1.90)	b	-0.83** (0.41)	0.04 (0.05)	4.19** (1.73)
1969 full-year earnings, 72	b	-182 (216)	b	-3 (46)	-5 (6)	-17 (196)

[a]Regressions control for SA, SEO, SMSA72, and FT72; collective bargaining (CB) and %FM,OCC72 *not* included. *General* curriculum is the excluded category. Wage and salary earnings regression further limited to respondents not enrolled in either 1971 or 1972.

[b]Coefficient *not* reported; inadequate sample cases.

Source: Tables A4.19, A4.20, A4.22, and A4.23.

Each coefficient is statistically significant. Our equations for longer-term potential earnings also indicate for white women (but not black) a positive effect for B&O. WEXP—measured not by age but by the actual number of years in which the respondent worked at least half a year—is positive for whites, but negative for blacks. Once again, we speculate that a sharp secular rise in the earnings of blacks, especially those with little work experience, may be a factor here. Tenure on current job is also related positively to rate of pay and earnings, although the effects are small. Some postschool training seems to add about $.10 per hour to rate of pay. The longer-term consequence of training may be more substantial, judging by the positive and significant coefficient for the TNG variable in the Bose index equation.

Among employed women with 12 years of schooling, collective bargaining (CB) makes less difference than it did for young men. (Tables A4.19 and A4.20.) Once again, CB adds more to the wage rate and earnings of whites than of blacks: $.44 vs. $.11 in the hourly-wage equation. The coefficients of the curriculum variables remain essentially unchanged. We included in each regression a measure of full-time/part-time status in order to adjust for the fact that B&O graduates were more likely than were their peers to have worked full time (35 or more hours per week). The coefficient for FT (1 = 35+; 0 otherwise) is consistently positive, and is both large and significant in the annual earnings equations.

Among employed women who either dropped out of high school after completing grade 10 or 11, or left college before graduation, there are insufficient sample cases to warrant a conclusion as to the relationship between having taken an occupational (rather than a general) program, and economic outcomes (Table A4.24). Those from a business and office curriculum are relatively unlikely to either drop out or go to college. As with young men, having had some postschool training bears a strong positive relationship with hourly wage rate in the case of women who left high school before graduation: $.28 per hour, a coefficient that is statistically significant.

Finally, it is interesting to note the effects on women's wages and earnings of holding stereotypically female jobs.

As shown in Table 4.8, both wages and earnings rise with level of education, and so does the index of typicality of occupation.[7] For instance, the mean values of the index for respondents with 10 to 11 years, 12 years, and 13 to 15 years of school are 69 percent, 75 percent, and 78 percent, respectively. However, the relationship between wages (or earnings) and the index varies by level of schooling. This can be illustrated by taking a literal interpretation of the regression results to derive estimated effects of a change from a job in which 33 percent of all the incumbents are females to a "typically female" one (i.e., one in which 66 percent are females). Among high school dropouts, this change would result in a *loss* of $.33 per hour and $639 per year. Among high school graduates, the *loss* in hourly wage would be $.10, but there would be no significant difference in annual earnings. Among those with some college but less than a baccalaureate degree, there would be no significant difference in hourly wage, but a *gain* of $529 in annual earnings. Also, as shown in Table 4.8, the effects vary by race. These results suggest that those who criticize vocational programs on the basis of occupational sex-segregation would be wise to consider carefully the alternatives available now or in the future for the employment of young women.

Career Mobility

We examine here only the early work experience of young men. Our regression results point to little or no difference between men from occupational and general curricula in initial rate of pay or earnings; but, as we have seen, longer-term prospects for the former appear less bright than for the latter. This observation, however, is based on Duncan scores and 1969 full-year earnings for the respondent's *current occupation.* Our conclusion would be strengthened if we discovered lesser mobility (especially upward) among occupational graduates than among others.

In the early stages of their careers, the extent of movement between occupations is extremely high. Between 1966 and

---

[7]This measure is the percentage that women represented of all persons employed in each occupation in 1970.

Table 4.8. **Effects of employment in stereotypically female occupations on hourly rate of pay and annual wage and salary earnings of women in 1972, by level of education and race** (Standard errors in parentheses)

	10–11 years, all races	12 years Total	12 years Whites	12 years Blacks	13–15 years, All races
Results from wage regressions					
Mean hourly wage	$2.25	$2.58	$2.58	$2.54	$3.35
Mean % female[a]	69.3	74.8	75.2	69.3	77.6
Simple correlation	-0.305	-0.049	-0.062	0.081	0.009
Partial regression coefficient	-0.010**	-0.003**	-0.003**	0.000	+0.002
(standard error)	(0.003)	(0.001)	(0.001)	(0.000)	(0.007)
Regression n	80	599	474	119	171
Results from earnings regressions					
Mean earnings	$3215	$4174	$4158	$4284	$5510
Mean % female[a]	69.4	74.5	75.0	68.3	75.5
Simple correlation	-0.263	-0.014	-0.021	0.063	0.052
Partial regression coefficient	-19.2**	-2.9	-3.5	2.1	15.9*
(standard error)	(8.46)	(2.9)	(3.3)	(6.4)	(8.3)
Regression n	77	558	445	109	135
Estimated effects of change of occupation from one that is 33% female to one that is 66%					
in hourly wage	-0.33	-0.10	-0.10	n.s.	n.s.
in annual earnings	-639	n.s.	n.s.	n.s.	+529

[a]Each respondent was assigned a value according to her 1972 occupation—namely, the proportion of all workers in that occupation who are females, taken from 1970 Census data.

n.s. refers to "no significant difference."

*Significant at 0.10 level (2-tailed t test).
**Significant at 0.05 level.

1973, nearly four out of five respondents who were *not* enrolled either year were in a different detailed (three-digit) occupation (Table 4.9). Over a two-year period, from 1971 to 1973, more than half of the young men were in different occupations. Furthermore, over three-fourths of the occupational changes involved different major occupational (one-digit) groups. In general, vocational students display slightly less movement than do their general counterparts, and the moves of the occupational graduates are less frequently to a different one-digit category.

Table 4.10 shows cross-sectional relationships between median Duncan score of current (last) job in 1966, and job in 1973. Three observations are in order. First, median Duncan scores are uniformly lower for blacks than for whites, controlling for highest year of school completed. Second, scores are considerably higher for young men with "some college" than for respondents with less education. Finally, the change in median Duncan scores over the seven-year period is consistently less for former occupational students than for their general peers.[8]

At the one-digit level, among those with exactly 12 years of school, all curriculum groups experienced a great deal of movement from first job after high school to 1973 job (Table A4.25). With the possible exception of black vocational and white commercial graduates, similarity of movement is evident in the early work histories of former occupational and general students. Over time, fewer young men work in clerical jobs; more are in the craftworker category; fewer are farm workers or nonfarm laborers.[9] Substantial numbers remain in operative jobs.

Summary

The first few years out of school are a time for "testing" the job market. The vast majority of young men changed employers at

---

[8] While there is considerable overlap, the composition of the 1966 and 1973 groups is not precisely the same.

[9] Regarding the movement of young men out of clerical positions, it is interesting that as time goes by, women move, on average, toward occupations that are traditionally dominated by women (table not shown).

Table 4.9. Comparison of occupation of current (last) job, 1966, 1971, and 1973: men, *not enrolled* 1973, by highest year of school completed 1973, most recent high school curriculum, and race[a]

(N in thousands)

	1966-67			1971-73		
	N	Percent who changed 3-digit occupation	Percent of changes involving different 1-digit	N	Percent who changed 3-digit occupation	Percent of changes involving different 1-digit
Whites						
12, total (or average)	1,879	75%	81%	3,087	53%	75%
Vocational	291	76	76	500	46	67
Commercial	109	70	79	181	59	82
General	1,196	78	83	1,876	56	75
College preparatory	283	66	76	529	50	78
Blacks						
12, total (or average)	196	86	81	317	57	66
Vocational	46	91	75	63	52	73
General	129	83	83	201	55	67
College preparatory	17	b	b	42	76	54
Total, all races						
10-11, total (or average)	488	80	75	653	42	94
Voc and com	66	b	b	112	38	71
General	392	81	77	489	55	76
12, total (or average)	2,079	76	81	3,409	54	74
13-15, total (or average)	562	79	82	1,572	56	78
-10-15, total (or average)	3,377	78	80	5,950	54	76

[a]Restricted to respondents *not* enrolled either year.
[b]Percent not reported; less than 25 sample cases.

Table 4.10. Median Duncan score of current (last) job, 1966 and 1973: young men, *not* enrolled but interviewed in relevant year, by highest year of school completed and most recent high school curriculum as of year in question[a]

	Whites			Blacks		
	1966	*1973*	*Arithmetic change*	*1966*	*1973*	*Arithmetic change*
10-11, total (or average)	19.4	20.5	1.1	15.7	16.0	0.3
Vocational or commercial	20.3	18.5	−1.8	22.8	18.4	−4.4
General	18.2	20.4	2.2	15.2	16.0	0.8
12, total (or average)	23.0	27.1	4.1	16.5	18.9	2.4
Vocational	21.7	24.3	2.6	15.8	17.1	1.3
Commercial	32.2	23.8	−8.4	b	b	—
General	20.6	25.6	5.0	15.8	19.3	3.5
College preparatory	28.8	36.3	7.5	23.7	20.2	−3.5
13-15, total (or average)	36.5	39.2	2.7	26.7	30.5	3.8
Vocational or commercial	b	33.3	—	b	b	—
General	29.1	36.7	7.6	b	23.8	—
College preparatory	40.7	42.3	1.6	b	40.5	—
10-15 total (or average)	22.4	29.1	6.7	16.7	18.4	1.7

[a]Calculated from grouped data.
[b]Not calculated; fewer than 25 sample cases.

least once between 1966 and 1973. Some entered military service during the Vietnam War, and subsequently returned to the sample. Only two of every three out-of-school women were in the labor force in 1968, and this proportion dropped by 1972 as many women took on added family responsibilities.

High school curriculum is clearly *not* a dominant factor in the unemployment of young men and women after they leave high school. Maturation and the business cycle are much more important. Nevertheless, white men from vocational programs, and white and black women who studied business and office subjects, experienced somewhat less unemployment than did their general peers. In some years, the survey week unemployment rate was lower for general than for occupational students, but on the whole, former occupational students were less likely to be jobless. Moreover, despite the fact that occupational men report more spells of unemployment, they were less likely than were their general counterparts to have suffered multiple spells, and the duration of their current, survey week spell was shorter. Unemployment of shorter average duration also characterized the experience of business and office women. Stated reasons for being unemployed (lost job, left job, or "other") indicate that occupational males were somewhat more likely than were their general counterparts to have *lost* their previous job. This was especially true during the 1970-71 recession.

Approximately seven out of ten young men who graduated from vocational programs were employed in craftworker or operative occupations in 1973—a fraction somewhat higher than the average for all men with exactly 12 years of school. Differences among women graduates are more substantial. About seven in ten from business and office programs were clerical workers in 1972, as compared with less than 60 percent from the other curricula. Interestingly, black women graduates from college preparatory programs were somewhat more likely than were respondents from business and office studies to be employed in clerical jobs.

By level of education, it is surprising to find how similar the pattern of occupational assignments is between white male dropouts and graduates. In fact, a slightly higher proportion of the former are in the skilled craftworker category. On the whole, the higher the level of education, the more likely a young man is to be in a white-collar job, and the less likely he is to be a laborer. "Some college" increases substantially the probability of being a white-collar worker. In the case of young women, the occupational distributions are considerably different for dropouts and graduates. Dropouts from the general track are much less likely than are their business and office or academic peers to hold clerical jobs: 22 vs. over 50 percent. Only among respondents with "some college" do black women do about as well as white in terms of the proportion employed in white-collar jobs. In general, higher educational attainment is associated with a greater likelihood of white-collar work, and a lesser likelihood of holding a blue-collar or service job.

Perhaps insufficient time has passed to warrant a conclusion as to whether occupational studies enhance the likelihood of working for oneself. Very few women or black men were self-employed at the most recent follow-up survey. Among white men, 8 percent of the graduates from vocational and 9 percent from general programs were self-employed, a finding of some interest, since some vocational educators argue that occupational skills enhance possibilities for self-employment.

As pointed out in Chapter 2, occupational students are more likely than are their peers to aspire to an occupation for which pre-employment training below the baccalaureate is sometimes available. Interestingly, by 1972, except for black women, occupational graduates were no more likely to hold such jobs than were their general counterparts.

We examined the relationship between high school curriculum (VOC, COM, and CP versus GENERAL), work experience, military service, and postschool training, on the one hand, and several economic outcomes, on the other: hourly rate of pay, earnings, Duncan (or Bose) score, and 1969 full-year earnings for the respondent's occupation. Average earnings in 1969 apply to *all* men (or all women) in the experienced civilian labor force in 1970. We controlled statistically for SA, SEO, and current residence, and for other, related characteristics. Among male graduates in 1971, the coefficient for having been in a vocational curriculum is uniformly negative but not statistically significant for blacks; it is positive, although not significant, for hourly rate of pay ($.10) and earnings ($487) among whites. Even for white graduates, the coefficient is negative for Duncan score and 1969 full-year earnings, two measures of longer-term, potential earnings. Segmenting the sample by curriculum, our years-of-work-experience variable (WEXP) adds *less* to the rate of pay of former vocational than general or college preparatory students.

Among female graduates, the data point consistently to a beneficial effect of having been a business or office student. The coefficient for B&O in both the hourly-wage-rate and earnings regressions is positive and significant for both whites ($.27 per hour, $665 per year) and blacks ($.26 and $683).

Turning to other explanatory variables, we note that mili-

tary service is negatively related to the various economic out-
come measures for white graduates, but positive for blacks.
However, the coefficient of MLSVC is statistically significant in
only one instance, reducing Duncan score for white male graduates by about two points. Perhaps because of the GI bill,
MLSVC is consistently positive (although not statistically significant) for men with some college. The coefficient is uniformly
negative (but not significant) among high school dropouts.

Years of work experience is positive and significant for
both black and white male graduates, although the coefficient is
much smaller for blacks than for whites. The flatter age-earnings
profile among the former, however, may not reflect the trajectory of earnings over time. Our longitudinal analysis indicates
that between 1966 and 1971, hourly rate of pay grew nearly as
much for black as for white men. Indeed, in relative (but not
absolute) terms, black men gained on whites. We speculate,
therefore, that an especially rapid secular improvement in earnings for black men entering the labor market may have flattened
the age-earnings profile.

Postschool training is positive and statistically significant
in nearly all the equations, adding $.40 per hour to the 1971
wage rate of white male graduates, $.24 for black male gradu-
ates, and about $.10 to the hourly wage of white and black
women. Postschool training, for both men and women, makes
as much (or more) difference for high school dropouts as for
graduates or respondents with some college. In our longitudinal
analysis, having had training between 1967 and 1971 added
more to the rate of pay of black than of white male graduates.

Recent years have witnessed a great deal of concern for
occupational sex-segregation. The Education Amendments of
1976 for vocational education place heavy emphasis on reducing sex bias and stereotyping in occupational programs. Regardless of empirical observations as to the relationship between the
sex composition of employment in an occupation and how well
a young woman fares in the labor market, we of course support
the view that young men and women should be encouraged to
consider *all* occupations in making education and career decisions. In 1972, young employed women in the NLS were
heavily concentrated in "female occupations." Furthermore,

controlling for highest year of school completed, the sex composition of a woman's occupation made little difference for
rate of pay or earnings. Not only is the coefficient for typicality of occupation (%FM, OCC_{72}) generally small, but with rare
exceptions it is not statistically significant. Nevertheless, taking
the coefficients at face value, being assigned to an occupation in
which 33 percent of the incumbents are women (instead of 66
percent) adds a modest amount to the pay of women with 10 or
11 years of schooling ($\$.33$ per hour and $\$639$ per year); makes
practically no difference for high school graduates; and actually
subtracts from the earnings of women with 13 to 15 years of
schooling (- $\$.00$ per hour, but - $\$529$ per year).

Since the regression results point to slower growth in
earnings over time for men who were occupational students,
compared to their general and college preparatory peers, we
examined cross-sectionally the occupational assignments of respondents from various programs: first job after leaving school,
1966 job, and 1973 job. The extent of movement between
occupations is great. In 1973, for example, over half the male
graduates were in a different occupation from the one they held
in 1971, just two years earlier. Nevertheless, we note that former vocational students were slightly less likely than were their
general peers to have changed occupations. And of those who
did change, fewer moved to a different major (i.e., one-digit) occupational group. Finally, judging by median Duncan scores,
vocational graduates made less progress over time than did their
counterparts from the other curricula.

5

Psychological Outcomes

A balanced assessment of "curriculum effects" should take into account the psychological implications of having pursued a particular program of studies in high school. Economic well-being and psychological satisfaction are not the same thing, although the two may be related. Economists tend to stress the former, while guidance personnel, among others, typically emphasize the latter. At least one theory of career development (Holland, 1973) takes as its starting point the idea that people choose kinds of work consistent with their basic personalities. In this chapter, we rely on cross-tabulations in examining psychological responses of respondents from various high school curricula. As in the case of unemployment (Chapter 4), we decided against a multivariate analysis, for two reasons. First, we are not aware of a carefully-articulated theory of job satisfaction and of response to earlier education. Second, time and resource constraints led us to put our analytic efforts into other lines of inquiry.

Adequacy of Prior Education

Do young people who have left school feel that their education has been beneficial? Has it met their felt needs? In the base year surveys, young people out of school were asked, "Considering all the experiences you have had in working or looking for jobs since leaving school, do you feel that not having more education has hurt you in any way?" In three out of four sex-race groups, high school graduates from an occupational program were less likely than were their general curriculum counterparts to feel hurt by the absence of additional education (Table 5.1). Differences are especially striking among white men: 28 percent from occupational and 42 percent from general programs felt hurt. The comparable proportions for black women were 50 and 65 percent. The opposite pattern holds only for black men: 69 percent of those from an occupational program report being hurt, compared to 57 percent from a general program of studies. The proportions for white women are uniformly low, and exhibit little variation by curriculum.

Testifying, perhaps, to the value society places on education—in rhetorical terms, at least—an overwhelming majority of

Table 5.1. Perceived adequacy of education and attitude toward high school experience, by curriculum (most recent), sex, and race: men (1966) and women (1968) *not* enrolled, who had completed exactly 12 years of school.

Item and curriculum	Men		Women	
	White	Black	White	Black
Percent who feel not having more education has *hurt:*[a]				
Vocational and commercial (or business and office)	28%	69%	30%	50%
General	42	57	34	65
College preparatory	50	70	38	61
Percent who *desire* more education or training:[a]				
Vocational and commercial (or business and office)	86	97	69	93
General	85	91	71	90
College preparatory	89	100	79	97
Percent who *disliked* high school experience:[a]				
Vocational and commercial (or business and office)	11	0	5	2
General	7	3	10	4
College preparatory	11	0	8	7

[a]See text for precise wording of each question.

youth would like to have more education. More than seven of every ten respondents in each sex-race category responded affirmatively to the question, "If you could, would you like to get more education or training?" Across the board, blacks were more likely than whites to say "yes." And white men were more likely than women to respond affirmatively. Differences by curriculum, however, are slight.

A person's labor market experience is only one of several factors that presumably influence his or her response to the question, "All things considered, how do you feel about your high school experience? Did you like it very much? like it fairly well? dislike it somewhat? dislike it very much?" Very few respondents with exactly 12 years of school said they *disliked* high school.

What Lies Behind these Responses? Following the question as to whether the respondent felt hurt by not having more education or training, the interviewer asked, "Why do you feel this way (either hurt or not hurt)?" Four out of five male graduates who felt hurt by the absence of additional education offered as a reason, not being able to get as good a job as they would like (Table A5.1). Only 4 percent of those from an occupational program, and 9 percent from a general one, cited difficulty in getting *any job*. Miscellaneous "other" reasons accounted for the remainder.[1]

Those who said they wanted more education were asked, "Do you expect that you actually will get this (desired) education or training?" Three out of four male graduates said "yes." With the exception of blacks who had pursued occupational or college preparatory programs, the proportion *expecting* more education was 10 to 15 percentage points below the fraction *desiring* more. The gap between aspiration and expectation was

---

[1] In reason cited for feeling *not hurt,* differences by curriculum and race were minor. Three-quarters of the male graduates offered as a reason, "Have a good job" or "No trouble obtaining a job." One in ten said they didn't need more education (or training) for their job. Monetary advantages of present position and miscellaneous "other" reasons account for the remainder.

nearly 30 percentage points for blacks in the two categories mentioned.

Few high school graduates answered "no" to the questions as to whether they expected to get more education or training. It is possible to compare *reasons* for expecting less than desired by curriculum only for whites. Among white males, former vocational/commercial students were more likely than were their general counterparts to cite financial considerations, inconvenience, and various other reasons. Former general students, on the other hand, more often cited lack of time and family responsibilities. In any event, the precise differences in proportions, which are not reported here, were minor.

Do High School Dropouts and Those with Some College Feel the Same as Graduates? Until this point, nothing has been said about the responses of those with 10 to 11 or 13 to 15 years of school. School leavers were more likely than were graduates to dislike school. Regarding the other questions, male respondents with some college or some high school were slightly more likely than were graduates to feel hurt, to desire more, and to expect more education or training. Differences by curriculum were again minor.

Job Satisfaction

How satisfied are young people with their jobs? In the base years, as well as later, respondents were asked, "How do you feel about the job you have now? Do you like it very much, like it fairly well, dislike it somewhat, or dislike it very much?"[2] About half the youth with 10 to 15 years of school reported liking the jobs "very much" in the base survey years (Table 5.2). In view of the national attention that has been focused on the disadvantaged position of females in the labor market, it is interesting that in almost every race-education category, young women seemed more satisfied with their jobs than did young men. This was true at the base year and at the most recent

[2] For an extensive study of work attitudes based on NLS data, see Andrisani, Appelbaum, Koppel, and Miljus (1977).

follow-up survey. Among whites, 59 percent of women reported liking their jobs very much in 1968, compared to 52 percent of men in 1966. Among blacks, the figures are 49 percent for women and 35 percent for men in the base years. The same general pattern holds in the latest followup: among whites, 52 percent of women said they liked their jobs "very much" versus 42 percent of men; among blacks the comparable figures are 42 and 32 percent.

Among women, level of satisfaction varies directly with level of schooling. This is true for both white and black women at either survey. The mixed results for men are consistent with research by Quinn, Stains, and McCullough (1974), which denies a relationship between schooling and job satisfaction among workers with less than a college degree.

Table 5.2 shows that the proportion highly satisfied declined between the base year survey and the latest followup, especially among high school dropouts. Quinn and his associates reported that "in spite of public speculation to the contrary, there is no conclusive evidence of a widespread, dramatic decline in job satisfaction" (1974, p. 1). However, Andrisani and his colleagues (1977) concluded, on the basis of NLS data from four cohorts, including middle-aged men and women, that: "job satisfaction declined ... during the 1966-1972 period within seven of eight age-sex-race [NLS] groups." They explain that "since virtually all of the decline was from 'highly satisfied' to 'somewhat satisifed,' rather than from 'satisfied' to 'dissatisfied,' it is likely that the oft-cited absence of a downward trend in job satisfaction reported by Quinn *et al.* (1974) resulted from an aggregation bias in their classification of responses to the job satisfaction question."

Does job satisfaction bear a consistent relationship to high school curriculum? Among high school graduates, youth from occupational programs are consistently *more* satisfied with their jobs than are those from the general curriculum. This is true for men and women, blacks and whites. The percentage of graduates from a college preparatory program who like their jobs "very much" is neither consistently higher nor lower than the fraction from other curricula.

Table 5.2. Attitude toward current job, by highest year of school completed, high school curriculum (most recent), sex, and race: employed men (1966, 1971) and employed women (1968, 1972) *not* enrolled in year in question

	Whites			Blacks		
	% who like "very much"		*Percentage difference*	% who like "very much"		*Percentage difference*
	1966(68)	*1971(72)*		*1966(68)*	*1971(72)*	
Men						
10-11, total (or average)	56%	37%	-34%	42%	32%	-25%
12, total (or average)	51	39	-23	32	33	a
Vocational	50	44	-12	53	44	-16
Commercial	68	42	-37	b	b	b
General	48	37	-24	32	30	-5
College preparatory	53	40	-24	45	25	-44
13-15, total (or average)	51	50	-1	34	29	-12
10-15, total (or average)	52	42	-20	35	32	-7
Women						
10-11, total (or average)	53%	45%	-15%	47%	34%	-28%
12, total (or average)	60	52	-13	46	44	-4
Vocational	b	52	b	b	b	b
Business and office	66	54	-18	56	46	-18
General	56	48	-14	38	43	13
College preparatory	53	54	2	54	37	-31
13-15, total (or average)	60	58	-3	66	50	-24
10-15, total (or average)	59	52	-12	49	42	-14

aLess than ±0.5 percent.
bPercent not shown; base less than 25 sample cases.

Perceived Progress and Economic Well-being

Young men, but not women, were asked in 1971, "All in all, so far as your work is concerned, since October 1969, do you think you have progressed, moved backward, or just about held your own?" The higher the respondent's level of education, the larger the proportion who report they have "progressed" in their work and the smaller the fraction who perceive themselves as having "moved backward" (Table 5.3). The ratio of the two responses exceeds ten to one for whites, at each attainment level. Among young black men, however, the ratio exceeds five to one only for general program graduates, and is below three to one for high school dropouts. Fewer blacks than whites report progress; more say they moved backward. Among whites, vocational graduates perceive greater progress in their work than those from the general curriculum. The differences, however, are, on the whole, relatively small.

At various interviews, respondents were asked, "So far as your overall financial position is concerned, would you say you are better off, about the same, or worse off now than you were at this time last year?" Even as the economy entered a recession, most young men and women felt better off in 1971 than in 1970 (Table A5.2). A small number of male graduates (14 percent of the white and 11 percent of the black) felt worse off. Differences by curriculum, controlling for highest year of school completed, are minor.

Perceived Chance of Reaching Occupational Goal

In 1966, when they were 14 to 24 years of age, very few out-of-school young men were in the occupation to which they aspired by age 30: 28 percent of the whites with 10 to 15 years of education, and 11 percent of the blacks (Table 5.4).[3] Black men with 12 to 15 years of schooling were about 20 percentage points more likely than white to be in an occupation different from the one they would like to have (91 and 71 percent).

---

[3] A comparable analysis for women is precluded by the difference in questions asked. See Chapter 2.

Table 5.3. Whether respondents feel they progressed in their work between 1969 and 1971, by highest year of school completed 1971, curriculum (most recent) 1971, and race: men interviewed but *not* enrolled in school, 1971
(N in thousands)

| | Whites | | | | Blacks | | | |
| | | Percent[a] | | Ratio | | Percent[a] | | Ratio |
	N	Progressed	Moved backward	P:MB	N	Progressed	Moved backward	P:MB
10-11, total (or average)	869	58%	5%	11.6	219	38%	14%	2.7
12, total (or average)	3,112	65	6	10.8	408	43	11	3.9
Vocational	534	68	3	22.7	72	36	8	4.5
Commercial	189	61	7	8.7	22	b	b	–
General	1,869	62	6	10.3	275	43	3	14.3
College preparatory	519	70	8	8.8	39	61	15	4.1
13-15, total (or average)	921	72	5	14.4	67	53	11	4.8

a"Held own" is excluded in the percentaging.
bPercent not shown; base less than 25 sample cases.

Table 5.4. Whether occupation desired at age 30 is different from occupation on current (last) job, 1966, and *if so,* perceived chance of reaching goal, by highest year of school completed 1966, high school curriculum (most recent), and race: men *not* enrolled in school, base year
(N in thousands)

| | N | Occupational goal different | Perceived chances (%)[a] | | Ratio E:F or P |
			Excellent	Fair or poor	
Whites					
10-11, total (or average)	852	75%	15%	44%	0.34
12, total (or average)	2,514	71	24	30	0.80
Vocational/commercial	537	70	23	23	1.00
General	1,487	72	26	33	0.79
College preparatory	489	68	21	29	0.72
13-15, total (or average)	596	71	35	18	1.94
10-15, total (or average)	4,040	72	24	31	0.77
Blacks					
10-11, total (or average)	228	85%	14%	43%	0.33
12, total (or average)	324	91	16	34	0.47
Vocational/commercial	63	88	4	46	0.09
General	227	91	16	34	0.47
College preparatory	34	100	33	20	1.65
13-15, total (or average)	45	94	31	32	0.97
10-15, total (or average)	621	89	16	37	0.43

[a]"Good" is not included in the percentaging.

Among both color groups, the more education a person has, the more likely he is to rate his chances of obtaining his goal as "excellent" and the less likely to rate them "fair" or "poor." On the whole, blacks at each attainment level feel their chances are less good than those of whites. Black graduates from an occupational program are the most pessimistic, while blacks from a college preparatory program are among the most optimistic. In each instance, however, the base on which the percentage is calculated is quite small. Among white graduates, curriculum background is essentially unrelated to either being in the occupation to which one aspires, or to the average rating of chances. Although not reported here in detail, young men of either race who judge their chances "fair" or "poor" offer similar reasons when asked why they think their chances are not so good. Less than one percent cite "poor grades." About a third mention "lack of education." Approximately one in seven give "lack of experience" as a reason. Remaining reasons were simply coded as "other."

Summary

Among employed youth no longer attending school, there are several important differences in the likelihood that a person will express certain feelings or attitudes regarding satisfaction and progress at work, and feel satisfied with his or her prior education. Differences in psychological variables exist among youth with 10 to 15 years of school by sex, race, and level of formal education. Black youth, for example, are less likely than white to express dissatisfaction with their high school experience, but are more likely to want additional education or training. Blacks express less satisfaction with their jobs. And, at least among young men (such information is not available for women), black respondents perceive less progress in their work, and feel their chances of reaching their occupational goals at age 30 are not as good, compared to whites.

Regarding "curriculum effects," the findings presented in this chapter may be summarized as follows:

- Except for black male youth, those from occupational programs are *less* likely than are general graduates to feel hurt by not having more education. Of those who do feel hurt, not being able to get as good a job as they would like is the reason most frequently cited.
- Nearly everyone, when asked, says that he or she *wants* more education or training. Among graduates, differences by curriculum are slight. However, those from occupational programs are slightly less likely than are their general program counterparts to *expect* to get more. The small number of black male graduates from occupational programs are noticeably less likely to expect more education or training.

- Fewer than one in ten high school graduates express a *dislike* for their high school experience. Differences by curriculum are slight.

- Except for young white men, in the base year surveys high school graduates from occupational programs were more likely than were their general counterparts to say that they liked their jobs "very much." By 1971 (or 1972), these differences had narrowed.

- Only the men were asked whether they thought they had "progressed," "moved backward," or "held their own" at work between one year and the next. Responses, on the whole, were in the direction of "progressed." Among whites, graduates from vocational programs perceived themselves as making greater progress than did general curriculum graduates. The opposite pattern, however, holds for young black men.

- Again, necessarily restricting attention to the men, very few out-of-school graduates in the base year (1966) were in the occupation to which they aspired at age 30: 29 percent of the whites and 9 percent of the blacks. Asked about their chances of realizing their aspirations, blacks were more pessimistic than were whites, and black youth from occupational programs were especially so.

6

Individuals with
Special Needs

It is often assumed that occupational training is especially important for youth who are disadvantaged or handicapped, and federal vocational education funds are set aside for persons so designated. Manpower programs also target persons who are disadvantaged.

The NLS samples of youth are by no means ideal for assessing the implications of job-related education and training for groups with special needs. This is true for several reasons. First, given the low prevalence nationwide of both foreign language in the home and handicapping conditions, problems of sample size exist, even with a national sample of 5,000 persons. Second, while representative of youth broadly, NLS respondents within population subgroups may not be representative of all persons in such subgroups. Finally, except for race, information from the interviews is very limited concerning disadvantage or handicap. Nevertheless, with due regard to these caveats, we present in this chapter the results of our work on whether occupational education and training improve the employment and psychological well-being of groups with special needs. We begin with a discussion of definitions and measurement problems, followed by presentation of findings on wage rates and earnings. The next section examines occupational mobility patterns, and whether some young men are trapped in what dual labor market theorists call the *secondary labor market.* Finally, we call attention to psychological differences between high school graduates and dropouts.

Definitions and Measurement

Since 1968, Congress has imposed minimum "set-aside" requirements for federal vocational education funds to serve disadvantaged and handicapped persons (15 percent and 10 percent respectively). The Education Amendments of 1976 (Title II, Section 195(7)) define *handicapped persons,* for purposes of vocational education, as "persons who are mentally retarded, hard of hearing, deaf, speech impaired, visually handicapped, seriously emotionally disturbed, crippled, or other health impaired persons who by reason thereof require special education and related services, and who, because of their handicapping condition, cannot succeed in the regular vocational education program without special education assistance or who require a modified vocational education program."

The term *disadvantaged* has been used in many federal categorical programs since the early 1960s. The term is commonly employed, in legislation and elsewhere, in three ways. First, some persons are said to be *economically disadvantaged* if they live in low-income families or lack suitable employment (e.g., long-term unemployed). Second, persons having difficulty in school, or those with low educational attainment (e.g., out of school, with less than 12 years of education) are often said to be *educationally disadvantaged,* if no physical or mental impairment accounts for their lack of educational accomplishment. Finally, members of some minority groups are sometimes said to be *disadvantaged socially or culturally,* if they have grown up in households and neighborhoods outside the mainstream, majority culture, or have limited English-speaking ability.

The Vocational Education Provisions (Title II) of the Education Amendments of 1976 define *disadvantaged* (for vocational education program purposes) as "persons (other than handicapped persons) who have academic or economic handicaps and who require special services and assistance in order to

enable them to succeed in vocational education programs . . ."
Reflecting the absence of agreement on the precise meaning of
the term, the law goes on to say that criteria are to be developed by the Commissioner of Education "based on objective
standards and the most recent available data." It is worth noting
that Title II of the Education Amendments of 1976 does not
mention sociocultural disadvantagement. Other legislation (and
administrative rules), however, does. In the late 1960s and early
1970s, for example, programs under the Manpower Development and Training Act defined *disadvantaged* as persons with
low income and lack of suitable employment, plus one or more
of the following characteristics: school dropout, minority group
member, under 22 years of age (or 45 or older), or
handicapped.

Since passage of the Bilingual Education Act of 1967 (Title VII of the Elementary and Secondary Education Act), the
federal government has maintained a special interest in the
needs of youngsters who live in homes where a language other
than English is spoken. The Education Amendments of 1974
(P.L. 93-380) established a bilingual vocational education program for persons at least 16 years of age who have limited
English-speaking ability. This program was reauthorized by the
1976 Amendments.

Measures of disability (physical and mental impairments)
in the NLS are by no means ideal. Nevertheless, they permit
some examination of the relationship between health-related
conditions and labor market outcomes. A set of questions in the
1971 survey of young men reveals that at that time 299 respondents had functional limitations ranging from "functionally dependent" (36 cases) to "minor loss" (171 cases).[1] In that same
year, 298 respondents reported their work to be limited by
their health.

In this report, we must rely on proxies of disadvantagement. Among youth not enrolled in school, attention is paid to

---

[1] Analagous questions were asked of young women in the 1973 survey, but
only data through 1972 were available for this study.

those who completed 10 or 11 but not 12 years of school.[2]
Because blacks were deliberately oversampled, the NLS is rich
in information on this minority group. A more refined, but
altogether different measure of sociocultural background is
available from a question in the 1971 survey of men: whether a
language other than English was spoken regularly in the respondent's household when he was age 15.[3] In 1971, 85 respondents
named Spanish; 169 others mentioned a language such as Ger-
man or French, for a total of 254 sample cases.

Wage Rate and Earnings

Before considering differences in economic outcomes associated
with high school curriculum, it may be helpful to discuss data
for special needs groups as a whole. Table 6.1 shows average
earnings, rate of pay, and (for those employed at two consecu-
tive survey dates) estimated hours worked in the year preceding
the 1971 interview. To permit comparisons, averages are also
shown for high school dropouts and graduates, and for blacks
with 12 years of schooling.

Among employed individuals reporting health impairments
and health limitations—many of whom are, of course, the same
individuals—the average hourly rates of pay of male graduates
exceeded those of all male respondents with exactly 12 years of
school. Yearly earnings, however, were lower than average for
the group with health limitations, indicating that, on the whole,
health problems had less effect on rate of pay per hour than on
hours worked during the year. Division of annual earnings by
hourly rate of pay reveals that the average number of hours
worked in the year preceding the 1971 survey was 2,027 hours
for *all* graduates employed two years in a row; 1,957 hours for

[2]Those with 10 to 11 years of school represent, of course, only a portion
of out-of-school youth with less than 12 years of school. In 1966, among
young men in the NLS who were not enrolled, 12 percent of the whites
and 23 percent of the blacks had completed 8 years or less (Parnes et al.,
1970, p. 23). Comparable proportions of the out-of-school women in 1968
were 7 and 16 percent (Shea et al., 1971, p. 25).
[3]Again, the analagous question was not asked of the women until 1973.

Table 6.1. **Mean hourly rate of pay 1971, and wage or salary earnings in past
year 1971: selected groups of employed men,** *not* **enrolled in 1971**
(Standard deviations in parentheses)

	$ per hour		Earnings, past year[a]		Estimated hours worked, past year[b]
	N (sample cases)	Mean (SD)	N (sample cases)	Mean (SD)	
10-11 years					
All races, total (or average)	167	$3.37 (1.31)	153	$6,794 (3,190)	2,016
12 years					
Blacks, total (or average)	157	3.04 (1.22)	130	5,999 (2,774)	1,973
All races, total (or average)	803	3.60 (1.48)	724	$7,296 (3,820)	2,027
All races, functional loss[c]	64	3.74 (1.89)	57	7,321 (6,315)	1,957
All races, health limits work[d]	71	3.60 (1.75)	60	6,515 (4,742)	1,810
All races, foreign language in home at age 15	98	3.81 (1.75)	81	7,796 (4,386)	2,046

[a]Limited to those *not* enrolled in either 1970 or 1971.

[b]By division of column 4 by column 2.

[c]Ranges from minor loss to dependent, except that few, if any, of the latter were employed.

[d]Denotes a self-report of a health problem that limits either the kind or amount of work.

those with a functional loss; and 1,810 hours among those reporting health limitations.[4] Not included in the table are young men whose health problems precluded their employment at all. The dispersion of rate of pay and of earnings is much greater

[4]Since we restricted the regressions on which the data on earnings in Table 6.1 are based to those employed for wages or salary in both 1970 and 1971—an adjustment designed to eliminate respondents attending school at the time of the earlier survey—these averages doubtless understate the effect of poor health on hours worked. Not all health problems are chronic, and a disproportionate number experiencing difficulties are probably out of the labor force one year, but in it the next.

among the 60 to 70 employed respondents with health problems than among all respondents. It is probable that differences
in the severity of health difficulties account for this finding.

On the whole, young male graduates who grew up in
homes where a foreign language was spoken report higher-than-
average rates of pay and earnings. Indeed, it appears that no
other group worked as many hours. Since the dispersion in both
measures is great, however, the average hides a great deal of
variation, much of which may be a reflection of geography and
differences among ethnic groups.[5]

Because the experience of dropouts and black graduates
was discussed in Chapter 4, this section will concentrate on the
other groups shown in Table 6.1. However, it is worth noting
that male school leavers worked about the same number of
hours per year as all graduates, and the equivalent of at least
one week more (43 hours) than did blacks with 12 years of
schooling.

Men. Appendix Table A6.1 presents regression results for 1971
hourly rate of pay for each special needs and comparison group
of men, except for those who reported functional health impairments. (Results are included for the slightly larger group reporting health limitations.) For both this group and for those who
grew up in homes where a foreign language was spoken, inadequate numbers in each of the three curriculum categories prevent a conclusion about differences by high school program of
study. When wage or salary earnings are regressed on the same
set of explanatory variables, fewer coefficients are statistically
significant: 15 instead of 18 out of 50 (Tables A6.1 and A6.2).

Regarding relationships evident in Tables A6.1 and A6.2,
several points should be made. Years of work experience is
uniformly positive, and significant in nearly every case. Two
exceptions are in the earnings equation for those with health

---

[5]Most Mexican-Americans live in the Southwest; Puerto Ricans, in New
York City; Cubans, in Florida. The number of sample cases is too small to
permit a comparison based on the language spoken, much less of different
ethnic groups speaking a common language, such as Spanish.

limitations, and for those who grew up in homes where a foreign language was spoken. The first exception is readily understandable. The second exception may reflect the aggregation of ethnic groups with differing labor market experiences. Having had some postschool training is related to a higher rate of pay and earnings, again except for those with health limitations, the group for whom we have the fewest sample cases. It is important to note that training makes as much difference, or more, for dropouts and for graduates from foreign language homes as it does for *all* graduates.

Regarding military service, in none of the ten equations is the coefficient for this dummy variable statistically significant. However, the coefficient is positive for both rate of pay and for earnings among black graduates, and approaches statistical significance in the dollars-per-hour equation. Although they are speculative, we offer two final observations on the regression results. First, among graduates with health limitations, the strong positive influence of scholastic aptitude on rate of pay may mean that cognitive skills are especially useful for youth with health impairments, or that a combination of low aptitude and poor health creates special difficulties.[6] Second, the comparatively large, positive, and statistically significant coefficient for SEO in equations for respondents from foreign language homes may mean that such a language background leads to employment difficulties only in the case of young men from low socioeconomic origins.

Women. In the case of young women, we are not able to say anything about the implications of curriculum and training for groups with special needs. Only eight female respondents with health problems were employed at the time of the 1972 survey. And, as noted earlier, the foreign language question was not asked until 1973.

[6] In this regard, a recent study of the costs and effectiveness of vocational rehabilitation strategies for "individuals most severely handicapped" (IMSH) is of interest. Based on data from Michigan and Washington, Berkeley Planning Associates (1975, p. iv) reached the following conclusion: "The service strategy which emerges as particularly effective for IMSH is university and college education."

As discussed in Chapter 4, young black women who were employed in 1972 profited as much as did white women from business and office studies. The same may be said of women graduates from the lowest third of the mental ability distribution. Indeed, in the wage rate equation the coefficient for B&O is somewhat larger for them than it is for all graduates: $.35 versus $.30 per hour (Table 6.2). There are only 80 sample cases of employed women who dropped out of school after completing grades 10 or 11. Thus it is not possible to make a statement as to curriculum effects for this group. Once again, however, as in the case of young men, having had training makes as much (or more) of a difference for dropouts as it does for graduates.

Occupational Mobility and Growth in Earnings Over Time

From data presented in Chapter 4, and in Tables A6.1 and A6.2, it appears that a year of labor market experience makes considerably less difference for rate of pay and annual earnings of black male graduates and of all dropouts than it does for majority whites with 12 years of schooling. The coefficients in the wage rate equation are 10 cents per hour in the first two instances, and 20 cents in the third.[7] However, this generalization is based on an age-earnings profile. The implicit assumption is that, other things being equal, the typical person at the age of 21 can look forward the next year to what a 22-year-old received this year.

The relatively flat age-earnings relation for blacks and early school leavers seems to support arguments that some culturally or otherwise disadvantaged groups are trapped in a *secondary labor market,* in jobs characterixed by Doeringer and Piore (1971, p. 165) as having "low wages and fringe benefits, poor working conditions, high labor turnover, little chance of advancement, and often arbitrary and capricious supervision." In earlier work using the NLS data for young men, Andrisani (1973) constructed a dual labor market variable, which was added to the public-use tapes. As other researchers before and

[7]The comparable coefficients for earnings are $217, $366, and $585. (See Table A6.2)

Table 6.2. Hourly rate of pay, 1972: regression results for
selected groups of women, not enrolled, employed as
wage or salary workers 1972
(Standard errors in parentheses)

Explanatory variables and statistics	Completed exactly 12 years			Completed 10-11 years
	Total (all races)	Blacks only	Low IQ third	
SA	0.01** (0.003)	0.01** (0.005)	0.01 (0.01)	0.01 (0.01)
SEO	0.03 (0.02)	0.06 (0.04)	−0.01 (0.02)	0.05 (0.05)
	b	b	b	b
$B\&O_{72}{}^a$	0.30** (0.07)	0.27** (0.13)	0.35** (0.09)	b
$CP_{72}{}^a$	0.24** (0.09)	0.02 (0.22)	0.29** (0.13)	b
$WEXP_{72}$	0.09** (0.02)	−0.05 (0.03)	0.08** (0.02)	0.03 (0.02)
TNR_{72}	0.01** (0.002)	0.02** (0.003)	0.002 (0.002)	−0.00 (0.00)
$SMSA_{72}$	0.29** (0.07)	0.13 (0.21)	0.19** (0.09)	0.29** (0.14)
TNG_{72}	0.12* (0.06)	0.14 (0.12)	0.09 (0.10)	0.28** (0.14)
FT_{72}	0.07 (0.08)	0.18 (0.18)	0.09 (0.10)	0.01 (0.14)
CB_{72}	0.42** (0.08)	0.11 (0.12)	0.54** (0.10)	0.93** (0.14)
Constant	0.31 (0.30)	0.47 (0.50)	0.92 (0.49)	0.38 (0.71)
R^2	0.27	0.25	0.23	0.40
F	21.35**	4.60**	8.47**	5.75**
N	599	119	281	80
Mean (Y)	2.58	2.54	2.41	2.25
SD (Y)	0.88	0.69	0.73	0.69

[a]Reference group: general curriculum

[b]Coefficient not reported; inadequate sample cases.

 *Significant at 0.10 level (1 tailed t-test except for curriculum)

**Significant at 0.05 level

since, Andrisani encountered understandable difficulty in constructing a useful proxy for the dual labor market construct. The NLS tapes do not contain measures of career possibilities within the firm, or of "arbitrary and capricious supervision."

Andrisani classified each three-digit Census occupation and industry as "primary," "intermediate," or "secondary," based on median 1959 earnings in the occupation (and industry) in relation to the median earnings of the male labor force, except that all apprentices were defined as "primary," as were all jobs in the construction industry, and the top one-fourth of the 1959 male labor force irrespective of industry.

Among those out of school in 1966, with 10 to 15 years of schooling, 34 percent of the whites but only 18 percent of the blacks had a first job after leaving school in Andrisani's "primary" sector; 39 and 52 percent, respectively, had "secondary" jobs (Table 6.3). The remainder (27 percent of the whites and 30 percent of the blacks, not shown in the table) held first jobs in an "intermediate" category. Because of initial differences in the percentage with jobs in the "primary" and "secondary" sectors, we calculate entry to the primary sector (and escape from the secondary) as a percentage of the maximum *potential* increase (or decrease).

While the data presented in Table 6.3 suggest that the hypothesized barrier between "secondary" and "primary" jobs is not impenetrable, even over a short period of time, differences by race and education do exist that are consistent with arguments advanced by segmented-labor market theorists. Since the data were collected in the initial wave of interviews, the typical youth, not enrolled, had been out of school a very few years. The longest period would apply to dropouts; for example, a 24-year-old who had left school at age 16 would have had 8 years of labor market exposure. A 17-year-old who had dropped out in 1965 would have had one year of labor market experience.

Aside from curriculum differences, to be discussed later in this chapter, the most striking relationships in Table 6.3 are: (1) the absence of much difference between the experience of white dropouts and graduates (both made substantial progress);

Vocational Education and Training

Table 6.3. Dual labor market status, first job after leaving school and current or last job, 1966, by highest year of school completed, high school curriculum (most recent), and race: men *not* enrolled, 1966

	Primary job[a]			Secondary job[a]		
	Percent		Change as % of potential increase[b]	Percent		Change as % of potential decrease
	1st job	1966 job		1st job	1966 job	
Whites						
10-11, total (or average)	24%	61%	49%	52%	22%	−58%
Vocational/commercial	20	62	52	51	14	−73
General	24	60	47	54	24	−56
12, total (or average)	33	59	39	39	21	−46
Vocational	34	55	32	37	24	−35
Commercial	27	70	59	52	13	−75
General	30	57	39	42	22	−48
College preparatory	45	67	40	27	18	−33
13-15, total (or average)	51	74	47	22	11	−50
General	46	76	56	22	9	−59
College preparatory	52	74	46	23	12	−48
10-15, total (or average)	34	62	42	39	20	−49
Blacks						
10-11, total (or average)	12	26	16	57	48	−16
Vocational/commercial	20	32	15	64	28	−56
General	12	26	16	53	55	*
12, total (or average)	20	48	35	48	36	−25
Vocational	20	42	28	56	48	−14
General	15	44	34	47	37	−21
College preparatory	52	72	42	37	24	−35
13-15, total (or average)	27	45	25	39	13	−67
10-15, total (or average)	18	41	28	52	37	−29

[a]See text for description of the variable; jobs in a third, "intermediate" category are excluded from the table.

[b]$\dfrac{1966 \text{ job} - 1\text{st job}}{100 \quad - 1\text{st job}} \times 100$

[c]$\dfrac{- (1\text{st job} - 1966 \text{ job})}{1\text{st job}} \times 100$

*Increase

and (2) the lack of much improvement in the position of many black dropouts, especially the very large number from a general program of studies. While comparable percentages of black general and occupational dropouts gained access to "primary" jobs, the latter were much more likely to escape from Andrisani's "secondary" sector. Black dropouts from occupational programs moved in sizable numbers to the "intermediate" category.

Understandably, on the basis of age alone the first jobs of dropouts were inferior to those of graduates. Despite the unequal start, however, white dropouts caught up to graduates. In 1966, 61 percent of the dropouts and 59 percent of the graduates were in "primary" jobs; 22 and 21 percent, respectively, held "secondary" labor market jobs. Whites from occupational programs did as well as their general counterparts.

Looking at the experience of blacks, one is struck by the near absence of any improvement in the job positions of the 136,000 black dropouts from a general program, who represent nearly three-quarters of the total with 10 to 11 years of schooling. While the proportion in primary jobs rose from 12 to 26 percent, the number in secondary jobs remained essentially unchanged (from 53 to 55 percent). The gap between white and black school leavers widened considerably in the first few years out of school. Black high school graduates made greater progress over (what must be, because of their comparable age) a shorter period of time. However, except for black graduates from a college preparatory program, blacks started quite low and experienced less movement out of the secondary job sector than did their white counterparts. We observe that the small number of black dropouts from occupational programs made considerably more progress than did the general curriculum student in escaping from the secondary category; but that among high school graduates, blacks from a general program reported slightly more progress than did their vocational counterparts.

By and large, the data presented in Table 6.3 conform to expectations based on Andrisani's more thorough analysis of early occupational mobility in the NLS sample of young men. For example, among respondents with 12 or fewer years of schooling, Andrisani found scholastic aptitude to be the only consistently important predictor of "primary" first job status for blacks. As we have shown, graduates from college preparatory curricula, with their higher mental ability scores, did considerably better than did other blacks (Table 6.3).

What about the period since 1966? Despite differences in age-earnings profiles evident in cross-sectional data, longitudinal analysis reveals comparable wage-rate gains for young white and black men over the period 1966 to 1971, by and large a period of economic expansion and firm commitment to progress for minority groups. Table 6.4 shows estimated wage rate increases for out-of-school respondents who were employed at both the 1966 and 1971 survey dates, and whose level of education did not change. The hourly wage rate rose by $.35 per year, on the average, among young white men with 12 years of schooling. It increased nearly as much, by $.31, among comparable blacks. A difference of only four cents per hour per year also separates increases for white and black dropouts. Over the five-year period, hourly rate of pay rose by $.28 per hour per year among whites, and by $.24 among blacks.

While the gap in dollars and cents between young black and white men grew slightly over the five-year period (from $.72 to $.94 per hour among dropouts, and from $.52 to $.70 per hour for graduates), the *relative* gap closed. The difference between graduates and dropouts, on the other hand, increased in both absolute and relative terms, suggesting that graduates are better able than are dropouts to profit from work experience.

What accounts for the apparent inconsistency in the effects of work experience in cross-sectional and longitudinal data? We offer as one hypothesis that relative gains by blacks were especially great for *new* entrants to the work force, generating a relatively flat age-earnings profile over the age range from roughly 16 to 31. Longitudinal data suggest that black male youth, as a group, shared in the economic expansion of the late 1960s. In a recent article on black-white wage differentials, Smith and Welch (1977, p. 325), note that cross-sectional data have encouraged the development of theories that "some

Table 6.4. Comparison of hourly rate of pay, 1966 and 1971, by race and educational attainment: men not enrolled either year, whose highest year of school completed remained unchanged, employed both years as wage or salary worker

(N in thousands)

Educational attainment and year	Whites	Blacks	Ratio B:W	Gap in dollars	Gap as % of black
10-11 years completed (N)	343	30	—	—	—
1966	$2.36	$1.64	0.69	$0.72	44%
1971[a]	3.76	2.82	0.75	0.94	33
1971 - 1966 (5 years)	1.40	1.18	0.84	0.22	19
(1971 - 1966) ÷ 5	0.28	0.24	—	—	—
12 years completed (N)	1,291	101	—	—	—
1966	$2.49	$1.97	0.79	$0.52	26%
1971[a]	4.23	3.53	0.83	0.70	20
1971 - 1966 (5 years)	1.74	1.56	0.90	0.18	12
(1971 - 1966) ÷ 5	0.35	0.31	—	—	—

[a]Calculated; mean of arithmetic change, 1966-71, added to mean rate of pay, 1966.

jobs, those dubbed 'secondary,' are dead-end, with little prospect for career progress in wages and jobs status .... Persons who seemed likely candidates for secondary careers were disproportionately black and less schooled." Relying on Census data, however, Smith and Welch argue persuasively that "cohort effects" lie behind the apparent inconsistency between cross-sectional and longitudinal data:

In [cross-sectional data for 1960 and 1970], black-white wage ratios clearly deteriorate [fall] as experience increases or vintage decreases and the rate of decline is more pronounced at higher levels of school completion. But, the within-cohort changes between 1960 and 1970 are the mirror image of the cross section. Not only did the relative position of blacks improve as they added 10 years of work experience, but this improvement was greatest at higher schooling levels.

Smith and Welch suggest that improvements in the quality of education in the South, which helps blacks disproportionately, may be an important reason for the recent economic gains of young blacks. We wish to add that for young men enrolled in grades 10 to 12 in 1966, and out of school in 1973, years of schooling had a bigger influence for black than for white men on the Duncan score of their 1973 job.[8]

Psychological Outcomes

In Chapter 5, we noted several differences in attitudes and other psychological states of graduates from different curricula. Without going into great detail, we comment briefly here on differences between graduates and dropouts, and within the latter category, between the small number who were enrolled in occupational programs and the much larger number from a general program. Compared to graduates, young men who left school early were: (1) about 7 percentage points more likely to feel hurt by not having more education, and to expect more; and (2) 4 percentage points more likely to want more education. Dropouts from an occupational area—regardless of race—were more likely than were former general students to feel hurt, but less likely to expect more education or training.

We observed in the last chapter that black male graduates were considerably less likely than were white to express a dislike for school: 2 versus 8 percent. The same pattern holds for dropouts, but the proportions who dislike their school experience are considerably larger: 29 percent for whites, and 15 percent for blacks. The most noticeable curriculum difference applies to blacks; 24 percent of the dropouts who had been in an occupational program disliked their schooling, compared to only 13 percent of those from the general program. Although the difference is smaller among white dropouts, the opposite pattern holds: 30 percent of the general, but only 23 percent of the occupational dropouts said they disliked school.

In the case of young women interviewed in 1968, the same intercolor difference in retrospective attitude toward school

---

[8]The regression controlled for SA, SEO, curriculum, and 1966 educational aspirations.

holds. Among graduates, 8 percent of the white women but only 4 percent of the black expressed a dislike for school. Once again, young women who left school early are considerably more likely to say they disliked school: 31 percent for white, and 12 percent for black. By curriculum, there are sufficient cases only for general and for business and office students to detect a difference by curriculum. Among women dropouts, however, the pattern by race is just the opposite of that for men. Among white women who left school after the tenth or eleventh grade, nearly half (47 percent) of those from business and office programs disliked school, compared to 28 percent from the general program. Of black women with comparable school attainment, only 6 percent of the occupational graduates, but 12 percent of the general, expressed dislike.

Regarding job satisfaction, it was noted in Chapter 5 that, across the board, white youth were more likely than were black to say they liked their jobs "very much." It was also pointed out that, among graduates, respondents from occupational programs consistently reported greater job satisfaction than did general curriculum graduates. This is true among dropouts as well; but by 1971, men who had dropped out of occupational programs expressed *less* satisfaction than did their general counterparts. In brief, the sharpest reduction in job satisfaction, as measured by the percent "very much" satisfied, took place among male dropouts from occupational programs.[9] No such reversal is evident in data for young women, but the number of sample cases is small.

As pointed out in Chapter 5, very large proportions of young men *not* enrolled in school aspired to an occupation at age 30 different from the one they held at the initial interview in 1966. Compared to high school graduates of the same race, white dropouts were slightly less likely to be in the job to which they aspired, while black dropouts were slightly more likely. At the same time, however, dropouts were more pessimistic than were graduates about their chances. With respect to curriculum

---

[9] Between 1969 and 1971, dropouts from vocational programs were also three times more likely than general to say they "moved backward" in their work: 15 versus 5 percent.

differences among dropouts, for both color groups, those from occupational programs were slightly more likely than were their general counterparts to want a different occupation by age 30.

Summary

Inadequate numbers of sample cases prevent a conclusion regarding "curriculum effects" on rate of pay and earnings of male high school graduates who reported health limitations on their work or who, at age 15, lived in a home where a foreign language was spoken. In comparison with all graduates, these two "special needs" groups reported higher mean hourly rate of pay. Average annual earnings for the health-limited group, however, were lower than average, presumably as a consequence of adverse effects of poor health on hours worked. Considerable variation around the averages suggests the presence of health problems differing in severity, and inter-ethnic (or geographic) differences as well. The larger number of cases for dropouts and black graduates warrants a more confident assertion regarding curriculum differences within these groups. With respect to dropouts, the coefficient for VOC is positive in both the wage and earnings equations, but not statistically significant. Thus we conclude that vocational program experiences do not hurt, and perhaps help some young men who fail to complete grade 12.

Postschool training generally adds to rate of pay and earnings, and makes as much (or more) difference for male and female dropouts and for male graduates from foreign language homes as it does for all graduates. Having had military experience bears a positive relationship to earnings of black graduates, and is nearly statistically significant in the dollars-per-hour equation. In cross-sectional data, controlling for highest year of school completed, the coefficient for age is uniformly positive and, in most instances, significant. However, the coefficient for dropouts and black graduates is roughly half the size of that for all graduates. This difference seems to support the dualist conception of the labor market—that institutionalized discrimination consigns large numbers of dropouts and blacks to a secondary labor market of jobs, with little opportunity for upward mobility.

Relying on Andrisani's dual labor market variable, black men are more likely than are whites with equivalent years of schooling to have had first jobs in the secondary job sector, and less likely to have had primary jobs. Comparing first job with 1966 job indicates that the boundaries between the primary and secondary labor market are not impenetrable. Yet blacks with 10 to 12 years of school made less progress than did whites in entering primary jobs by 1966. Indeed, black dropouts made the least progress of any group. White dropouts, on the other hand, experienced substantial gains. Indeed, for all practical purposes, they caught up to white graduates. Among those with exactly 12 years of school, large numbers of men of both races moved up occupationally, with the small number of blacks from college preparatory programs doing about as well as their white counterparts. Blacks from a general program were more likely than were those from an occupational curriculum to enter the primary sector, or to escape the secondary. The opposite was true for white graduates, except that the small number of former commercial students did better than the students from a general program. Among dropouts, whites and blacks from occupational programs experienced greater upward mobility than did their general counterparts.

The extent of upward occupational movement seems inconsistent with the small coefficient for work experience among blacks in cross-sectional regressions. Limiting attention to respondents out of school in both 1966 and 1971, rates of pay increased (in absolute terms) nearly as fast for blacks as for whites, and for dropouts as well as for graduates. Indeed, while the gap in dollars-and-cents increased moderately, the *relative* increase for blacks was considerably greater than for whites. In 1966, young black men reported pay rates equal to 69 and 79 percent of those for white dropouts and graduates, respectively. By 1971, the percentages had risen to 75 and 83 percent. In light of recent work by Smith and Welch (1977), we speculate that especially rapid economic gains for black youth entering the labor market over the period 1966 to 1971 may account for the apparent discrepancy between longitudinal and cross-sectional findings.

With respect to psychological measures, several differences exist by level of education and curriculum. Among dropouts, several race-sex-curriculum interactions can be reported, although they defy ready explanation and might even be attributable to sampling error. Men who left high school early are more likely than are graduates to feel that not having more education has hurt them, to want more, and (except for those from an occupational program) to expect more education or training. The differences in proportions, however, are relatively small. The gap between graduates and dropouts is much greater in attitude toward school. While whites were more inclined than blacks to say they disliked school, dropouts in all sex-race groups more frequently expressed dislike than did graduates. Members of the following groups of dropouts were especially likely to say they disliked school: (1) black men and white women from occupational programs; and (2) white men and black women from the general curriculum.

In 1966, male dropouts from occupational programs reported greater job satisfaction than did their general counterparts. However, this pattern was reversed by 1971. Finally, we note that in 1966, white dropouts were more likely than were graduates to aspire to a different occupation at age 30; black dropouts were less likely. All dropouts, however, were more pessimistic than were graduates in judging their chances of reaching their goal.

7

Systemic Effects: In the Labor Market and at Home

So far, our analysis of outcomes has been limited to self-reported earnings and employment and to selected psychological states, such as job satisfaction and attitude toward school. In attempting to assess the economic impact of vocational education, the employer's perspective and do-it-yourself activities deserve more attention than they are usually given. Unfortunately for our purposes, there is nothing in the NLS on the latter, and only indirect evidence bearing on the former.

This chapter begins with a general discussion of the importance of the employer's perspective and of the likelihood that types of education may differ in their difficult-to-measure productivity effects. We then examine the nature and perceived usefulness of postschool training, to see whether such training seems to be complementary with or substitutable for regular schooling. In the next section, we draw attention to the relationship between high school curriculum and characteristics of the respondent's occupation. To be specific, for each respondent's occupation, we examine: (1) its educational requirements and training opportunities; and (2) its specific vocational preparation (SVP) characteristics. We then look at the average size of establishments (i.e., number of workers per unit) in the industry to which the respondent is attached to see if occupational graduates tend to be employed by small firms. Once again, a brief concluding section summarizes our findings.

Do-It-Yourself and Diffused Productivity Effects

There is reason to believe that practical arts and occupational studies may develop skills that are often useful outside an employment relationship. Typewriting for the college student is one example; automobile mechanics and the construction crafts are two others. Most adults have cars, and home improvements are a way to increase assets or avoid expenditures on home maintenance. Aside from studies by home economists, we have not been able to locate research on the implicit value individuals derive from acquiring the ability to meet some of their consumption needs through do-it-yourself activities.

Regarding measured economic outcomes, it is sometimes assumed that if programs of formal occupational preparation were to vanish overnight, employers would provide such training and perhaps do it better, at no cost to the general taxpayer. It has been pointed out that nearly any skill can be learned on the job, but that many skills cannot be learned off the job (Evans, Holter, and Stern, 1976). Several issues are involved here. First, would employers have the incentive to provide the kinds of training schools now provide? Second, who would be selected for such training? Third, would employers be able to provide such training efficiently?

Gordon (1964, 1965) feels that the willingness of employers to engage in training depends, in part, on the tightness of the labor market. She points out that serious issues of equality of opportunity (in access to training) arise any time reliance is placed on company-sponsored training, and that only large firms are inclined to provide much training. The inclination of employers to train may reflect greater incentives or greater training capacity and efficiency in large than in small firms. Based on a review of the training literature, as well as interviews with Air Force and private sector employers, Evans and his associates concluded that the cost-effectiveness of off-the-job and on-the-job training options weigh heavily in employer training decisions.

In their study of employment problems encountered by low-income youth in Houston, Texas, Champagne and Prater (1969) asked company officials to "assess the importance of vocational training when considering a teenager for a full-time job" (p. 159). Of the 63 companies that responded to the question, approximately 43 percent were inclined to give vocational training some weight. The authors noted (p. 160) that: " . . . the establishments surveyed were selected from a manufacturer's directory and each employed a minimum of 100 workers. The vocational graduates of the secondary school level are not traditionally employed in great numbers by such firms, but rather by small establishments, often nonmanufacturing in nature." Hamburger and Wolfson (1969) surveyed 1,000 employers in the New York City area in the mid-1960s, and found that small firms were more likely than medium and large to want their employees to have had vocational courses in the schools.[1] In a Conference Board survey, Lusterman (1976, p. 43) found that only 30 percent of the firms that gave training did so for *new* employees. He writes, "The prevalence of courses for new employees varies, and quite markedly, with company size (small firms often finding it necessary or economical to recruit persons already trained by larger ones), and is well above average in companies engaged in banking, insurance, transportation, or communications, and in utilities."[2] Lusterman (p. 44) notes that the need for theoretical understanding, and the consequences of errors or misjudgments while learning, are two key criteria for where training occurs. "But the main determinant of whether instruction takes place on or off the

[1] A minority were in favor of on-the-job training. Most considered a school-job partnership optimal. One percent said "prefer school training only;" 9 percent "prefer OJT only;" 37 percent, "theory in school and practice OJT;" and 53 percent, "practice training in school and on the job."

[2] At least in transportation, communications, and utilities, there are many skills (e.g., telephone installer, railroad fireman) that are found in few other sectors. Presumably this fact—and its implication that skills, once acquired, are unlikely to be taken eslewhere—provides incentive for both employees and employers to develop specialized occupational skills at work. Moreover, firms in each sector are typically quite large, and thus able to conduct training efficiently.

job, and how the two modes are blended, may simply be cost-efficiency."

It is readily apparent that the most widely-offered vocational programs develop skills for large occupations where tasks are rather standard from employer to employer, and where it would be difficult and costly to develop skills on the job. It is much easier and far less expensive to teach typewriting, bookkeeping—or for that matter television repair and welding—in a shop or classroom than to have to learn the same things on the job. The likely consequences of pre-employment training may be some combination of a slightly higher salary, greater productivity for establishments (and suppliers and others), lower labor costs, and lower prices of goods and services that establishments produce. In other words, the pattern of education in the formal school system may be *rational*, and inattention to these "systemic," more diffused effects of having occupational studies in the schools may understate their economic contribution to the well-being of society.

Regular Schooling and Postschool Training: Complements or Substitutes?

In Chapter 3, we reviewed briefly the relationship between high school curriculum and the extent of postschool training. We observed that:

- Nearly two-thirds of non-college graduate men in 1971, and about half of the out-of-school women in 1972, reported having received some postschool training;
- Dropouts were less likely than were high school graduates to have received training since they left school; and
- Slightly fewer men in occupational programs, but proportionately more business and office women, report postschool training than did their general program counterparts; but among the men, former occupational students were more likely to report company or "other vocational" training, a category that includes apprenticeship.[3]

---

[3] In other words, proportionately more general graduates obtained off-the-job training in technical institutes or took courses in part-time, adult education programs.

Fewer than one in five male respondents who received military training beyond the basic (or recruit) stage reported using such training in their civilian employment, a finding that may account for the apparent absence of a positive effect of military service in the rate-of-pay and earnings equations in Chapter 4. For the other kinds of training, less than half the men reported using such training on their current (or last) job in 1966. Despite this rather low perceived usefulness, training bore a consistently positive relationship to economic outcomes. Black men with 12 to 15 years of schooling acquired a great deal of training between 1966 and 1971, and evidence in Chapter 4 indicates that postschool training was especially beneficial to young black men over this period.

To supplement what was reported earlier, we now consider the nature and perceived usefulness of postschool training. In 1966, 26 percent of the white young men and 14 percent of the blacks who had completed 10 to 15 years of school reported having served in the military; 85 percent of this group reported some post-basic training. The largest fraction (40 percent) received training in the "clerical" area. "Managerial" or "professional" training was reported by 22 percent; military specialties 13 percent; and only 10 percent received training in what the Census Bureau classified as "semi-skilled manual" areas. Thus, specialized military training does not appear to have duplicated the kinds of subjects studied in high school.

Business college or technical institute training may well have complemented occupational subject matter studied by men in the high school. Four-fifths of the training from this source was "professional, technical, or skilled manual." Inadequate numbers of sample cases prevent a statement about the nature of other kinds of postschool training reported by young men. Among young women out of school in 1972, who had exactly 12 years of education, several differences in postschool training are related to high school curriculum. Women from college preparatory programs are more likely than are other graduates to report training: whites, 64 percent, and blacks, 66 percent. They are followed by business and clerical (54 and 60 percent), general (46 percent of both color groups), and other vocational (42 and 46 percent) graduates. This pattern suggests the possibility that some skills acquired in school reduce the need for later training. White women from the academic track are more likely than are their classmates to report professional, technical, and managerial training. The same may be said of black women with business and office backgrounds. Substantial fractions of both business and office and college preparatory graduates received clerical training after leaving school; it is probable that these skills build on or complement the work undertaken in high school (Table 7.1).

It is interesting to examine the nonvocational high school graduates according to whether they received typing or shorthand in high school. Having taken typing courses in high school is related to a greater likelihood of receiving additional training. In fact, the proportions receiving postschool clerical or secretarial training are invariably higher for those with typing or shorthand during school than for those without such courses: for college preparatory white women the figures are 34 versus 21 percent; for general curriculum, white graduates they are 24 versus 15 percent; and the analogous figures for blacks are 56 versus 18, and 23 versus 17 percent. Thus, postschool training received by young women is often related to the program of study taken in school. Yet the bulk of the training was clearly outside of the clerical field, the dominant area of training for women in the high school.

Are skills acquired in formal training programs outside of regular school used in the respondent's line of work? Survey data may not be ideal for answering this question, but the general pattern of perceived use is probably fairly valid. In only one educational attainment category are there sufficient sample cases—and then only for total, all races—to examine a difference by high school curriculum. Among those with exactly 12 years of schooling, respondents from an occupational program are the least likely to say they use skills obtained in their military training on their current (or last), civilian job: 13 percent versus 16 and 40 percent of the general and college preparatory graduates, respectively. This relatively high proportion for former college preparatory students may indicate that some picked up skills not acquired earlier in school.

Table 7.1. Percentage of respondents reporting training based outside regional
school, by highest year of school completed 1972, high school
curriculum (most recent), and race: women *not* enrolled, 1972

(N in thousands)

			Percent reporting			
		Some training (unduplicated count)	Type			
Highest year end curriculum	N		Professional/ technical, managerial	Clerical	Skilled manual	Other
Whites						
10-11, total (or average)	2,303	33%	5%	10%	6%	20%
12, total (or average)	6,501	52	16	26	7	18
Vocational	129	42	11	14	3	25
Business and office	2,061	54	14	31	5	19
General	2,844	46	12	22	8	16
w/typing, shorthand	2,071	49	12	24	8	19
w/o typing, shorthand	768	36	12	15	6	8
College preparatory	1,354	64	27	30	10	20
w/typing, shorthand	913	70	28	33	12	26
w/o typing, shorthand	441	52	27	21	8	8
13-15, total (or average)	1,643	51	31	18	4	17
Blacks						
10-11, total (or average)	661	38	8	9	5	27
12, total (or average)	771	51	15	25	9	18
Vocational	39	46	9	17	3	27
Business and office	160	60	21	29	9	22
General	454	46	14	20	9	15
w/typing, shorthand	278	45	14	22	7	14
w/o typing, shorthand	175	46	13	18	12	18
College preparatory	112	66	16	45	9	18
w/typing, shorthand	80	72	17	56	11	15
w/o typing, shorthand	32	50	14	18	3	24
13-15, total (or average)	141	66	26	33	7	30

The most striking patterns in perceived use of training received outside regular school are:

- Much greater use of company training (61 percent) than of
  training received from other sources, especially military (20
  percent);
- Significantly lower use rates for blacks than for whites, especially for company training (67 vs. 29 percent), business college or technical institute (51 vs. 31 percent), and for other
  vocational training, such as apprenticeship (53 vs. 16 percent).

We are not sure what to make of this second observation, especially in light of the positive relationship between training and
labor market success and the fact that training seems to benefit
blacks as much as whites. It could be that having received training is a sign (a "credential") that influences occupational assignment. In only one case—part-time non-degree-credit course
work taken at schools and colleges—are black youth as likely as
white to perceive that training is used in their civilian occupation (Table 7.2). In general, for both men and women, the
closer the training is to employment, the greater the likelihood
that it is perceived as useful in the respondent's job. Company
training, except for young black men, stands out in this regard.

Training Characteristics of Occupations

Scoville (1969, pp. 80-90), in analyzing the changing job content of the U.S. economy, presented for each three-digit Census
occupation of 1960, two ratings of the skill demands of jobs,
which he obtained from material on workers' traits from the
Dictionary of Occupational Titles (Manpower Administration,
1965, pp. 651-653). The first of the two ratings, called General
Educational Development (GED), is designed to embrace "those
aspects of education (formal and informal) which contribute to
the worker's (a) reasoning development and ability to follow
instruction, and (b) acquisition of 'tool' knowledge, such as language and mathematical skills. It is education of a general nature." The second, termed Specific Vocational Preparation
(SVP), represents the time needed to facilitate "average performance in a specific job-worker situation," and encompasses

Table 7.2. Percentage of respondents with postschool training who report using their training on current (last) job, by type and source of training, sex and race; men *not* enrolled 1966 with 10-15 years of schooling; and women *not* enrolled 1972, with exactly 12 years of schooling

Source and type	Men		Women	
	Whites	*Blacks*	*Whites*	*Blacks*
Source				
Military training	20%	9%	a	a
Business college or technical institute	51	31	40%	26%
Company training	67	29	69	62
Correspondence school	a	a	30	25
Other vocational training	53	16	46	40
Regular courses	47	48	28	22
Type				
Professional, technical	c	c	51%	35%
Managerial	c	c	70	b
Clerical	c	c	51	29
Skilled manual	c	c	45	43
Other	c	c	43	49

aNot included in questionnaire as a specific item; such training included in "other" category.

bNot calculated; base less than 25 sample cases.

cData not reported; items not included on specially-constructed data tape used for analysis

training received in vocational education, apprenticeship programs, in-plant and on-the-job training, and experience in other jobs. Both measures are designed to reflect occupational skill level by estimating the general (GED) and specific (SVP) preparation required for average performance in jobs in the given occupational category.[4]

[4] The measures, while not based on an analysis of the characteristics of workers, are undoubtedly influenced by realities of the labor market. Eckaus (1964) and Scoville (1966) are apparently the first to make use of these measures in empirical application. Subsequent criticism has concentrated on the interpretation of GED scoring as "years of school required" (Fine, 1968). We recognize the legitimacy of this criticism, and urge the reader not to infer that *young* workers in jobs with GED ratings below their attainment are "overqualified." Such a conclusion is *not* warranted.

Judged by median GED and SVP scores, the occupational assignments of young black men in 1971 were noticeably inferior to those of white at each educational attainment level (Table 7.3). Only among white graduates from vocational programs are GED and SVP scores higher, on the average, than those of their general counterparts. Thus, aside from this important exception, it appears that former vocational students are no more likely to obtain jobs calling for extensive specific vocational preparation. Among young women in 1972, who had exactly 12 years of schooling, average (mean) GED and SVP scores are again higher for whites than for blacks: 10.30 and 0.89 in the case of white women, versus 9.96 and 0.86 for black. Multiple regression analysis suggests that graduates of business and office programs take jobs with higher GED and SVP ratings than is typical of their peers who graduated from

Table 7.3. Median General Educational Development (GED) and Specific Vocational Preparation (SVP) scores for occupation of current (or last) job 1971, by highest year of school completed, high school curriculum (most recent), and race: men *not* enrolled (N in thousands)

	Whites			Blacks		
	N	GED	SVP	N	GED	SVP
10-11, total (or average)	905	9.8	1.05	228	8.5	0.71
Vocational	129	8.8	0.78	34	8.6	0.76
General	94	9.4	0.87	11	a	a
College preparatory	662	10.0	1.10	169	8.5	0.76
12, total (or average)	3,650	10.4	1.24	487	8.9	0.75
Vocational	581	10.6	1.64	86	8.7	0.69
Commercial	209	10.1	0.91	25	9.7	0.76
General	2,169	10.3	1.07	321	8.7	0.75
College preparatory	692	10.8	1.52	56	9.6	0.87
13-15, total (or average)	1,458	11.1	1.78	90	10.1	0.77
Vocational	107	10.8	1.50	10	a	a
General	776	11.1	1.65	35	10.3	0.84
College preparatory	545	11.3	2.05	44	10.0	0.68

[a]Median not shown; base less than 25 sample cases.

the general curriculum. However, only the B&O coefficient of 0.40 for white women is statistically significant. Former academic students are especially likely to be in jobs with higher-than-average SVP scores, a finding that is somewhat suprising, since presumably their high school curriculum was not intended to develop specific occupational skills.

GED and SVP scores for each 1960 Census occupation are presented in Appendix C. Listed below are illustrative occupations with SVP scores in the general vicinity of the average SVP scores for high school graduates in the two cohorts:

Mechanics and repairmen, automobile	1.66
Bakers	1.54
Structural metal workers	1.47
Firemen, fire protection	1.26
Janitors and sextons	1.21
Farm laborers, wage workers	1.20
Rollers and roll hands, metals	1.02
Packers and wrappers, n.e.c.*	0.98
Millers, grain, flour, feed, etc.	0.97
Housekeepers	0.94
Salesmen and sales clerks, n.e.c.*	0.82
Excavating, grading, and machinery operatives	0.82
Postal clerks	0.79
Stock clerks and storekeepers	0.79
File clerks	0.79
Bus drivers	0.75
Laundry and dry cleaning operatives	0.63
Welders and flame-cutters	0.61
Waiters and waitresses	0.61
Secretaries	0.58
Typists	0.58
Laborers, n.e.c.*	0.46

*n.e.c.—not elsewhere classified

We draw attention to the low scores for typists and secretaries. We suspect that job analysts have rated the SVP characteristics of these occupations based on the kinds of competencies that people bring to the job market from regular school. If a person learns secretarial work in high school, it may take no more than six-tenths of a year to reach "average performance" in secretarial work. Nevertheless, our intuition tells us that SVP scores may be significantly off the mark for many occupations.

In the most recent interview for which data are available, male graduates from occupational programs are no more likely than are their general peers to hold occupations for which some preemployment preparation is available (Table 7.4). Women from business and office programs, on the other hand, are somewhat more likely than are their general counterparts to hold such jobs.

Size of Employing Establishments

Following from our earlier discussion of human capital theory and the socially optimal division of training responsibility between schools and employers, we now look at the size-of-establishment characteristics of the industries within which respondents work. Unfortunately for our purposes, the NLS questionnaires through 1973 did not elicit information on the size of the establishment or company for which respondents worked. (This has been remedied in later surveys, the results of which are not available to us at this time.) We use as a proxy the number of employees per establishment in each industry. Since 1964, the Bureau of the Census has issued an annual report on *County Business Patterns*. We used 1973 data, based on reports of employers covering 61.3 million workers, or 69 percent of total employment in that year.[5] Appendix B shows employees per establishment for each of the three-digit Census industries for which information is available.

The average size of establishments is small in agriculture, construction, in several sectors within transportation and public

---

[5] Employment and payroll information is reported to the Social Security Administration on Treasury Form 94. Excluded from the count were 8.2 million self-employed persons, nearly 14 million government workers, and employees of the nation's railroads.

Table 7.4. Pre-employment educational requirements and opportunities for occupation on current (or last) job by highest year of school completed, high school curriculum (most recent), sex and race: men (1973) and women (1972) *not* enrolled in school[a]

(N in thousands)

	N	Occupation requires college 4+	Other pre-employment training available	No special requirements
			Men	
Whites				
10-11, total (or average)[b]	602	10%	41%	49%
12, total (or average)	3,441	15	48	37
Vocational	564	11	49	40
Commercial	194	18	34	48
General	2,085	16	48	36
College preparatory	597	19	48	33
13-15, total (or average)	1,738	29	41	30
10-15, total (or average)	6,664	18	45	37
Blacks				
10-11, total (or average)[b]	174	2	32	66
12, total (or average)	394	6	45	48
Vocational	77	4	45	51
Commercial	13	c	c	c
General	251	4	49	47
College preparatory	53	14	35	51
13-15, total (or average)	118	13	30	57
10-15, total (or average)	864	6	40	54
			Women	
Whites				
12, total (or average)[b]	3,597	6%	62%	32%
Vocational	106	11	62	26
Business and office	1,180	4	64	32
General	1,384	7	62	31
College preparatory	854	8	57	35
Blacks				
12, total (or average)[b]	408	3	60	37
Vocational	16	c	c	c
Business and office	98	3	70	37
General	233	3	61	37
College preparatory	51	0	44	56

[a]Data for women restricted to employed full-time wage or salary workers.

[b]Detail may not add to 100 percent due to rounding.

[c]Percent not shown; base less than 25 sample cases.

utilities, in trade, in finance, insurance, and real estate, and in most services. Industries with an average of 300 or more employees per unit include: (1) blast furnaces, steel works, and rolling and finishing mills (537); (2) manufacturers of aircraft and parts (473); (3) manufacturers of synthetic fibers (934); and (4) hospitals (377).

Interestingly, the average establishment size within industries to which young black men with exactly 12 years of school are attached is higher than it is for whites: 91 versus 68 (Table 7.5). We had expected, on the basis of dual labor market theory, that young black men would be congregated in industries characterized by small average size of firm. The larger the firm, presumably the greater the chance for a person to find a place on an internal promotion ladder. We suspect that for the present generation of young blacks, being located in major metropolitan areas is a factor explaining the large average size of industries in which they are employed. In addition, affirmative action and manpower programs may have helped young blacks to get jobs in sectors with relatively large establishments.

We regressed the average size of establishment of the respondent's industry on the same set of explanatory variables used in our earlier analysis of rate of pay and earnings. For black men but not white, with exactly 12 years of schooling, the coefficient for VOC is not only negative, but statistically significant. For black men, having been a vocational student is associated with 35 fewer employees per establishment, a finding consistent with our theoretical expectations. The VOC coefficient among white graduates, while negative, is small and not statistically significant.

The relationship between having had postschool training and size of establishment is positive, although statistically significant only for blacks. The positive sign is consistent with the supposition that larger firms have greater capacity as well as incentive to provide training internally. Other than the positive SEO coefficient for black graduates, the only variable in the model strongly related to size of firm is collective bargaining coverage.

Table 7.5. Number of employees per establishment in 3-digit
industry to which attached: regression results for men
with exactly 12 years of education, *not* enrolled
in 1971
(Standard errors in parentheses)

	Total all races	Whites	Blacks
SA	-0.11 (0.32)	0.14 (0.41)	0.18 (0.70)
SEO	-1.17 (2.28)	-1.93 (2.73)	11.65** (5.80)
VOC_{71}[a]	-6.99 (10.46)	-2.13 (12.19)	-35.23* (23.72)
COM_{71}[a]	12.95 (16.63)	8.00 (18.91)	52.29 (40.52)
CP_{71}[a]	-0.42 (14.71)	-0.53 (12.24)	1.41 (29.48)
$WEXP_{71}$	0.91 (1.72)	1.20 (1.95)	1.57 (4.15)
$MLSVC_{71}$	-0.73 (8.04)	-3.83 (9.04)	26.95 (19.27)
$SOUTH_{71}$	9.37 (8.87)	13.03 (10.30)	-26.60 (20.96)
$SMSA_{71}$	8.87 (8.68)	4.83 (10.49)	-10.56 (20.67)
$TNG(IM)_{71}$	5.93 (8.08)	0.97 (9.22)	34.89** (17.82)
CB_{71}	57.79** (8.02)	60.43** (9.11)	20.10 (18.99)
Constant	55.56	37.83	-47.33
R^2	0.07	0.07	0.13
F	5.84**	4.25**	2.21**
N	836	645	180
Mean (Y)	70.58	67.88	90.77
SD (Y)	113.05	111.97	120.23

[a]Reference group: *general* curriculum.

*Significant at 0.10 level (2-tailed t test except for VOC_{71} and $TNG(IM)_{71}$).

**Significant at 0.05 level.

Summary

‿‿apter, we have explored possible "curriculum effects," which are difficult to measure, and about which we have relatively little information from the NLS. Although conceivably very important—given the volume of economic activity that takes place outside the marketplace—we can do little more than speculate as to the do-it-yourself implications of high school curriculum. Many skills developed in occupational programs may be useful at home: typewriting, automobile repair, construction crafts, cooking and sewing, hairdressing, and so forth.

We doubt seriously that skills acquired after high school are redundant, or that postschool training options are to any substantial degree duplicative. Postschool training is pervasive; men from vocational programs are about as likely as are their general peers to have received postschool training. However, the form is often different. Former general students are more likely to have received school-based training (e.g., in technical institutes); former vocational students more frequently report company training or "other vocational," a category that includes apprenticeship. Very little specialized military training is "semiskilled manual," an area that is the heart of high school vocational experiences for men. Only about one-quarter of the postschool training reported by women is "clerical," the field in which most high school girls report having had courses. Proportionately more college preparatory than other women report postschool training. We suspect the reason is that many academic women simply postponed acquisition of special occupational skills until after high school, at least among those who did not go to college.

It is of interest that less than half the respondents feel that they use their postschool training in their jobs. Except for black men, respondents more often view company-sponsored training as being used than training from other sources. In 1966, black men less often than white saw their training as useful. Nevertheless, as pointed out in Chapter 4, such training (especially from 1966 onward) seems to have been at least as valuable for blacks. Since the GED and SVP scores for the occupations held by black men remain considerably lower than for their white counterparts, many black men may find themselves in jobs that fail to utilize their acquired skills.

We find SVP ratings suspect in many cases. In particular, the score accorded typists and secretaries (0.6 of a year) seems low. Despite this observation, white women graduates from business and office programs, and white men from vocational programs, have occupations that, on the average, have higher SVP scores than do their general peers. The acquisition of occupational skills in school may have helped them obtain more demanding jobs.

As would be expected, occupational students in high school are more likely than are their peers to aspire to jobs for which some pre-employment training opportunities below the baccalaureate are available. Yet, by the early 1970s, former occupational students were no more likely than were their general peers to hold jobs in this category, and were as likely to have jobs for which there are "no special requirements." The same statement, however, does not apply to the women. Female respondents from business and office programs are more likely than are their peers to hold jobs for which pre-employment training may be required or preferred.

Both human capital theory and past research suggest that the kinds of occupational skills developed in schools may be socially rational in the sense that (1) school-based training is more cost-effective, or (2) employers would not have sufficient incentives to develop skills at the work place. Specialized occupational competencies (such as typewriting and welding) are by no means *specific,* in Becker's sense, if these skills are common to a large number of employers. Reflection suggests that it is cheaper and probably more effective to teach 25 students how to operate a typewriter in a classroom than to leave the acquisition of this skill to the workplace. In general, one would expect smaller firms, in particular, to be less efficient than large firms in developing skills at the work place. This line of reasoning suggests that schools may tend to develop skills commonly employed in smaller establishments. Our measure of size of firm— an overall average from each industry—is not ideal. Nevertheless, we find that, at least for young black men, students from vocational programs are employed in industries with lower-than-average mean size of establishment. Consistent with past research, on the other hand, having had some postschool training is positively associated with industry average size of establishment. While our analysis of difficult-to-measure productivity effects is necessarily limited by the absence of appropriate measures, we judge this exploratory analysis to be of sufficient interest to stimulate additional research.

8

Conclusions and Recommendations

We began this research project in the hope of answering three basic questions about occupational training:

- Who gets it?
- Why? (For example, to what extent does a person's curriculum reflect informed choice, rather than "tracking" by school personnel?)
- What difference does it make?

So far, we have described the study's methods and presented our empirical results. In this chapter, we briefly highlight several findings, offer interpretations of them, and assess some of the implications of our work for improved education and training, and for further research.

First, however, a brief review is in order. This study is based on data from two of four cohorts in the National Longitudinal Surveys (NLS) of Labor Market Experience: men 14 to 24 years of age when first interviewed in 1966, and women of the same age in 1968. The data used in this study were collected in the surveys of men from 1966 to 1973, and in the surveys of women from 1968 to 1972. This study expands on earlier work by the authors (Grasso and Shea, 1973; Grasso, 1975), which confined analysis to data from the men's surveys through 1969. The present study not only includes more recent data, but expands the earlier work in three basic ways. First, this study is based on data for women as well as for men. Second, it includes analysis of topics not addressed earlier, such as the effects of curriculum on persistence in school and on the transition to college. Third, while the earlier work was confined to high school graduates who did not attend college, this study includes selected analyses for high school dropouts, and for those with from one to three years of college but less than a baccalaureate degree.

Highlights: What did we find?

Some critics of high school vocational programs have claimed that they serve as a "dumping ground" for low-status and low-ability youth. Evidence from Project Talent, based on a 1960 sample of high school students (Evans and Galloway, 1973), and from the Youth-in-Transition sample of 1966 high school sophomore boys (Bachman, 1972) reveals that, for young men at least, the average vocational student ranked below the average student in a general program in academic aptitude and in family socioeconomic level.

Our data, however, show that vocational and general students do not differ very much, on the average, with respect to social class background and mental ability. Judging from our NLS data, and ignoring college preparatory students, neither the vocational nor the general program seems to be a dumping ground. Our results, incidentally, agree with those based on the National Longitudinal Study of the High School Class of 1972 (Echternacht, 1975), where differences in academic ability between vocational and general students were not statistically significant.

The NLS data shed new light on the probable reasons that some students find their way into vocational programs. Students from all curricula tend to enjoy vocational classes, although students in occupational curricula and those with relatively low scholastic aptitude are somewhat more likely than are others to feel this way. In short, vocational offerings are psychologically congenial for many young people.

Is curriculum assignment congruent with educational and occupational goals? On the whole, the answer is yes. Nearly all the white girls in business and office studies in the late 1960s wanted only to complete high school. Among young black men in high school, however, 40 percent of vocational and over 50 percent of commercial students aspired to four or more years of college—a level of education presumably better facilitated by a more academic program.

Wise curricular choices require adequate information about career opportunities and about the consequences of pursuing alternative education and training options. Unfortunately, the NLS data do not permit detailed analysis of the breadth and depth of students' understanding of available options. However, respondents were questioned to elicit their knowledge of occupations. At least among the boys, vocational students had less information about career opportunities than did their counterparts from the general curriculum. Not only does this finding raise a serious question about the adequacy of guidance counseling, but it also implies that "tracking" and nonvocational purposes may be among the reasons why many male students enter a vocational program.

Proponents of vocational education have long claimed that practical studies encourage young people to complete at least a high school education. Our findings for young women support this claim, but our analysis of the experience of young men yields mixed results. The NLS data show that between the ninth and twelfth grades, some students move from one curriculum to another, with a net increase in vocational enrollments from one year to the next. This "net flow" toward vocational studies, among those who stay in school, contributes to a positive association between enrollment in a vocational program and grade in high school. The shift also imparts a positive bias to any cross-sectional regression results linking most recent curriculum to highest year of school completed (through grade 12). Longitudinal data make it possible to trace students from one year to the next. In the NLS, among the young men who began a high school year in a certain curriculum, those in a general program were somewhat more likely than were their vocational peers to complete that year. In other words, longitudinal and cross-sectional results for men (but not for women) disagree on whether vocational programs seem, on balance, to prevent dropping out of high school.

On the related matter of transition to college, enrollment in a vocational program, among women as well as men, reduces the likelihood of high school graduates completing at least one year of college. This finding holds even after taking account of the lower educational goals of vocational than of general students.

A related point is the way in which aspirations change among students in various curriculum groups. For some vocational students, relatively low educational goals undoubtedly precede their enrollment in a vocational program. Among high school boys in the NLS who started with lower-than-average goals, staying in a vocational program for two years in a row was more often associated with a reduction than with an increase in aspirations from one year to the next. (The reverse was true for young men in college preparatory programs, whose exceedingly high goals went even higher.)

The long-run, secular increase in educational attainment of the population is applauded by most Americans. By this logic, the lower goals and attainments of vocational students might be regarded as a shortfall. We suggest, however, that as long as choice is exercised, and as long as vocational programs serve the psychological and economic needs of individuals, lower goals and educational attainment should not necessarily be considered negative factors.

We failed to find convincing evidence of an alleged labor market advantage of vocational education for young men. We did, however, find consistent labor market benefits of occupational training for young women. On the whole, the experience of the average male graduate of a vocational program who did not go on to college was not substantially different from that of the average general program graduate. Differences were either inconsistent or were not statistically significant on virtually every criterion measure: unemployment, occupation, hourly rate of pay, annual earnings, and so on. On the other hand, young women who had graduated from high school in business and office programs reported, on the average, higher hourly wages and higher annual earnings than did their counterparts from general programs. Moreover, young women from occupational programs with exactly 12 years of school reported less unemployment than did their general program peers. Nevertheless, the curriculum difference in joblessness was small, and the year-to-year pattern of unemployment reveals the predominant influence of general economic conditions from the mid-1960s to the early part of this decade.

Despite the absence of a clear economic advantage to male high school graduates from a vocational program, they were less likely than were their peers from a general program to "feel hurt" by a lack of additional education. This statement, however, does not apply to young black men. It is also true that, as of our latest follow-up data, vocational graduates were more likely than were their general curriculum counterparts to report enjoying their jobs. Thus we can say that for those young men who do not go on to college (at least for the white majority), vocational programs represent a choice at the high school level that meets at least psychological needs, both immediately and in their first few years out of school.

Implications for Policy and Practice

As we see it, our research has practical importance for guidance personnel, educators, those in charge of employment and training programs, and policymakers at state and federal levels. We make this assertion in full awareness that conditions have changed over the past fifteen years, and that some relationships found in the experience of youth in the late 1960s and early 1970s may no longer hold. With this caveat, we advance recommendations for change in policy and practice in the following four areas:

- We would urge educators and policymakers to avoid an overly narrow definition of program "success," and to ask for multidimensional indicators in evaluative research on curricula. Judgments of the worth of curricular options should go well beyond expressions of intent (e.g., to develop "marketable skills") and training-related placement rates to embrace such matters as: (1) congruence with an individual's career objectives; (2) differences in learning styles; (3) nonvocational purposes; (4) psychological satisfaction; (5) influence on eventual educational attainments; (6) short- and longer-term economic benefits to the individual; (7) social efficiency at the work place; (8) ability to fulfill the aspirations of persons with special needs (e.g., the physically handicapped); and (9) cost-effectiveness.

Consistent with this perspective, we feel it would be myopic to condemn vocational education for boys in high school either because there seems to be no obvious economic advantage over peers from a more general program, or because vocational education may dampen aspirations and highest year of school eventually completed. Our perspective on student satisfaction with courses in school is the same. We would not advocate expansion of vocational education for boys on the basis of any single indicator, economic or psychological.

With respect to young women, however, the bulk of the evidence is clearly favorable for those who took business or office studies, and we would take a stronger stand in favor of occupational training. We fully realize that some observers may reach different conclusions. For example, those who believe that "occupational crowding" of women into a small subset of occupations is detrimental to women generally—and to men as well—may take a different view. We favor expansion of career horizons, but recognize the value of business and clerical skills.

- Our research points up the perennial need for greater sophistication in career guidance work. Informed education and career choices depend, in part, on accurate, useful information about opportunities. Yet among both white and black males, those students from vocational programs possessed somewhat less information about occupations than did their counterparts from a general curriculum. Although we believe that some "unrealism" in the aspirations of youth in school is a good thing, in part because it encourages completion of high school, our research also shows that among black males, those enrolled in vocational programs possessed, on the average, higher scholastic aptitude and higher educational goals than did their general peers. Despite this fact, their enrollment in vocational programs seems to have depressed their educational attainment. We suspect that, at least in the late 1960s, many young black men were in programs not fully congruent with their educational goals, and that such programs did not serve their needs as well as more general offerings would. We admit, however, that other plausible explanations exist—one being that attractive employment opportunities in urban areas in the mid-1960s may have induced some vocational students to cut short their educational plans. Needless to say, there is room for further research on this topic.

In some ways, our finding that out-of-school young women from business and office programs received higher hourly wages and annual earnings than did their general peers is ironic. Especially in recent years, vocational programs in general, and business and office programs specifically, have been sharply criticized on grounds of sex bias. The logic of the criticism is that secondary-level vocational programs are largely sex-stereotypic, and lead to occupational sex-segregation and ultimately to an earnings disadvantage for women.

Our data confirm that enrollments in occupational programs during the period were largely sex-stereotypic and may have contributed to occupational sex-segregation. However, our data also reveal that business and office graduates enjoyed an earnings advantage over their peers from the general curriculum. In a separate analysis of the influence on earnings of the sex-typicality of the occupations in which young women were employed, we found that sex-stereotyping was not necessarily associated with an earnings disadvantage. In fact, among the NLS women with some college, but less than a baccalaureate degree, those in more traditional occupations earned more per year than those in less traditional jobs. For high school graduates, there was no significant difference in annual earnings.

We feel strongly that sex-stereotyping and bias *per se* should be eliminated wherever it exists. It is unfair, frequently illegal, and unnecessarily constrains freedom of choice for both women and men. It can have pernicious economic effects on individuals and on society. Yet there is at least short-run value for some (perhaps many) women in some typically-female jobs, and guidance of individuals should be sensitive to this fact. At least in the early 1970s, many young women with business and office skills enjoyed abudant employment opportunities and good chances for reentry to the labor force.

It may be extremely difficult for a young women in high school to orient herself to and actually enter a traditionally-male, high-school-level occupation, such as a blue-collar skilled trade. (Of course, we are not against trying.) But failure to enroll in some kind of occupational program may later lead to a job somewhere between the typically-male and typically-female occupations, and to an earnings disadvantage. We suggest, therefore, that counselors consider all of the alternatives facing young women in high school, and not expend their energies on merely dissuading young women from entering traditional fields. Such a stance would be a disservice, if "nontraditional" alternatives are not available.

• At least since 1963, many commentators on American education have expressed a belief that vocational education is especially important for boys and girls with "special needs" stemming from a handicap of some sort, or from economic, educational, or social disadvantages. In this study we tried (largely unsuccessfully, for reasons of sample size) to analyze the effects of vocational education on disadvantaged and handicapped youth. We were forced to rely on rather crude measures to identify these populations. Small numbers of cases—for example, of those with physical disabilities—thwarted completion of much of the planned analysis. Only in comparing the experience of blacks with that of whites were there sufficient sample cases to draw worthwhile conclusions.

In this regard, we did not uncover any evidence indicating that vocational programs of the 1960s were especially beneficial for young black men. On the other hand, black female business and office graduates enjoyed the same wage advantage as did young white females from the same programs.

It may make sense, of course, to allocate extra federal or state funds for vocational education to areas with high concentrations of handicapped or disadvantaged persons. In light of above-average unit costs, one can argue for such a position on purely fiscal grounds. It is not clear, however, that minority groups are especially in need of vocational education, nor that students operating substantially below grade level, or from low-income families, or with handicaps, would be especially well served by existing vocational education efforts. Vocational education may or may not be especially helpful to and desired by such persons.

- This study supports proponents of greater encouragement of post-high-school, noncollegiate forms of training. (It supports collegiate forms as well.) Most young men and women in the NLS who completed their formal schooling upon completion of high school reported having received some type of training after graduation. Such training was acquired in business colleges and technical institutes, in apprenticeships, in the military service, in company-sponsored programs, and elsewhere. Much of the postschool training seems to have complemented skills acquired in high school. Among the women, for example, those who had received instruction in typing and shorthand in high school were more likely than were their peers to receive additional postschool clerical and secretarial training. Among the men, general curriculum graduates were especially likely to receive business school and technical institute training, while vocational graduates were likely to get company-sponsored and other vocational training.

Postschool training for out-of-school youth in the NLS was important for three reasons. First, non-formal education and training opportunities added a degree of egalitarianism. When educational attainment is defined in terms of level of formal schooling completed, such attainment is strongly related to socioeconomic origin and scholastic aptitude. The influence of social class background and mental ability is much less potent when "attainment" is viewed more broadly to include both collegiate and noncollegiate forms of training. Second, among the NLS men at least, blacks were less likely than were whites to have had any postschool training in 1966, but the relative gap closed considerably over the next five years, attesting perhaps to the success of equal opportunity efforts and manpower training programs. Finally, postschool training was associated with clear economic benefits in terms of hourly rate of pay, and the benefits were distributed in such a way as to reduce economic inequalities. Specifically, postschool training for men in the NLS contributed to a larger percentage increase in pay for blacks than for whites, and helped to close, in relative but not absolute terms, the wage gap between these two color groups over the period 1966 to 1971.[1] Moreover, among both men and women, postschool training appears to have yielded benefits, as measured by hourly wages, at least as high for high school dropouts as for graduates. Although an absence of data on the costs of training prevents comparison of benefits with costs, training appears to have been a significant factor in career preparation and career establishment of young people over the period for which we have data.

Before turning to the matter of what additional research would be especially useful, we would like to review briefly the main reasons for caution in basing policy decisions solely on the findings we have presented and on our interpretation of them. One reason for caution is inherent in nearly all studies of curriculum impact—namely, the fact that most students select their own program. This raises a question as to whether inferences about the impact of a program are correct. Self-selection into programs may mask "effects" inferred from a comparison of ostensibly similar students in occupational and general programs. A second problem is in drawing policy implications from findings based on long-run followups. The extent to which past conditions currently apply is uncertain. This point is important

---

[1] The postschool training data for women were not analyzed in as much detail for two interrelated reasons: less time had passed since the first survey, and the number of sample cases for out-of-school employed women was inadequate.

in view of the continual evolution of school curricula since the 1960s in various areas of the country. Our findings should be seen in their historical context. The institution of vocational education, as well as the youth labor market, has undergone change since the mid-1960s, necessitating periodic reassessment of results.

Additional Research

At various points in the report, we have pointed out lines of research that we consider potentially fruitful in understanding access to and the impact of occupational training. In concluding our report, we summarize these suggestions.

- For reasons of sample size, we have not been able to say much about the appropriateness of vocational education for youth with special needs (e.g., handicapped or disadvantaged persons). Yet we feel that it is especially important to know what kinds of education and training experiences are most useful for persons in such categories, and for others such as young women who leave school early due to marriage or pregnancy.

- On a related point, the NLS data do not contain information that might be used to investigate the effects of curriculum on achievement in basic skills. Vocational programs may have both a positive influence, through demonstrating the real-world applicability of academic subjects, and a negative influence, by virtue of less time spent directly on the development of basic skills. Business and office programs often build on basic competencies in language and mathematics, whereas this may not be as true of some skilled manual training. Could this fact partially account for the sex difference in the usefulness of occupational studies reported here? In our judgment, the importance of basic skills, and their relationship to occupational know-how, warrants further research. Any comprehensive assessment of the effects of high school curriculum should take account of findings concerning achievement in all important areas.

- Since longitudinal and cross-sectional studies seem to disagree on the probable influence of curriculum on completion of high school (for boys, but not for girls), a matter attributable at least in part to year-to-year shifts between programs, we feel that additional research in this topic would be helpful. This is an especially important area because such an effect is generally considered to be an important reason for supporting occupational training in the high school.

- We also feel that a multivariate analysis of curriculum and its relation to unemployment among women would be helpful. We regret that time did not permit us to examine this matter in detail, since the bivariate relationship (Chapter 4) suggests the possibility that occupational studies may reduce unemployment slightly for young women with exactly 12 years of school.

- Somewhat more blacks in high school than whites report their curriculum as vocational. More importantly, perhaps, black men in such programs tend to be "more able" and to hold higher aspirations than do their general curriculum counterparts. Nevertheless, a vocational program experience for them depresses their average educational attainment. The reasons for this pattern are not entirely clear. We speculate that among black youth in school, with higher-than-average mental ability as measured by standardized tests, a disproportionately large number may live in large cities where well-established vocational programs are available. Job opportunities may be greater in such areas too. We believe that further examination of location and opportunity variables (both jobs and schooling options) might assist in understanding the intriguing black-white patterns presented in this report.

- We suspect that there may be substantial unmeasured benefits to society that stem from much occupational training. Some critics of vocational education implicitly assume that, in the absence of publicly-supported training programs, employers and private institutions would provide the desirable volume and mix of vocational training. However, the willingness of firms to engage in training, and the specific nature of the training, seem to vary by size of firm. Since much of vocational education is directed at developing fairly general skills—in the sense of being relevant to a large number of potential employers—it is not clear how eager firms would be, especially small firms, to undertake this training function. Thus publicly-supported education in occupational skills may be rational and more efficient than alternatives. Indeed, a socially optimal level may be impossible, otherwise. This line of reasoning argues that even if occupational training were found to impart no obvious wage advantage to graduates, it might be socially beneficial in an economic sense. We would urge further research on the public benefits of vocational education that may be captured by employers and by society at large.

- On a related point, a lack of information in the NLS has prevented us from investigating nonmarket outcomes, such as the value of do-it-yourself activities that may stem from skills gained in school. In home economics, automobile mechanics, typing, and other skill areas, we believe that there may be substantial nonmarket payoffs to graduates. We feel that this topic deserves further research, and that findings in this regard should be taken into account in assessing the impacts of various programs of study.

Bibliography

Andrisani, P. "An Empirical Analysis of the Dual Labor Market Theory." Columbus, Ohio: Center for Human Resource Research, Ohio State University, 1973.

Andrisani, P., and Kohen, A. *Career Thresholds.* Vol. 5, Manpower Research Monograph No. 16. Washington, D.C.: U.S. Government Printing Office, 1975.

Andrisani, P. J., Appelbaum, E., Koppel, R., and Muljus, R.C. *Work Attitudes and Labor Market Experience: Evidence from the National Longitudinal Surveys.* Philadelphia: Center for Labor and Human Resource Studies, Temple University, 1977.

Bachman, J. G. *Young Men in High School and Beyond: A Summary of Findings from the Youth in Transition Project.* Final Report, Project No. 5-0196, Contract No. 0E-5-85-054. Washington, D.C.: Bureau of Research, Office of Education, U.S. Department of Health, Education, and Welfare, 1972.

Becker, G. S. *Human Capital.* New York: Columbia University Press, 1964.

Berkeley Planning Associates. *An Evaluation of the Costs and Effectiveness of Vocational Rehabilitation Service Strategies for Individuals Most Severely Handicapped.* Berkeley, Calif.: Author, 1975.

Bose, C. E. *Jobs and Gender: Sex and Occupational Prestige.* Baltimore: Johns Hopkins University Center for Metropolitan Planning and Research, 1973.

Carnegie Council on Policy Studies in Higher Education. *The Federal Role in Postsecondary Education.* San Francisco: Jossey-Bass, 1975.

Center for Human Resources, Ohio State University. *The National Longitudinal Surveys Handbook.* Columbus, Ohio: Author, 1977.

Champagne, J. E., and Prater, R. L. *Teenage Employment: A Study of Low Income Youth in Houston, Texas.* Houston: Center for Human Resources, University of Houston, July 1969.

Creech, F., et al. *Comparative Analysis of Postsecondary Occupational and Educational Outcomes for the High School Class of 1972.* Final Report. Princeton, N. J.: Educational Testing Service, 1977.

Decker Associates. *Information About the World of Work, Job Corpsmen, and High School Students.* Silver Springs, Md.: Louis R. Decker Associates, 1967.

Doeringer, P. B., and Piore, M. J. *Internal Labor Markets and Manpower Analysis.* Lexington, Mass.: D. C. Heath, 1971.

Duncan, O. D., et al. *Socioeconomic Background and Achievement.* New York: Seminar Press, 1972.

Echternacht, G. L. *A Vocational Re-Evaluation of the Base Year Survey of the High School Class of 1972: Part II, Characteristics Distinguishing Vocational Students from General and Academic Students.* Princeton: Educational Testing Service, 1975.

Eckaus, R. S. "Economic Criteria for Education and Training." *Review of Economics and Statistics*, 46(2), 1964, pp. 181-190.

Employment and Training Report of the President, 1977. Washington, D.C.: U.S. Government Printing Office, 1977.

Evans, R. N., and Galloway, J. D. "Verbal Ability and Socioeconomic Status of 8th and 12th Grade College Preparatory, General, and Vocational Students." *Journal of Human Resources*, 8 (1), 1973, pp. 24-36.

Evans, R. N., Holter, A., and Stern, M. "Criteria for Determining Whether Competency Should Be Taught On-the-Job or in a Formal Technical Course." *Journal of Vocational Education Research*, 1 (2), Spring 1976, pp. 21-38.

Fetters, W. B. *National Longitudinal Study of the High School Class of 1972: Student Questionnaire and Test Results by Sex, High School Program, Ethnic Category, and Father's Education.* Washington, D.C.: National Center for Education Statistics, 1975.

Fine, S. A. "The Use of the Dictionary of Occupational Titles as a Source of Estimates of Educational and Training Requirements." *Journal of Human Resources*, 3 (3), 1968, pp. 363-375.

Freedman, M. *Labor Markets: Segments and Shelters.* New York: Allan, Osmun and Co., 1976.

Gallup, G. H. "Report of the Gallup Youth Survey." *The Phi Delta Kappan*, 58 (2), October 1976.

Gordon, M. S. "U.S. Manpower and Employment Policy." *Monthly Labor Review*, 87, Part 2, November 1964, pp. 1314-1321.

Gordon, M. S. *Retraining and Labor Market Adjustment in Western Europe.* Berkeley, Calif.: Institute of Industrial Relations, University of California, 1965.

Grasso, J. T. *The Contributions of Vocational Education, Training, and Work Experience to the Early Career Achievements of Young Men.* Columbus, Ohio: Center for Human Resource Research, Ohio State University, July 1975.

Grasso, J. T., and Shea, J. R. "The Effects of High School Curriculum on Age-Earnings Profiles." *Proceedings of the Social Statistics Section, American Statistical Association* (1973).

Hamburger, M. and Wolfson, H. T. *1000 Employers Look at Occupational Education.* Occupational Curriculum Project, Report No. 1. New York: Board of Education of the City of New York, 1969.

Hill, C. R. "Capacities, Opportunities, and Educational Investments: The Case of the High School Dropout." (Unpublished paper, 1977)

Holland, J. L. *Making Vocational Choices: A Theory of Careers.* Englewood Cliffs, N. J.: Prentice-Hall, 1973.

Jencks, C., et al. *Inequality: A Reassessment of the Effect of Family and Schooling in America.* New York: Basic Books, 1972.

Kohen, A. I. *Determinants of Early Labor Market Success Among Young Men: Race, Ability, Quantity and Quality of Schooling.* Columbus, Ohio: Center for Human Resource Research, Ohio State University, 1973.

Lusterman, S. "Education for Work: Business Views and Company Programs." *The Conference Board Record,* 13(5), May 1976, pp. 39-44.

Manpower Administration, *Dictionary of Occupational Titles (Vol. II): Occupational Classification and Industry Index* (3rd ed.). Washington, D.C.: Author, U.S. Department of Labor, 1965.

Marland, S. P., Jr. "Education for the Real World," An Address to the Jefferson County Chamber of Commerce at Harpers Ferry, West Virginia, May 26, 1971.

National Assessment of Educational Progress. *What Students Know and Can Do: Profiles of Three Age Groups.* Denver: NAEP, March 1977.

National Planning Association, *Policy Issues and Analytical Problems in Evaluating Vocational Education.* Project No. 8-0643, Grant No. OEG-0-71-3707, unpublished report, July 1972.

Parnes, H. S., et al. *Career Thresholds.* Vol. 1, Manpower Research Monograph No. 16. Washington, D.C.: U.S. Government Printing Office, 1970.

Quinn, R. P., Staines, C. L., and McCullough, M. R. *Job Satisfaction: Is There a Trend?* Manpower Research Monograph No. 3. Washington, D.C.: U.S. Government Printing Office, 1974.

Reubens, B. G. "Vocational Education for All in High School?" Chapter 13 in J. O'Toole (Ed.), *Work and the Quality of Life: Resource Papers for Work in America.* Cambridge, Mass.: The MIT Press, 1974a.

Reubens, B. G. "Vocational Education: Performance and Potential." *Manpower,* (7), 1974b.

Scoville, J. G. "Education and Training Requirements for Occupations." *Review of Economics and Statistics,* 48(4), 1966, pp. 387-394.

Scoville, J. G. *The Job Content of the U.S. Economy, 1940-1970.* New York: McGraw-Hill, 1969.

Shea, J. R., et al. *Dual Careers.* Vol. 1, Manpower Research Monograph No. 21. Washington, D.C.: U.S. Government Printing Office, 1970.

Shea, J. R., et al. *Years for Decision.* Vol. 1, Manpower Research Monograph No. 16. Washington, D.C.: U.S. Government Printing Office, 1971.

Simon, K. A., and Grant, W. V. *Digest of Educational Statistics* (1972 ed.). Washington, D.C.: U.S. Department of Health, Education, and Welfare, 1973.

Smith, J. P., and Welch, F. R. "Black-White Wage Ratios: 1960-70." *The American Economic Review,* 67(3), June 1977, pp. 323-338.

Somers, G. G., Sharp, L. M., Myint, T., and Meives, S. F. *The Effectiveness of Vocational and Technical Programs: A National Follow-up Survey.* Madison, Wisc.: Center for Studies in Vocational and Technical Education, University of Wisconsin, 1971.

U.S. Bureau of the Census. *Census of Population 1970,* Subject Report PC(2)-7A, *Occupational Characteristics.* Washington, D.C.: U.S. Government Printing Office, 1973.

U.S. Bureau of the Census. *County Business Patterns, 1973 U.S. Summary.* Washington, D.C.: U.S. Government Printing Office, 1974.

U.S. Bureau of Labor Statistics. *Jobs for Which a College Education is Usually Required.* Washington, D.C.: U.S. Government Printing Office, 1976a.

U.S. Bureau of Labor Statistics. *Jobs for Which Junior College, Technical Institute, or Other Specialized Training is Usually Required.* Washington, D.C.: U.S. Government Printing Office, 1976b.

U.S. Bureau of Labor Statistics. *Jobs for Which Apprenticeships Are Available.* Washington, D.C.: U.S. Government Printing Office, 1976c.

U.S. Bureau of Labor Statistics. *Jobs for Which a High School Education is Usually Required.* Washington, D.C.: U.S. Government Printing Office, 1976d.

U.S. Bureau of Labor Statistics. *Jobs for Which a High School Education is Preferred, but Not Essential.* Washington, D.C.: U.S. Government Printing Office, 1976e.

Appendix A

Appendix Tables

Table A1.1 Percentage of women (1968) 14 to 24 years old who
have completed one or more typing courses, by
enrollment status, highest year of school
completed, and race

	Grade enrolled					Not in high school		
	Total, 9-12	9	10	11	12	Total	Dropouts	Graduates
					Whites			
All curricula (average)	55%	18%	50%	72%	82%	83%	63%	87%
Vocational	67	b	b	b	b	52	b	66
Business and office	85	24	82	99	99	99	93	99
General	52	20	50	86	87	79	57	89
College preparatory	45	12	34	51	71	79	63	79
					Blacks			
All curricula (average)	49%	15%	42%	68%	75%	65%	42%	76%
Vocational	47	b	b	b	b	48	b	61
Business and office	86	b	79	92	99	92	78	97
General	41	12	31	71	69	59	38	70
College preparatory	47	5	42	51	74	66	b	76

[a] Includes high school graduates enrolled in college in 1968.

[b] Percent not shown; base less than 25 sample cases.

Table A2.1 Percentage distribution by socioeconomic origin (SEO) and scholastic aptitude (SA), thirds[a] by sex and race: men (1966) and women (1968) enrolled in grades 10–12, base year (N in thousands)

	Whites			Blacks		
	Hi SA	Mid SA	Lo SA	Hi SA	Mid SA	Lo SA
		Men				
N[b]		3,745 (= 100%)[c]			326 (= 100%)[c]	
Hi SEO	19%	12%	7%	1%	3%	2%
Mid SEO	13	15	10	3	6	22
Lo SEO	6	8	11	1	15	46
		Women				
N[b]		3,605 (= 100%)[c]			354 (= 100%)[c]	
Hi SEO	20%	14%	9%	3%	1%	3%
Mid SEO	12	15	11	1	6	22
Lo SEO	4	6	9	3	10	51

[a]SEO and SA thirds are approximate, and are based on all respondents in each sample (male, female) for whom SEO and SA were ascertained.

[b]Excludes those for whom curriculum SEO or SA were not ascertained.

[c]Detail may not add to 100 percent due to rounding.

Table A2.2 Percentage in college preparatory curriculum,[a] by socioeconomic origins (SEO) and scholastic aptitude (SA) thirds, sex, and race: men (1966) and women (1968) enrolled in grades 10–12, base year

	Whites			Blacks		
	Hi SA	Mid SA	Lo SA	Hi SA	Mid SA	Lo SA
		Men				
Hi SEO	79%	54%	44%	b	b	b
Mid SEO	69	40	23	b	b	35%
Lo SEO	50	16	6	b	35%	13
		Women				
Hi SEO	76%	64%	40%	b	b	b
Mid SEO	59	37	10	b	69%	20%
Lo SEO	34	16	7	b	22	20

[a]Excludes those for whom curriculum, SEO, or SA were not ascertained.

[b]Percent not shown; base less than 25 sample cases.

Table A2.3 Percentage, excluding college preparatory students, in occupational curricula,[a] by socioeconomic origins (SEO) and scholastic aptitude (SA) thirds, sex, and race: men (1966) and women (1968) enrolled in grades 10–12, base year

	Whites			Blacks		
	Hi SA	*Mid SA*	*Lo SA*	*Hi SA*	*Mid SA*	*Lo SA*
	Men					
Hi SEO						
Vocational	11%	19%	15%	b	b	b
Commercial	0	8	5	b	b	b
Mid SEO						
Vocational	9	18	27	b	b	21%
Commercial	2	13	3	b	b	8
Lo SEO						
Vocational	24	15	27	b	16%	23
Commercial	4	5	1	b	0	3
	Women					
Hi SEO						
Vocational	0%	9%	0%	b	b	b
Business and office	16	25	27	b	b	b
Mid SEO						
Vocational	7	0	8	b	b	2%
Business and office	38	36	28	b	b	39
Lo SEO						
Vocational	b	7	1	b	0	7
Business and office	b	47	22	b	49%	18

[a] Excludes those for whom curriculum, SEO, or SA were not ascertained.

[b] Percent not shown; base less than 25 sample cases.

Table A2.4 Attitude toward high school, by scholastic aptitude (SA), curriculum, sex, and race: men (1966) and women (1968) enrolled in grades 10 to 12

(N in thousands)

| | Men | | | | Women[a] | | | |
| | Whites | | Blacks | | Whites | | Blacks | |
	N	% like school very much	N	% like school very much	N	% like school very much	N	% like school very much
All curricula, total (or average)	4,367	42%	571	59%	4,364	53%	584	61%
High SA	1,390	48	31	42	1,336	61	22	52
Middle SA	1,263	40	79	64	1,306	53	63	58
Low SA	1,013	36	265	56	1,084	46	288	60
Occupational, total (or average)[b]	545	30	116	56	751	50	100	56
High SA	72	c	15	c	136	54	6	c
Middle SA	204	36	10	c	280	52	15	c
Low SA	219	25	63	54	324	48	57	76
General, total (or average)	1,833	37	303	59	1,663	48	312	59
High SA	339	46	2	a	306	58	3	c
Middle SA	580	39	37	65	427	53	20	c
Low SA	581	35	148	55	628	44	161	57
College preparatory, total (or average)	1,875	50	134	63	1,830	60	149	67
High SA	979	51	14	c	868	64	13	c
Middle SA	479	44	32	55	565	56	28	76
Low SA	213	50	54	61	190	50	59	50

[a]"Other vocational" not shown; inadequate number of sample cases.

[b]Vocational or commercial for men, and business and office for women.

[c]Percent not shown; base less than 25 sample cases.

Table A2.5 Occupation (major group) desired or preferred at age 30 (or 35),
by curriculum and race: men (1966) and women (1968) *not* enrolled in
base year, who had completed 10–12 years of school

(N in thousands)

| | Total (or average)[a] | Curriculum | | |
		Occu-pational[b]	General	College preparatory
		Men		
Whites (N)	3,366	666	2,154	546
Professional, technical	22%	18%	20%	34%
Nonfarm manager	17	21	13	25
Craft	27	27	31	15
Other	34	35	36	26
Don't know[c]	(15)	(16)	(16)	(11)
Blacks (N)	552	102	399	51
Professional, technical	23%	18%	24%	28%
Nonfarm manager	15	23	9	45
Craft	27	39	25	23
Other	35	20	42	5
Don't know[c]	(23)	(31)	(21)	(22)
		Women		
Whites (N)	5,409	2,055	2,427	912
Professional, technical	11%	5%	7%	35%
Clerical	54	69	44	46
Services	16	12	22	8
Other	19	13	27	11
Don't know[c]	(20)	(18)	(24)	(17)
Blacks (N)	767	194	481	92
Professional, technical	15%	18%	13%	20%
Clerical	45	67	33	57
Services	19	10	26	4
Other	21	5	28	19
Don't know[c]	(25)	(22)	(29)	(15)

[a]Each N includes "don't know" and related categories. However, the percentages citing an occupation in the four categories add to 100 (except for rounding errors), where the base (not shown) is N minus the "don't know" and "missing data" cases.

[b]Vocational and commercial for men; vocational, business and office for women.

[c]"Don't know" and no data cases for men; "don't know," other plans, married and not working, or possibly working at unknown type of work in case of women.

Table A2.6. Plans at age 35, by curriculum and race: women *not* enrolled in 1968, who had completed 10–12 years of school
(N in thousands)

| | | | Percent[a] | | | | |
| | | | Married, keeping house, raising family, and . . . | | | | |
	N	Working	Occupation preference specified	Unknown type of work	Not working	Don't know	Other
Whites							
Vocational	135	20	41	13	12	13	0
Business and office	1,920	22	61	4	2	9	2
General	2,427	29	49	9	5	8	2
College preparatory	912	30	52	3	6	6	2
Total (or average)	5,409	26	54	6	4	8	2
Blacks							
Vocational	43	34	56	7	0	3	0
Business and office	151	44	30	7	2	13	4
General	481	45	28	9	2	15	3
College preparatory	92	40	44	5	0	8	2
Total (or average)	769	43	32	8	1	13	3

[a]Detail may not add to 100 percent due to rounding.

Table A2.7. Knowledge of the World of Work (KWW) (total score and part-scores for college-level jobs and non-college jobs separately): regression results for men enrolled in grades 10 to 12 in 1966
(Standard errors in parentheses)

Explanatory variables and statistics	Whites			Blacks		
	Total KWW score	College part-score	Non-college part-score	Total KWW score	College part-score	Non-college part-score
SA	0.12** (0.01)	0.01** (0.001)	0.02** (0.003)	0.18** (0.03)	0.02** (0.004)	0.03** (0.006)
SEO	0.03** (0.01)	0.01 (0.007)	0.01* (0.0055)	0.08** (0.02)	0.01* (0.006)	0.01 (0.006)
VOC_{66}[a]	−1.07* (0.63)	−0.31** (0.08)	0.03 (0.12)	−1.54 (1.00)	−0.17 (0.15)	−0.44* (0.23)
COM_{66}[a]	0.23 (1.05)	−0.02 (0.17)	−0.11 (0.21)	−1.77 (1.59)	−0.21 (0.23)	0.22 (0.37)
CP_{66}[a]	0.49 (0.42)	0.08 (0.05)	−0.10 (0.09)	0.15 (0.93)	0.02 (0.11)	−0.12 (0.20)
Grade, 66	1.82** (0.23)	0.11** (0.03)	0.31** (0.05)	1.29** (0.43)	0.01 (0.04)	0.27** (0.10)
Ever worked, 66	0.39 (0.51)	0.12* (0.07)	0.30** (0.10)	2.77** (0.95)	0.41** (0.13)	0.32 (0.22)
A14RNF[b]	1.48* (0.76)	0.06 (0.09)	0.26* (0.15)	2.54* (1.51)	0.04 (0.24)	0.63* (0.35)
A14SC[b]	1.00 (0.61)	−0.03 (0.07)	0.11 (0.12)	2.73** (1.37)	0.32* (0.19)	0.45 (0.32)
A14MT[b]	1.17* (0.68)	0.10 (0.08)	0.07 (0.12)	2.10 (1.43)	0.42** (0.20)	0.68** (0.33)
A14CTYS[b]	1.38** (0.62)	0.17** (0.08)	0.16 (0.12)	3.08** (1.28)	0.43* (0.18)	0.72** (0.30)
Constant	−4.44	−0.77	−1.51	−13.15	−1.07	−3.41
R^2	0.19	0.14	0.12	0.33	0.20	0.20
F	21.96*	15.60*	13.44*	12.79*	7.20*	6.89*
N	1,003	1,003	1,003	268	268	268
Mean	33.18	2.27	4.91	28.90	1.82	4.03
SD	6.21	0.76	1.20	6.77	0.88	1.43

[a]Reference group: *general* curriculum.

[b]Reference group: respondents living on a rural farm at age 14.

*Significant at 0.10 level (2-tailed t test except for SA and SEO).

**Significant at 0.05 level.

Table A2.8. High school curriculum assignments judged inappropriate to educational and occupational goals

Educational and occupational goals	Curriculum			
	Vocational	Commercial (or B&O)	General	College preparatory
Aspires to HS 12 or less:				
Occup requires coll 4+	I_O	I_O	I_O	I_E
Other pre-employment preparation available	A	A	A	I_B
No special requirements	A	A	A	I_B
"Don't know," other	A	A	A	I_E
Aspires to Coll 2:				
Occup requires coll 4+	I_O	I_O	I_O	A
Other pre-employment preparation available	A	A	A	A
No special requirements	A	A	A	I_O
"Don't know," other	A	A	A	A
Aspires to Coll 4+:				
Occup requires coll 4+	I_B	I_B	I_B	A
Other pre-employment preparation available	I_E	I_E	I_E	A
No special requirements	I_E	I_E	I_E	I_O
"Don't know," other	I_E	I_E	I_E	A

Note: I_E = Curriculum inappropriate to educational goal.
I_O = Curriculum inappropriate to occupational goal.
I_B = Curriculum inappropriate to both goals.
A = Curriculum appropriate to both goals.

Table A3.1. Percentage of school leavers who bore a child within one year of leaving school, by race, highest year of school completed, and high school curriculum (most recent): women (1968) *not* enrolled in school, base year

	Highest year completed		
	10 & 11	12	13 to 15
Whites (average)	35%	11%	16%
Vocational	a	a	a
Business and office	34	8	a
General	32	11	18
College preparatory	47	14	17
Blacks (average)	44%	28%	22%
Vocational	a	32	a
Business and office	31	23	a
General	41	29	28
College preparatory	a	29	21

aPercent not shown; base less than 25 sample cases.

Table A3.2. Educational attainment and postschool training: regression
results for men in low SA third (1973)
(Standard errors in parentheses)

Explanatory variables and statistics	Whites				Blacks			
	$Y = 12+$ (1,0)	$Y = 13+$ (1,0)[a]	$Y = 13+/$ TNG (1,0)[a]	$Y = HSC$ (yrs)[a]	$Y = 12+$ (1,0)	$Y = 13+$ (1,0)[a]	$Y = 13+/$ TNG (1,0)[a]	$Y = HSC$ (yrs)[a]
SA	0.006** (0.002)	0.002 (0.002)	0.001 (0.003)	0.03** (0.01)	0.004 (0.003)	0.006** (0.003)	0.01** (0.003)	0.02** (0.01)
SEO	0.04** (0.01)	0.06** (0.01)	0.06** (0.01)	0.22* (0.05)	0.02 (0.02)	0.05** (0.02)	0.06** (0.02)	0.25** (0.07)
VOC73[b]	0.03 (0.04)	-0.12** (0.05)	0.04 (0.06)	-0.32 (0.21)	0.04 (0.08)	0.08 (0.08)	0.01 (0.10)	0.28 (0.28)
COM73[b]	0.18** (0.07)	0.10 (0.08)	0.09 (0.10)	0.75** (0.36)	-0.204 (0.126)	0.13 (0.12)	-0.14 (0.15)	0.13 (0.46)
CP73[b]	0.10** (0.04)	0.34* (0.05)	0.15** (0.06)	1.67** (0.20)	0.19** (0.08)	0.20** (0.08)	0.05 (0.10)	1.44** (0.31)
A14R[c]	-0.02 (0.04)	-0.04 (0.05)	-0.087 (0.059)	-0.19 (0.21)	0.08 (0.09)	0.12 (0.09)	0.03 (0.11)	0.57* (0.33)
A14T[c]	-0.05 (0.04)	0.01 (0.05)	-0.03 (0.06)	-0.11 (0.20)	-0.05 (0.09)	0.10 (0.09)	0.06 (0.11)	0.18 (0.34)

A14CTY[c]	-0.02	0.01	-0.02	-0.04	-0.06	0.01	0.08	-0.23
	(0.05)	(0.05)	(0.06)	(0.23)	(0.07)	(0.08)	(0.10)	(0.29)
Constant	-0.06	-0.58	-0.002	7.67	0.27	-0.86	-0.54	8.15
R^2	0.09	0.24	0.09	0.26	0.07	0.13	0.09	0.21
F	6.75**	19.20**	5.86**	20.91**	2.29**	3.65**	2.63**	6.90**
N	526	494	494	494	239	211	211	211
Mean (Y)	0.84	0.22	0.66	12.46	0.78	0.21	0.56	12.23
SD (Y)	0.37	0.42	0.47	1.86	0.42	0.40	0.50	1.59

[a]Restricted to those out of school who had completed 10 or more years of school.

[b]Reference group: *general* curriculum.

[c]Reference group: respondents living in small city or suburb at age 14.

*Significant at 0.10 level (2-tailed t test except for SA and SEO).

**Significant at 0.05 level.

Table A3.3. Educational attainment and postschool training: Regression results for women, low SA third, 1972

Explanatory variables and statistics	Whites				Blacks			
	$Y = 12+$ (1,0)	$Y = 13+$ (1,0)	$Y = 13+1$ TNG (1,0)[a]	$Y = HSC$ (yrs)[a]	$Y = 12+$ (1,0)	$Y = 13+$ (1,0)	$Y = 13+1$ TNG (1,0)[2]	$Y = HSC$ (yrs)[a]
SA	0.001 (0.002)	0.006** (0.002)	0.002 (0.003)	0.01 (0.01)	0.001 (0.002)	0.007** (0.002)	0.002 (0.003)	0.01 (0.01)
SEO	0.03** (0.008)	0.04** (0.007)	0.03** (0.01)	0.10** (0.02)	0.03** (0.01)	0.06** (0.01)	0.05** (0.02)	0.11** (0.04)
VOC_{72}[b]	0.15* (0.08)	0.02 (0.07)	0.06 (0.12)	0.26 (0.23)	0.03 (0.10)	-0.19** (0.10)	0.01 (0.13)	-0.28 (0.29)
$B\&O_{72}$[b]	0.15** (0.03)	-0.08** (0.03)	0.03 (0.04)	0.16** (0.09)	0.03 (0.05)	-0.15** (0.05)	0.01 (0.07)	-0.18 (0.15)
CP_{72}[b]	0.19** (0.04)	0.33** (0.04)	0.30** (0.06)	1.11** (0.12)	0.11** (0.01)	0.23** (0.06)	0.12 (0.08)	0.62** (0.19)
A14R[c]	0.08* (0.04)	0.07** (0.35)	-0.04 (0.06)	0.30** (0.11)	0.09 (0.06)	0.16** (0.05)	-0.15** (0.07)	0.31* (0.17)
A14T[c]	0.07* (0.04)	0.03 (0.03)	-0.05 (0.05)	0.25** (0.11)	0.03 (0.06)	0.004 (0.06)	-0.12 (0.08)	-0.02 (0.19)

	(1)	(2)	(3)	(4)	(5)	(6)	(7)	(8)
A14CTY[c]	0.03	0.06*	0.03	0.20*	-0.05	-0.03	-0.04	-0.20
	(0.04)	(0.04)	(0.06)	(0.12)	(0.05)	(0.05)	(0.07)	(0.16)
Constant	0.36	-0.89	-0.04	9.49	0.45	-0.91	-0.005	9.93
R^2	0.07	0.27	0.08	0.19	0.02	0.19	0.07	0.09
F	7.79**	32.80**	7.44**	19.47**	2.26**	13.43**	4.28**	5.16**
N	677	677	634	634	413	413	354	354
Mean (Y)	0.84	0.15	0.52	11.99	0.82	0.23	0.57	12.09
SD (Y)	0.36	0.36	0.50	1.07		0.42	0.50	1.15

[a]Restricted to those out of school who had completed 10 or more years of school.

[b]Reference group: *general* curriculum.

[c]Reference group: respondent living in small city or suburb at age 14.

*Significant at 0.10 level (2-tailed t test except for SA and SEO).

**Significant at 0.05 level.

Table A3.4. Highest year of school completed, 1973: regression results
for men enrolled in grades 10 to 12 in 1966, out of school but
interviewed in 1973 (Standard errors in parentheses)

	Whites	*Blacks*
SA	0.03**	0.02**
	(0.005)	(0.008)
SEO	0.15**	0.08
	(0.04)	(0.07)
VOC/COM$_{66}$ and EDASP Coll 4+[a]	0.38	−0.07
	(0.32)	(0.41)
VOC/COM$_{66}$ and EDASP Coll 2 or less[a]	−0.04	−0.42
	(0.20)	(0.41)
CP$_{66}$ and EDASP Coll 4+[a]	1.67**	1.01**
	(0.17)	(0.35)
CP$_{66}$ and EDASP Coll 2 or less[a]	0.14	1.21*
	(0.33)	(0.77)
GEN$_{66}$ and EDASP Coll 4+[a]	0.80**	0.96**
	(0.19)	(0.32)
Constant	7.20	9.42
R^2	0.40	0.25
F	59.54**	6.67**
N	637	147
Mean (Y)	13.23	12.48
SD (Y)	1.88	1.54

[a]Reference group: *general* curriculum student who aspired to college 2 or less.

*Significant at 0.10 level (1-tailed t test except for VOC/COM$_{66}$ who aspired to college 2 or less).

**Significant at 0.05 level.

Table A3.5. Completion of high school and highest year of school
completed, 1973: regression results for men, all races,
enrolled in nonacademic curricula in grades 10 to 12
in 1966, who aspired to four or more years of
college, not enrolled in 1973
(Standard errors in parentheses)

Explanatory variables and statistics	$Y = HSC_{73}$ (yrs)	$Y = 12+$ (1,0)
SA	0.04**	0.0018
	(0.01)	(0.0012)
SEO	0.16*	0.25*
	(0.07)	(0.01)
VOC_{66}[a]	−0.54*	−0.03
	(0.31)	(0.04)
COM_{66}[a]	−0.29	−0.06
	(0.49)	(0.07)
A14R[b]	0.38	−0.01
	(0.39)	(0.05)
A14T[b]	0.32	−0.01
	(0.29)	(0.04)
A14CTY[b]	−0.07	−0.02
	(0.30)	(0.04)
Constant	7.13	0.52

[a]Reference group: *general* curriculum.

[b]Reference group: respondent living in small city or suburb at age 14.

*Significant at 0.10 level (2-tailed t test except for SA and SEO).

**Significant at 0.05 level.

Table A3.6. The educational attainment process: regression results for men, all races, enrolled in grades 10 to 12 in 1966 (except in college preparatory curriculum), not enrolled but interviewed in 1973 (Standard errors in parentheses)

Explanatory variables and statistics	$Y = SA$	$Y = EDASP_{66}$		$Y = VOC/COM_{66}$		$Y = HSC_{73}$	
		1	2	1	2	1	2
SEO	1.93** (0.34)	0.21** (0.05)	0.21** (0.05)	0.001 (0.01)	0.004 (0.01)	0.15** (0.03)	0.11** (0.03)
A14R[a]	-0.50 (1.74)	-0.59** (0.25)	-0.61** (0.25)	-0.04 (0.06)	-0.05 (0.06)	-0.15 (0.16)	-0.34 (0.15)
A14T[a]	-0.29 1.67	-0.31 0.23	-0.33 0.23	-0.05 0.06	-0.06 0.06	-0.046 0.15	0.02 0.15
A14CTY[a]	-4.44** (1.82)	0.34 (0.27)	0.33 (0.27)	-0.024 (0.06)	-0.016 (0.06)	-0.01 (0.16)	-0.08 (0.16)
SA	b	0.04** (0.01)	0.04** (0.01)	-0.002 (0.002)	-0.0014 (0.002)	0.031** (0.01)	0.023** (0.004)
VOC/COM$_{66}$[c]	b	b	-0.45** (0.18)	b	b	-0.32** (0.12)	-0.23* (0.12)
EDASP$_{66}$	b	b	b	b	-0.25** (0.01)	b	0.20** (0.03)
Constant	79.99	8.18	8.42	0.54	0.74	8.01	6.33
R^2	0.08	0.16	0.17	0.007	0.02	0.20	0.28
F	9.60**	18.45**	16.33**	0.66	1.44**	19.69**	26.09**
N	473	473	473	473	473	473	473
Mean (Y)	98.30	14.04	14.04	0.27	0.27	12.44	12.44
SD (Y)	13.65	2.08	2.08	0.44	0.44	1.34	1.34

[a]Reference group: respondents living in small city or suburb at age 14.

[b]Variable *not* included in the equation.

[c]Reference group: *general* curriculum.

*Significant at 0.10 level (2-tailed t test).

**Significant at 0.05 level.

Table A3.7. The educational attainment process: regression results for *white* men enrolled in grades 10 to 12 in 1966 (except in college preparatory curriculum), not enrolled but interviewed in 1973 (Standard errors in parentheses)

Explanatory variables and statistics	Y = SA	Y = EDASP$_{66}$ 1	Y = EDASP$_{66}$ 2	Y = VOC/COM$_{66}$ 1	Y = VOC/COM$_{66}$ 2	Y = HSC$_{73}$ 1	Y = HSC$_{73}$ 2
SEO	1.55** (0.39)	0.30** (0.06)	0.30** (0.06)	-0.004 (0.01)	0.003 (0.01)	0.18** (0.04)	0.12** (0.04)
A14R[a]	-0.29 (1.90)	-0.48* (0.28)	-0.50* (0.28)	-0.04 (0.07)	-0.05 (0.07)	-0.15 (0.18)	-0.06 (0.18)
A14T[a]	-0.65 (1.81)	-0.25 (0.27)	-0.26 (0.27)	-0.03 (0.06)	-0.04 (0.06)	-0.07 (0.17)	-0.02 (0.16)
A14CTY[a]	-4.26** (1.99)	0.45 (0.30)	0.42 (0.30)	-0.06 (0.07)	-0.04 (0.07)	0.07 (0.19)	-0.07 (0.19)
SA	b	0.04** (0.008)	0.04** (0.008)	-0.003 (0.002)	-0.002 (0.002)	0.04** (0.005)	0.03** (0.005)
VOC/COM$_{66}$[c]	b		-0.45** (0.22)	b	b	-0.27* (0.14)	-0.18 (0.14)
EDASP$_{66}$	b	b	b	b	-0.03** (0.01)	b	0.18** (0.03)
Constant	84.78	6.58	6.89	0.69	0.86	7.29	6.02
R^2	0.05	0.20	0.21	0.01	0.02	0.22	0.28
F	5.03**	18.20**	15.98**	0.85	1.40**	16.55**	19.91**
N	363	363	363	363	363	363	363
Mean (Y)	99.59	14.01	14.01	0.27	0.27	12.47	12.47
SD (Y)	12.86	2.08	2.08	0.45	0.45	1.35	1.35

[a]Reference group: respondents living in small city or suburb at age 14.

[b]Variable *not* included in the equation.

[c]Reference group: *general* curriculum.

*Significant at 0.10 level (2-tailed t test).

**Significant at 0.05 level.

Table A3.8. Marginal contribution of explanatory variables to highest year of school completed, by race: *white* men enrolled in grades 10 to 12 (except college preparatory curriculum) in 1966, *not* enrolled but interviewed 1973

| | Indirect effect | | | | | Direct effect | Total effect in year (=100%) |
| | Via SA through $EDASP_{66}$ | Via SA or $EDASP_{66}$ through VOC/COM_{66} | Through | | | | |
			SA	$EDASP_{66}$	VOC/COM_{66}		
Basic model							
SEO	—	—	0.06(26%)	—		0.18(74%)	0.24
A14CTY	—	—	-0.17(100%)	—			-0.17
SA	—	—	—	—		0.04(100%)	0.04
VOC/COM_{66}	—	—	—	—		-0.27(100%)	-0.27
Goal-directed model							
SEO	0.01(5%)		0.05(20%)	0.05(23%)		0.12(52%)	0.23
A14R	—	—		-0.09(100%)			-0.09
A14CTY	—	—	-0.13(81%)	-0.03(19%)			-0.16
SA	—	—		0.01(19%)		0.03(81%)	0.04
$EDASP_{66}$	—	—		—	0.01(4%)	0.18(96%)	0.19
VOC/COM_{66}	—	—		—			
Tracking model							
SEO	0.01(6%)		0.05(26%)	-0.09(100%)		0.12(68%)	0.18
A14R	—	—		0.03(19%)			-0.09
A14CTY	—	—	-0.13(81%)	0.01(19%)			-0.16
SA	—	—		-0.08(100%)		0.03(81%)	0.04
VOC/COM_{66}	—	—		—			-0.08
$EDASP_{66}$	—	—		—		0.18(100%)	0.18

Note: Dashes (−) designate causal linkages ruled out by the model.

Table A5.5. The educational attainment process: regression results for *black* men enrolled in grades 10 to 12 in 1966 (except in college preparatory curriculum), not enrolled but interviewed in 1973 (Standard errors in parentheses)

Explanatory variables and statistics	Y = SA	Y = EDASP66		Y = VOC/COM66		Y = HSC73	
		1	2	1	2	1	2
SEO	-0.77 (0.97)	0.10 (0.14)	0.10 (0.14)	0.02 (0.03)	0.02 (0.03)	0.12* (0.09)	0.09 (0.08)
A14R[a]	-10.10** (3.73)	-0.95* (0.57)	-0.95* (0.57)	0.006 (0.12)	0.003 (0.13)	-0.04 (0.35)	0.23 (0.32)
A14T[a]	-5.28 (3.95)	-0.40 (0.59)	-0.41 (0.60)	-0.20 (0.13)	-0.20 (0.13)	0.18 (0.37)	0.30 (0.33)
A14CTY[a]	-3.21 (4.08)	-0.53 (0.60)	-0.51 (0.61)	0.17 (0.13)	0.17 (0.13)	-0.16 (0.38)	-0.01 (0.34)
SA	b	0.04** (0.01)	0.04** (0.015)	0.005* (0.003)	0.005* (0.003)	0.02** (0.009)	0.01 (0.01)
VOC/COM66[c]	b	b	-0.08 (0.47)	b	b	-0.53* (0.29)	-0.51** (0.26)
EDASP66	b	b	b	b	-0.004 (0.02)	b	0.29** (0.05)
Constant	96.81	10.84	10.82	-0.33	-0.29	9.82	6.72
R²	0.07	0.11	0.12	0.12	0.12	0.09	0.29
F	1.93**	2.52**	2.08**	2.66**	2.20**	1.59**	5.47**
N	103	103	103	103	103	103	103
Mean (Y)	85.17	14.19	14.19	0.27	0.27	12.17	12.17
SD (Y)	13.64	2.05	2.05	0.45	0.45	1.25	1.25

[a]Reference group: respondents living in small city or suburb at age 14.

[b]Variable *not* included in the equation.

[c]Reference group: *general* curriculum.

*Significant at 0.10 level (2-tailed t test).

**Significant at 0.05 level.

Table A3.10. Marginal contribution of explanatory variables to highest year of school completed, by race: *black* men enrolled in grades 10 to 12 (except college preparatory curriculum) in 1966, *not* enrolled but interviewed 1973

| | Indirect effect | | | | | | |
	Via SA through EDASP$_{66}$	Via SA or EDASP$_{66}$ through VOC/COM$_{66}$	Through SA	Through EDASP$_{66}$	Through VOC/COM$_{66}$	Direct effect	Total effect in year (=100%)
Basic Model							
SEO	—		-0.20(100%)			0.12(100%)	0.12
A14R	—	—					-0.20
SA	—	—	—		a(-15%)	0.02(115%)	0.02
VOC/COM$_{66}$	—	—	—		—	-0.53(100%)	-0.53
Goal-directed model							
SEO	-0.12(32%)	0.03(-7%)	—	-0.28(75%)	—		-0.37
A14R	—	—	—	0.01(128%)	a(-28%)		0.01
SA	—	—	—	—	—	0.29(100%)	0.29
EDASP$_{66}$	—	—	—	—	—	-0.51(100%)	-0.51
VOC/COM$_{66}$	—	—	—	—	—		
Tracking model							
SEO	-0.12(32%)	0.03(-7%)	—	-0.28(75%)	—		-0.37
A14R	—	—	—	0.01(128%)	a(-28%)		0.01
SA	—	—	—	—	—		
VOC/COM$_{66}$	—	—	—	—	—	-0.51(100%)	-0.51
EDASP$_{66}$	—	—	—	—	—	0.29(100%)	0.29

a Less than 0.01 year.

Note: Dashes (—) designate causal linkages ruled out by the model.

Table A3.11. The educational attainment process: regression results for women, by race, enrolled in grades 10 to 12 in 1968, (except college preparatory curriculum), not enrolled but interviewed in 1972 (Standard errors in parentheses)

Explanatory variables and statistics	$Y=SA$ Whites	$Y=SA$ Blacks	$Y=EDASP_{68}$ Whites	$Y=EDASP_{68}$ Blacks	$VOC/B\&O_{68}$ Whites	$VOC/B\&O_{68}$ Blacks	$Y=HSC_{72}$ Whites	$Y=HSC_{72}$ Blacks
SEO	1.96** (0.35)	0.52 (0.70)	0.25** (0.05)	0.23** (0.09)	-0.003** (0.01)	0.04 (0.03)	0.06** (0.02)	0.04 (0.04)
A14R[a]	1.11 (1.75)	3.07 (3.10)	-0.13 (0.23)	0.59 (0.41)	0.13** (0.06)	0.01 (0.11)	-0.06 (0.11)	0.02 (0.16)
A14T[a]	-0.71 (1.53)	-0.72 (3.42)	0.24 (0.20)	0.91** (0.45)	0.05 (0.05)	-0.18 (0.12)	-0.12* (0.09)	-0.07 (0.18)
A14CTY[a]	-1.26 (1.78)	7.06** (2.83)	0.46** (0.23)	0.22 (0.38)	0.08 (0.06)	-0.03 (-0.10)	-0.15 (0.11)	-0.20* (0.15)
SA	b	b	0.03** (0.01)	0.03** (0.01)	0.001 (0.002)	0.01** (0.003)	0.01 (0.00)	0.00 (0.00)
VOC/B&O$_{68}$[c]	b	b	b	b	b	b	0.00 (0.00)	-0.00 (0.00)
EDASP$_{68}$	b	b	b	b	-0.06** (0.01)	-0.05** (0.02)	-0.12** (0.02)	0.04 (0.03)
Constant	82.66	78.39	8.10	9.41	1.07	0.25	9.20	10.74
R^2	0.06	0.04	0.15	0.08	0.06	0.05	0.12	0.00
F	8.52**	2.63**	17.85**	3.80**	6.58**	2.38**	10.26	0.91
N	493	160	493	160	493	160	493	160
Mean (Y)	103.32	85.91	13.98	14.16	0.29	0.33	12.02	11.84
SD (Y)	12.92	13.21	1.75	1.78	0.45	0.47	0.81	0.66

[a]Reference group: respondents living in small city or suburb at age 14.

[b]Variable not included in the equation.

[c]Reference group: general curriculum.

*Significant at 0.10 level (2-tailed t test).

**Significant at 0.05 level.

Table A3.12. Percentage of respondents reporting training outside regular school, by highest year of school completed 1966, high school curriculum (most recent), and race: men *not* enrolled, 1966 (N in thousands)

Highest year completed and curriculum	N	Some training (unduplicated)	Military training	Business college or tech institute	Company training	Other vocational training	Regular courses
				Percent reporting — *Source*			
Whites							
10-11, total (or average)	852	37%	16%	12%	6%	7%	8%
12, total (or average)	2,514	52	18	23	6	14	9
Vocational	401	46	16	13	8	16	6
Commercial	136	36	20	24	6	14	8
General	1,487	54	17	28	7	11	16
College preparatory	489	54	18	22	8	6	14
13-15, total (or average)	596	51	18	20	7	11	10
10-15, total (or average)	4,040	48	18	20	7	11	10
Blacks							
10-11, total (or average)	228	23%	4%	4%	9%	9%	6%
12, total (or average)	324	32	14	9	5	5	4
Vocational	54	35	15	4	7	10	5
Commercial	9	a					
General	227	34	15	10	5	4	3
College preparatory	34	18	4	14	4	0	4
13-15, total (or average)	45	42	0	0	3	14	25
10-15, total (or average)	621	29	9	6	6	8	6

aPercent not calculated; base less than 25 sample cases.

Table A3.13. Mean educational attainment and postschool training (including military) by race, sex, and scholastic aptitude: various groups of men (1966, 1973) and women (1968, 1972)

	Men			Women		
	Whites	Blacks	Ratio B:W	Whites	Blacks	Ratio B:W
1966 (1968)						
Not enrolled, total:[a]						
Highest grade completed	12.3	11.7	0.95	12.4	12.2	0.98
13+ years or some training	61%	36%	0.59	55%	50%	0.90
Not enrolled, low SA third:[a]						
Highest grade completed	11.8	11.7	0.99	11.8	12.0	1.02
13+ years or some training	46%	33%	0.72	42%	46%	1.11
1973 (1972)						
Not enrolled, total:[a]						
Highest grade completed	13.7	12.4	0.91	12.8	12.3	0.96
13+ years or some training	78%	55%	0.71	67%	60%	0.90
Not enrolled, low SA third:[a]						
Highest grade completed	12.5	12.2	0.98	12.0	12.1	1.01
13+ years or some training	47%	56%	1.19	52%	57%	1.09
In- or out-of-school, total:						
12+ years	93%	78%	0.84	91%	85%	0.93
13+ years	49%[a]	25%[a]	0.51[a]	40%	30%	0.74
In- or out-of-school, low SA third:						
12+ years	84%	78%	0.93	84%	82%	0.97
13+ years	22%[a]	21%[a]	0.95[a]	15%	23%	1.48

[a]Restricted to those who had completed 10 or more years.

Vocational Education and Training

Table A4.1. Labor force participation rates (LFPR) and percentage of
the employed who work full-time, by high school curriculum
(most recent), and race: women (1968, 1972) *not* enrolled
in relevant year who had completed 10 to 15 years
of school (' ɩ in thousands)

	1968			1972		
	N	LFPR	% full-time	N	LFPR	% full-time
Whites						
10-11, total (or average)	1,067	40%	64%	1,422	47%	64%
Vocational	43	a	a	53	a	a
Business and office	239	46	a	287	44	80
General	682	40	66	909	45	61
College preparatory	92	a	a	131	56	a
12, total (or average)	4,343	66	79	6,501	63	73
Vocational	92	a	a	187	63	87
Business and office	1,681	70	83	2,214	62	75
General	1,746	63	74	2,697	61	72
College preparatory	820	69	77	1,304	70	71
13-15, total (or average)	930	69	82	1,643	66	73
Vocational	5	a	a	10	a	a
Business and office	70	a	a	132	69	a
General	203	74	78	344	59	74
College preparatory	639	66	80	1,148	66	71
Blacks						
10-11, total (or average)	261	58	62	357	51	68
Vocational	11	a	a	8	a	a
Business and office	46	48	a	50	48	a
General	195	60	63	267	52	75
College preparatory	9	a	a	19	a	a
12, total (or average)	508	71	75	771	66	81
Vocational	33	61	a	42	44	a
Business and office	104	74	78	163	69	90
General	286	70	70	450	67	78
College preparatory	83	74	86	111	63	75
13-15, total (or average)	107	82	78	141	77	90
Vocational	0	a	a	4	a	a
Business and office	11	a	a	14	a	a
General	51	71	62	63	78	89
College preparatory	46	89	89	60	71	89

aPercent not reported; base less than 25 sample cases.

Table A4.2. Survey week unemployment rates, curriculum (most recent), sex: men (1966-73) and women (1968-72), *not* enrolled in relevant year, who had completed exactly 12 years of school

| | Curriculum (most recent) | | | |
	Vocational	*Commercial (or B&O)*	*General*	*College preparatory*
		Men		
Whites				
1966	3.0	0.0	2.1	0.8
1967	3.5	2.3	1.5	1.9
1968	0.8	2.9	2.5	1.5
1969	1.7	4.2	3.3	6.0
1970	3.9	6.0	5.9	7.3
1971	5.7	7.4	5.9	11.1
1973	0.7	1.9	2.4	2.8
Blacks				
1966	0.0	a	5.0	3.1
1967	9.0	a	10.5	2.3
1968	3.5	a	1.0	2.7
1969	6.9	a	3.4	2.2
1970	10.6	a	11.7	8.3
1971	8.0	8.1	8.7	12.6
1973	5.0	a	6.4	1.5
		Women		
Whites				
1968	0.0	5.7	14.3	4.6
1969	7.9	8.5	7.5	6.8
1970	16.6	4.9	11.7	8.6
1971	11.3	7.6	9.7	9.4
1972	8.9	8.1	11.6	8.7
Blacks				
1968	12.6	8.7	18.0	21.3
1969	15.4	7.0	14.6	18.0
1970	9.7	11.8	16.1	12.8
1971	23.9	16.9	23.3	25.6
1972	12.8	4.2	21.7	23.8

[a]Percent not reported; base less than 25 sample cases.

Table A4.3. Average number of weeks unemployed as of the reference week, 1966-71, by highest year of school completed and high school curriculum (most recent) in the relevant year, and race: unemployed men interviewed but not enrolled in the relevant year (N in thousands)

	Whites			Blacks		
		Percent (weighted average)^b			Percent (weighted average)^b	
	N^a	unemployed 1-4 weeks	unemployed 15 + weeks	N^a	unemployed 1-4 weeks	unemployed 15 + weeks
10-11, total (or average)	306	54%	13%	155	59%	12%
12, total (or average)	734	53	16	159	44	17
Vocational/commercial	141	63	11	32	47	20
General	409	51	18	111	43	17
College preparatory	185	48	13	15	c	c
13-15 total (or average)	199	51	22	32	54	0

^{a}Cumulative number of observations, not necessarily different respondents.

^{b}5-14 weeks excluded from the percentaging.

^{c}Percentages not shown; base less than 25 observations.

Table A4.4. Cumulative number of spells of unemployment, 1966-70,
by highest year of school completed 1970, high school curriculum
(most recent) 1970: men *not* enrolled in 1970
but interviewed in that year
(N in thousands)

| | N^b | Percent who experienced[a] | | | |
		1 or more spells	1 spell	2-4 spells	5 or more spells
Whites					
10-11, total (or average)	661	50%	13%	25%	13%
12, total (or average)	2,269	48	17	22	10
Vocational	377	60	27	22	11
Commercial	149	54	17	22	15
General	1,345	45	15	23	8
College preparatory	398	45	14	18	14
13-15, total	775	46	20	18	8
Blacks					
10-11, total (or average)	123	73%	16%	42%	14%
12, total (or average)	266	69	22	30	18
Vocational	51	71	30	20	22
Commercial	10	c	c	c	c
General	167	69	21	31	17
College preparatory	38	64	17	27	21
13-15, total	57	65	26	11	28

[a]Detail may not add to total due to rounding.

[b]Excludes those for whom number of spells was not ascertained for one or more years.

[c]Percent not shown; base less than 25 sample cases.

Table A4.5. Reason seeking employment at the time of each survey,
1967-71,[a] by highest year of school completed and high school
curriculum (most recent) in the relevant year, and race:
unemployed men interviewed but not enrolled
in the relevant year (N in thousands)

| | N[b] | Reason (percent) | | |
		Lost job	Quit job	Other
Whites				
10-11, total (or average)	231	32%	41%	27%
12, total (or average)	573	26	28	46
General	339	27	28	45
College preparatory	153	19	26	55
13-15, total (or average)	157	20	20	60
Blacks				
10-11, total (or average)	104	41%	26%	33%
12, total (or average)	147	33	32	36
General	104	39	31	30
13-15, total (or average)	295	31	25	44
All races				
10-11, total (or average)	339	35%	36%	29%
12, total (or average)	731	27	29	44
Vocational/commercial	111	32	31	37
General	454	29	29	41
College preparatory	167	18	27	55
13-15, total (or average)	188	22	21	57

[a]Information not available for 1966.
[b]Cumulative number of observations, not necessarily different respondents.

Table A4.6. Ratio of *involuntary* to all other reasons for leaving first job after school and current job 1966, 1970, and 1971, by highest year of school completed, high school curriculum (most recent), and race: Men (1966, 1971, 1973), not enrolled in relevant year, who had changed employers (N in thousands)

	First job to 1966 job		1970 job to 1971 job		1971 job to 1973 job	
	Number who changed	Ratio involuntary to all other	Number who changed	Ratio involuntary to all other	Number who changed	Ratio involuntary to all other
Whites						
10-11, total (or average)	414	0.29	262	0.61	244	0.27
VOC/COM	67	a	31	a	47	a
General	325	0.25	219	0.78	174	0.27
College preparatory	22	a	12	a	22	a
12, total (or average)	1,148	0.37	780	0.52	1,203	0.26
Vocational	154	0.28	107	0.70	187	0.17
Commercial	86	a	49	a	76	a
General	674	0.39	460	0.55	730	0.28
College preparatory	234	0.31	164	0.18	210	0.33
13-15, total (or average)	226	0.14	319	0.46	620	0.15
VOC/COM	24	a	30	a	81	a
General	99	0.13	115	0.64	239	0.12
College preparatory	103	0.14	174	0.46	300	0.15
10-15, total (or average)	1,826	0.32	1,421	0.55	2,281	0.23
Blacks						
10-11, total (or average)	124	0.39	50	0.61	42	0.28
VOC/COM	20	a	5	a	7	a
General	92	0.45	44	0.80	31	0.27
College preparatory	12	a	1	a	4	a
12, total (or average)	179	0.20	95	0.62	124	0.12
Vocational	34	0.23	16	a	27	0.11
Commercial	4	a	2	a	7	a
General	129	0.19	59	0.69	72	0.15
College preparatory	12	a	18	a	18	a
13-15, total (or average)	21	a	21	a	28	0.21
VOC/COM	3	a	8	a	3	a
General	13	a	9	a	23	a
College preparatory	5	a	4	a	3	a
10-15, total (or average)	338	0.28	174	0.68	236	0.18

aRatio not reported; base less than 25 sample cases.

Table A4.7. Selected measures of employment stability, 1966-70, 1970-71, and 1971-73, by highest year of school completed and high school curriculum (most recent) as of the end of each period: men *not* enrolled but interviewed at the end of each period (N in thousands)

| | 1966-70 | | | 1970-71 | | 1971-73 | | |
| | | Percent with 1+ interfirm shifts | | | Percent with employer in 1971 | | Percent with different employer in 1973 | |
	N^a	Total	Per year[b]	N^a		N^a	Total	Per year[c]
Whites								
10–11, total (or average)	877	77%	19%	710	37%	602	40%	20%
12, total (or average)	3,342	68	17	2,836	27	3,446	35	17
Vocational	504	71	18	448	24	560	33	17
Commercial	200	69	17	165	30	194	39	20
General	1,987	67	17	1,735	26	2,090	35	18
College preparatory	650	69	17	489	34	601	35	17
13–15, total (or average)	1,188	68	17	1,105	29	1,735	36	18
Blacks								
10–11, total (or average)	200	79%	20%	133	38%	174	24%	12%
12, total (or average)	427	75	19	340	28	395	32	16
Vocational	72	77	19	62	25	77	35	18
Commercial	21	d	d	14	d	13	d	d
General	283	76	19	224	26	252	29	14
College preparatory	50	66	16	39	46	53	34	17
13–15, total (or average)	85	71	18	59	33	120	24	12

[a]Includes only those interviewed both years.
[b]Estimated by dividing total percentage by 4.
[c]Estimated by dividing total percentage by 2.
[d]Not calculated, base less than 25 sample cases.

Table A4.8. Occupation (major group) on current (or last)
job (1972, 1973) by highest year of school completed
(1972, 1973) and race: men and women *not*
enrolled, but interviewed (1972, 1973)
(N in thousands)

	Men			Women		
	10–11 years	*12 years*	*13–15 years*	*10–11 years*	*12 years*	*13–15 years*
Whites (N)	602	3,441	1,738	532	3,597	1,614
Prof, tech[a]	1%	4%	10%	2%	5%	30%
Managerial	8	11	20	2	2	4
Clerical	4	7	11	38	60	43
Sales	2	5	9	4	7	4
Craftsmen	34	31	20	3	1	0
Operatives	32	26	16	17	9	3
Pvt. H.H. Workers	0	0	0	6	3	2
Service	5	6	6	24	14	13
Farmers and farm mgrs.	3	3	2	0	0	0
Farm laborers and foremen	1	1	1	1	0	0
Laborers	9	6	5	1	0	0
Armed forces	0	0	*	b	b	b
Blacks (N)	173	394	118	149	408	163
Prof, tech[a]	1%	3%	10%	3%	2%	21%
Managerial	2	5	5	1	1	2
Clerical	1	6	21	22	50	54
Sales	1	3	5	1	1	2
Craftsmen	12	20	13	0	2	0
Operatives	52	44	26	24	20	9
Pvt. H.H. Workers	0	0	0	9	4	0
Service	8	7	9	38	20	10
Farmers and farm mgrs.	1	0	1	0	0	0
Farm laborers and foremen	6	1	1	0	0	0
Laborers	16	11	8	2	1	1
Armed forces	0	0	0	b	b	b

[a]Detail may not add to 100 percent due to rounding.

[b]Category was not included for women.

*Less than 0.5 percent.

Table A4.9. Major industry group, current (or last) job 1973, by highest year of school completed and high school curriculum (most recent), and race: men *not* enrolled (N in thousands)

	N	Agri, forestry, fisheries, and mining	Construction	Manufacturing	Trans, comm, and public utilities	Trade	Finance, ins, and real estate	Services
Whites								
10–11, total (or average)	598	6%	20%	30%	11%	19%	1%	13%
Voc and comm	109	5	27	29	12	18	0	9
General	441	7	17	32	11	19	0	13
12, total (or average)	3,430	7	15	36	8	18	2	14
Vocational	564	11	15	42	11	16	0	5
General	2,078	6	17	37	6	19	2	12
College preparatory	594	3	13	28	12	19	4	22
13–15, total (or average)	1,746	7	12	24	8	23	7	20
Voc and comm	198	4	8	31	8	24	8	17
General	637	2	14	21	10	24	7	22
College preparatory	911	8	12	26	7	21	7	19
Blacks								
10–11, total (or average)	174	8%	14%	36%	11%	20%	0%	12%
Voc and comm	30	8	15	20	5	32	0	20
General	138	9	12	38	12	18	0	11
12, total (or average)	393	2	11	46	8	15	3	16
Vocational	76	2	3	61	6	11	0	16
General	251	2	13	42	9	17	4	15
College preparatory	53	0	14	37	6	8	2	33
13–15, total (or average)	120	3	5	30	24	10	4	24
General	65	3	3	31	26	8	4	26
College preparatory	38	2	3	36	24	12	4	19

[a]Percent may not add to 100 due to rounding.

Table A4.10. Major industry group, current job 1972, by highest year of school completed and high school curriculum (most recent), and race: women *not* enrolled, employed for wages or salary (N in thousands)

	N	Agri, for, fish, mining and construction	Manufacturing	Trans, comm, and public utilities	Trade	Finance, ins, and real estate	Personal services	Professional and related services	Public administration	Other services
Whites										
10–11 total (or average)	532	2%	20%	5%	29%	6%	13%	16%	5%	4%
Business and office	117	0	24	12	12	12	5	24	7	4
General	284	3	22	3	32	3	20	10	5	1
12, total (or average)	3,597	2	19	8	21	14	7	21	5	4
Vocational	106	4	31	4	26	4	13	12	5	0
Business and office	1,180	1	20	10	16	16	3	23	7	5
General	1,384	2	19	6	24	11	10	18	5	3
College preparatory	854	2	16	10	21	16	6	23	3	3
13–15, total (or average)	1,614	1	9	3	18	5	4	49	5	6
Business and office	114	4	24	0	12	0	0	30	13	17
General	357	1	12	2	22	3	4	47	4	5
College preparatory	1,111	1	7	4	18	7	4	51	4	5
Blacks										
10–11, total (or average)	149	0%	21%	4%	15%	3%	14%	31%	8%	5%
General	102	0	22	4	17	0	17	29	6	5
12, total (or average)	408	0	23	6	15	9	8	26	7	6
Business and office	98	1	18	7	14	11	2	24	14	10
General	233	0	24	3	15	10	14	26	5	4
College preparatory	56	0	30	18	18	6	0	16	5	7
13–15, total (or average)	163	1	16	10	9	8	0	48	8	0
General	68	0	26	13	1	5	0	46	10	0
College preparatory	78	2	11	8	15	11	0	47	6	0

Percent [a]

[a]Percent may not equal exactly 100 due to rounding.

Table A4.11. Hourly rate of pay, 1971: regression results for men
with exactly 12 years of school, *not* enrolled, employed
for wages on salary, 1971
(Standard errors in parentheses)

Explanatory variables and statistics	Ignoring CB Coverage		Including CB Coverage	
	Whites	Blacks	Whites	Blacks
SA	0.01**	−0.004	0.01**	−0.004
	(0.005)	(0.01)	(0.005)	(0.01)
SEO	0.04	0.12**	0.05**	0.11*
	(0.04)	(0.06)	(0.03)	(0.06)
VOC_{71}[a]	0.10	−0.19	0.04	−0.19
	(0.16)	(0.25)	(0.15)	(0.24)
COM^{a}_{71}	−0.28	−0.34	−0.29	−0.33
	(0.24)	(0.45)	(0.22)	(0.44)
CP_{71}[a]	−0.14	−0.50	−0.10	−0.49
	(0.16)	(0.31)	(0.15)	(0.30)
$WEXP_{71}$	0.21**	0.10**	0.21**	0.09**
	(0.02)	(0.04)	(0.02)	(0.04)
$MLSVC_{71}$	−0.04	0.17*	−0.04	0.14
	(0.12)	(0.12)	(0.11)	(0.20)
$SOUTH_{71}$	−0.61**	−0.59**	−0.37**	−0.42**
	(0.13)	(0.20)	(0.12)	(0.21)
$SMSA_{71}$	0.17*	0.30*	0.16*	0.31*
	(0.13)	(0.21)	(0.12)	(0.21)
$TNG(IM)_{71}$	0.40**	0.24*	0.32**	0.21
	(0.12)	(0.18)	(0.11)	(0.18)
CB_{71}	b	b	1.03**	0.46**
			(0.11)	(0.19)
Constant	0.30	1.74	−0.26	1.57
R^2	0.19	0.22	0.30	0.25
F	14.59**	4.02**	23.61**	4.31**
N	625	157	625	157
Mean (Y)	$3.67	$3.04	$3.67	$3.04
SD (Y)	1.50	1.22	1.50	1.22

[a]Reference group: *general* curriculum.

[b]Variable *not* included in the model.

*Significant at 0.10 level (1-tailed t test except for curriculum variables).

**Significant at 0.05 level.

Table A4.12. Hourly rate of pay, 1971: regression results for men, all races, by highest year of school completed, *not* enrolled, employed for wages or salary, 1971 (Standard errors in parentheses)

Explanatory variables and statistics	Highest year of school completed		
	10–11 years	12 years	13–15 years
SA	0.01 (0.01)	0.01** (0.004)	-0.001 (0.01)
SEO	0.002 (0.05)	0.06** (0.03)	0.10* (0.06)
VOC_{71}[a]	0.13 (0.28)	0.05 (0.13)	0.53 (0.34)
COM_{71}[a]	0.61 (0.65)	-0.30 (0.21)	0.52 (0.66)
CP_{71}[a]	0.18 (0.35)	-0.20 (0.14)	0.01 (0.20)
$WEXP_{71}$	0.10** (0.04)	0.20** (0.02)	0.28** (0.05)
$MLSVC_{71}$	-0.02 (0.22)	-0.02 (0.10)	0.19 (0.20)
$SOUTH_{71}$	-0.75** (0.20)	-0.66** (0.11)	-0.54** (0.21)
$SMSA_{71}$	0.19 (0.20)	0.13 (0.11)	0.22 (0.19)
$TNG(IM)_{71}$	0.43** (0.20)	0.39** (0.10)	0.17 (0.19)
Constant	1.94	0.10	0.74
R^2	0.20	0.20	0.16
F	3.89**	20.13**	6.39**
N	167	803	336
Mean (Y)	$3.37	$3.60	$3.98
SD (Y)	1.31	1.48	1.76

[a]Reference group: *general* curriculum.

*Significant at 0.10 level (1-tailed t test except for curriculum variables).

**Significant at 0.05 level.

Vocational Education and Training

Table A4.13. Wage or salary earnings in past year, 1971: regression results for men with exactly 12 years of school, *not* enrolled in either 1970 or 1971, employed for wages or salary, 1971 (Standard error in parentheses)

Explanatory variables and statistics	Ignoring CB Coverage		Including CB Coverage	
	Whites	Blacks	Whites	Blacks
SA	33**	14	34**	12
	(15)	(20)	(14)	(20)
SEO	136	181	136	183
	(99)	(161)	(97)	(158)
VOC_{71}[a]	487	-376	363	-376
	(431)	(631)	(424)	(621)
COM_{71}[a]	-252	-234	-270	-433
	(639)	(1,267)	(627)	(1,249)
CP_{71}[a]	587	-236	608	-187
	(440)	(833)	(431)	(820)
$WEXP_{71}$	634**	217**	633**	181*
	(67)	(108)	(66)	(108)
$MLSVC_{71}$	-188	385	-213	400
	(332)	(556)	(326)	(547)
$SOUTH_{71}$	-689*	-1,366**	-310	-889
	(356)	(536)	(358)	(568)
$SMSA_{71}$	-152	-89	-142	-80
	(373)	(546)	(366)	(537)
$TNG(IM)_{71}$	588*	417	477	331
	(333)	(484)	(327)	(477)
CM_{71}	b	b	1,493**	1,152**
			(312)	(512)
Constant	-2,374	2,217	-3,058	1,782
R^2	0.17	0.07	0.21	0.17
F	11.68**	11.91**	13.11**	2.25**
N	567	130	567	130
Mean (Y)	$7,460	$5,999	$7,460	$5,999
SD (Y)	3,907	2,774	3,907	2,774

[a]Reference group: *general* curriculum.

[b]Variable *not* included in the model.

*Significant at 0.10 level (1-tailed t test except for curriculum variables).

**Significant at 0.05 level.

Table A4.14. Wage or salary earnings in past year, 1971: regression
results for men, by highest year of school completed, *not*
enrolled in either 1970 or 1971, employed for wages
or salary, 1971 (Standard error in parentheses)

Explanatory variables and statistics	Highest year of schooling completed		
	10–11 years	12 years	13–15 years
SA	24	32**	10
	(22)	(11)	(23)
SEO	7	144**	189
	(132)	(83)	(185)
VOC_{71}[a]	415	324	353
	(706)	(368)	(1,069)
COM_{71}[a]	20	−256	−518
	(1,683)	(565)	(2,001)
CP_{71}[a]	1,613*	502	108
	(927)	(382)	(625)
$WEXP_{71}$	366**	585**	613**
	(95)	(58)	(155)
$MLSVC_{71}$	−315	−122	208
	(574)	(288)	(655)
$SOUTH_{71}$	−1,300**	−893**	−425
	(514)	(300)	(699)
$SMSA_{71}$	−381	−214	208
	(522)	(301)	(584)
$TNG(IM)_{71}$	637	603**	966*
	(516)	(284)	(623)
Constant	1,426	−1,959	334
R^2	0.20	0.17	0.10
F	3.58**	14.71**	2.72**
N	153	724	255
Mean (Y)	$6,794	$7,296	$8,667
SD (Y)	3,190	3,820	4,599

[a]Reference group: *general* curriculum.

*Significant at 0.10 level (1-tailed t test except for curriculum variables).

**Significant at 0.05 level.

Table A4.15. Duncan index of current job, 1971: regression
results for men with exactly 12 years of school, *not*
enrolled, employed for wages or salary, 1971
(Standard errors in parentheses)

Explanatory variables and statistics	Ignoring CB coverage		Including CB coverage	
	Whites	Blacks	Whites	Blacks
SA	0.20**	0.32**	0.20**	0.32**
	(0.06)	(0.09)	(0.07)	(0.09)
SEO	1.30	−0.59	1.33**	−0.57
	(0.43)	(0.75)	(0.45)	(0.78)
VOC_{71}[a]	−1.82	−1.15	−1.27	−1.17
	(1.92)	(3.12)	(2.01)	(3.20)
COM_{71}[a]	4.96*	4.83	5.20*	4.82
	(2.99)	(5.34)	(3.13)	(5.48)
CP_{71}[a]	2.54	1.76	2.29	1.76
	(1.93)	(3.90)	(2.03)	(3.96)
$WEXP_{71}$	1.17**	−0.69	1.20**	−0.68
	(0.31)	(0.54)	(0.32)	(0.56)
$MLSVC_{71}$	−1.96*	−0.06	−1.91*	−0.06
	(1.43)	(2.52)	(1.49)	(2.70)
$SMSA_{71}$	4.09**	0.80	4.09**	0.84
	(1.66)	(2.56)	(1.72)	(2.64)
$TNG (IM)_{71}$	7.01**	8.32**	7.60**	8.33**
	(1.45)	(2.34)	(1.53)	(2.40)
CB_{71}	b	b	−6.98**	−0.40
			(1.47)	(2.40)
Constant	−15.62	0.49	−14.21	0.53
R^2	0.11	0.16	0.14	0.16
F	9.42**	3.91**	9.99**	3.72**
N	728	189	645	180
Mean (Y)	31.40	22.45	31.40	22.45
SD (Y)	19.25	16.78	19.25	16.78

[a]Reference group: *general* curriculum.

[b]Variable *not* included in the model.

*Significant at 0.10 level (1-tailed t test except for curriculum variables).

**Significant at 0.05 level.

Table A4.16. Duncan index of current job, 1971: regression
results for men, all races, by highest year of school
completed, *not* enrolled, employed for wages or
salary, 1971 (Standard errors in parentheses)

Explanatory variables and statistics	Highest year of school completed		
	10–11 years	12 years	13–15 years
SA	0.20** (0.08)	0.25** (0.05)	0.29** (0.09)
SEO	1.31** (0.59)	1.32** (0.35)	1.80** (0.74)
VOC_{71}[a]	−2.69 (3.07)	−1.84 (1.66)	−2.06 (4.48)
COM_{71}[a]	1.51 (6.37)	4.88* (2.61)	9.17 (8.28)
CP_{71}[a]	3.06 (3.78)	2.08 (1.70)	−1.73 (2.54)
$WEXP_{71}$	0.64* (0.40)	0.98** (0.27)	2.90** (0.62)
MIL_{71}	−1.52 (2.39)	−1.60 (1.25)	2.33 (2.46)
$SMSA_{71}$	−1.06 (2.21)	2.75** (1.35)	3.55** (2.34)
$TNG(IM)_{71}$	3.39* (2.18)	7.24** (1.25)	1.38 (2.41)
Constant	−12.10	−19.48	−29.89
R^2	0.12	0.12	0.11
F	2.95**	13.62**	5.17**
N	208	940	404
Mean (Y)	24.09	30.34	42.79
SD (Y)	15.65	19.18	23.43

[a]Reference group: *general* curriculum.

*Significant at 0.10 level (1-tailed t test except for curriculum variables).

**Significant at 0.05 level.

Table A4.17. 1969 earnings in occupation of current job, 1971:
Regression results for men with exactly 12 years of school,
not enrolled, employed for wages or salary, 1971
(Standard errors in parentheses)

Explanatory variables and statistics	Ignoring CB coverage		Including CB coverage	
	Whites	*Blacks*	*Whites*	*Blacks*
SA	20**	4	21**	4
	(11)	(12)	(12)	(13)
SEO	250**	41	256**	39
	(73)	(101)	(76)	(105)
VOC_{71}[a]	-140	-324	-33	-321
	(330)	(421)	(345)	(433)
COM_{71}[a]	434	-46	480	-45
	(514)	(719)	(535)	(740)
CP_{71}[a]	65	84	17	83
	(333)	(325)	(347)	(540)
$WEXP_{71}$	148**	8	154**	6
	(53)	(73)	(55)	(76)
MIL_{71}	-227	63	-217	51
	(246)	(340)	(256)	(352)
$SMSA_{71}$	391*	140	392*	130
	(286)	(345)	(297)	(357)
$TNG(IM_{71}$	346*	831**	461**	829**
	(250)	(315)	(261)	(324)
CB_{71}	b	b	-1,348**	87
			(253)	(326)
Constant	2,823	6,148	3,093	6,138
R^2	0.04	0.05	0.08	0.05
F	3.33**	1.08**	5.62**	0.92
N	728	189	645	180
Mean (Y)	$8,771	7,375	8,771	7,375
SD (Y)	3,196	2,121	3,196	2,121

[a]Reference group: *general* curriculum.

[b]Variable not included in the model.

*Significant at 0.10 level (1-tailed t test except for curriculum variables).

**Significant at 0.05 level.

Table A4.18. 1969 earnings in occupation of current job, 1971:
Regression results for men, all races, by highest year of
school completed, *not* enrolled, employed for wages
and salary, 1971 (Standard errors in parentheses)

Explanatory variables and statistics	Highest year of school completed		
	10–11 years	12 years	13–15 years
SA	46** (16)	25** (9)	14 (15)
SEO	174* (111)	263** (60)	336** (127)
VOC_{71}[a]	−351 (574)	−194 (279)	−957 (768)
COM_{71}[a]	−313** (119)	362 (439)	85 (1,419)
CP_{71}[a]	−71 (707)	2 (286)	−267 (435)
$WEXP_{71}$	83 (75)	135** (45)	374** (107)
MIL_{71}	−88 (448)	−185 (210)	340 (421)
$SMSA_{71}$	−299 (414)	149 (227)	367 (402)
$TNG(IM)_{71}$	91 (408)	427** (211)	336 (413)
Constant	1,816	2,236	3,555
R^2	0.09	0.05	0.06
F	2.11**	5.57**	2.81**
N	208	940	404
Mean (Y)	$8,078	8,601	10,168
SD (Y)	2,876	3,114	3,918

[a]Reference group: *general* curriculum.

*Significant at 0.10 level (1-tailed t test except for curriculum variables).

**Significant at 0.05 level.

Table A4.19. Hourly rate of pay, 1972: regression results for women with exactly 12 years of school, *not* enrolled, and employed for wages or salary, 1972 (Standard errors in parentheses)

Explanatory variables and statistics	*Ignoring CB coverage*		*Including CB coverage*		*Including %FM,OCC$_{72}$*	
	Whites	*Blacks*	*Whites*	*Blacks*	*Whites*	*Blacks*
SA	0.01** (0.003)	0.01** (0.005)	0.01** (0.003)	0.01** (0.005)	0.01** (0.003)	0.01** (0.005)
SEO	0.03 (0.02)	0.07* (0.04)	0.03 (0.02)	0.06 (0.04)	0.04* (0.02)	0.07** (0.04)
VOC$_{72}$[a]	0.11 (0.25)	-0.71 (0.36)	0.13 (0.24)	-0.67 (0.37)	0.07 (0.25)	-0.71* (0.37)
B&O$_{72}$[a]	0.27** (0.08)	0.26** (0.12)	0.30** (0.08)	0.27** (0.13)	0.28** (0.08)	0.26** (0.13)
CP$_{72}$[a]	0.24** (0.10)	0.03 (0.22)	0.25** (0.10)	0.03 (0.22)	0.23** (0.10)	0.03 (0.22)
WEXP$_{72}$	0.10** (0.02)	-0.06** (0.03)	0.10** (0.02)	-0.05* (0.03)	0.10** (0.02)	-0.06** (0.03)
TNR$_{72}$	0.01** (0.002)	0.02** (0.003)	0.01** (0.002)	0.02** (0.003)	0.01** (0.002)	0.02** (0.003)
SMSA$_{72}$	0.30** (0.08)	0.14 (0.21)	0.28** (0.08)	0.13 (0.21)	0.29** (0.08)	0.14 (0.22)

TNG_{72}	0.10* (0.07)	0.11 (0.11)	0.10* (0.7)	0.14 (0.12)	0.11* (0.07)	0.11 (0.12)
FT_{72}	0.07 (0.09)	0.20 (0.18)	0.08 (0.08)	0.18 (0.18)	0.07 (0.09)	0.20 (0.18)
CB_{72}	b	b	0.44** (0.10)	0.11 (0.12)	b	b
$\%FM,OCC_{72}$	b	b	b	b	-0.0003* (0.0002)	0.00 (0.0002)
Constant	0.27	0.48	0.19	0.47	0.35	0.48
R^2	0.25	0.25	0.28	0.25	0.25	0.25
F	16.75**	4.99**	17.83**	4.60**	15.68**	4.50**
N	474	119	474	119	474	119
Mean (Y)	2.58	2.54	2.58	2.54	2.58	2.54
SD (Y)	0.90	0.69	0.90	0.69	0.90	0.69

a Reference group: *general* curriculum.

b Variable *not* included in the model.

*Significant at 0.10 level (1-tailed t test except for curriculum variables).

**Significant at 0.05 level.

Table A4.20. Wage or salary earnings in past year, 1972: regression results for women with exactly 12 years of school, *not* enrolled in either 1971 or 1972, employed for wages or salary, 1972 (Standard errors in parentheses)

Explanatory variables and statistics	Ignoring CB coverage		Including CB coverage		Including %FM,OCC72	
	Whites	Blacks	Whites	Blacks	Whites	Blacks
SA	11 (7)	24* (14)	11 (7)	25* (14)	11 (7)	24* (14)
SEO	103** (50)	-2 (116)	100** (50)	-24 (118)	106** (50)	-5 (117)
VOC72[a]	890* (523)	-1,642 (1,032)	910* (521)	-1,477 (1,044)	845 (525)	-1,687 (1,045)
B&O72[a]	665** (181)	683* (365)	697** (181)	700* (366)	669** (181)	662* (373)
CP72[a]	225 (219)	-341 (640)	243 (218)	-378 (640)	213 (219)	-346 (643)
WEXP72	222** (38)	-54 (81)	226** (38)	-43 (81)	224 (38)	-50 (82)
TNR72	25** (4)	54** (10)	24** (4)	54** (10)	25** (4)	53** (10)
SMSA72	387** (172)	876* (612)	362** (171)	861* (612)	370** (172)	855* (619)

TNG$_{72}$	189	64	198	142	203	51
	(162)	(340)	(161)	(349)	(162)	(344)
FT$_{72}$	1,530**	1,411**	1,540**	1,358**	1,529**	1,426**
	(187)	(517)	(186)	(520)	(187)	(522)
CB$_{72}$	b	b	455**	360	b	b
			(208)	(354)		
%FM,OCC$_{72}$	b	b	b	b	-0.35	0.21
					(0.32)	(0.65)
Constant	-1,514	-1,119	-1,538	-1,178	-1,429	-1,472
R^2	0.40	0.32	0.41	0.32	0.40	0.31
F	30.65**	6.08**	28.54**	5.62**	27.98**	5.49**
N	445	109	445	109	445	109
Mean (Y)	$4,158	$4,284	$4,158	$4,284	$4,158	$4,284
SD (Y)	2,102	2,027	2,102	2,027	2,102	2,027

[a]Reference group: *general* curriculum.

[b]Variable *not* included in the model.

*Significant at 0.10 level (1-tailed t test except for curriculum variables).

**Significant at 0.05 level.

Table A4.21. **Wages and salary earnings for past year: regression results for women with exactly 12 years of school, *not* enrolled in either 1971 or 1972, employed for wages or salary, employed 39+ weeks, 1972 (Standard errors in parentheses)**

Explanatory variables and statistics	Ignoring CB coverage		Including CB coverage		Including %FM, OCC_{72}	
	Whites	Blacks	Whites	Blacks	Whites	Blacks
SA	8	34**	9	34**	8	34**
	(8)	(13)	(8)	(13)	(8)	(13)
SEO	68	164*	64	165*	69	156*
	(56)	(116)	(55)	(119)	(56)	(117)
VOC_{72}[a]	648	-1,669	666	-1,667	581	-1,731
	(571)	(1,154)	(566)	(1,174)	(572)	(1,170)
$B\&O_{72}$[a]	594**	469	647**	468	595**	453
	(198)	(349)	(198)	(353)	(198)	(353)
CP_{72}[a]	179	-738	205	-737	178	-716
	(244)	(623)	(241)	(627)	(243)	(628)
$WEXP_{72}$	142**	-147**	154**	-148**	148**	-142**
	(44)	(77)	(44)	(79)	(44)	(78)
TNR_{72}	20**	34**	18**	34**	20**	33**
	(4)	(10)	(4)	(10)	(4)	(10)
$SMSA_{72}$	385**	743	353**	745	345**	714
	(193)	(616)	(192)	(621)	(195)	(623)

TNG$_{72}$	216*	177	202	174	238*	168
	(178)	(331)	(177)	(339)	(179)	(333)
FT$_{72}$	1,540**	1,202**	1,573**	1,204**	1,542**	1,240**
	(218)	(582)	(216)	(588)	(218)	(591)
CB$_{72}$	b	b	609**	−17	b	b
			(223)	(343)		
%FM,OCC$_{72}$	b	b	b	b	−0.54*	0.27
					(0.36)	(0.63)
Constant	−89	1,797	−189	−1,794	102	−1,818
R^2	0.27	0.24	0.28	0.23	0.27	0.23
F	14.09**	3.75**	13.73**	3.36**	13.06**	3.39**
N	353	90	353	90	353	90
Mean (Y)	$4,733	$4,808	$4,733	$4,808	$4,733	$4,808
SD (Y)	1,854	1,655	1,854	1,655	1,854	1,655

[a]Reference group: *general* curriculum.

[b]Variable *not* included in the model.

*Significant at 0.10 level (1-tailed t test except for curriculum variables).

**Significant at 0.05 level.

Table A4.22. Bose index of current job, 1972: regression
results for women with exactly 12 years of school, *not*
enrolled, employed for wages or salary, 1972

Explanatory variables and statistics	Total	Whites	Blacks
SA	0.12**	0.10**	0.15**
	(0.03)	(0.03)	(0.07)
SEO	0.78**	0.71**	1.60**
	(0.21)	(0.23)	(0.58)
VOC_{72}[a]	−4.93**	−5.05**	−6.07
	(2.20)	(2.48)	(5.54)
$B\&O_{72}$[a]	3.16**	3.34**	−0.30
	(0.75)	(0.84)	(1.90)
CP_{72}[a]	−0.17	−0.03	−3.19
	(0.91)	(0.99)	(3.29)
$WEXP_{72}$	0.31**	0.40**	−0.83**
	(0.16)	(0.17)	(0.41)
TNR_{72}	0.01	0.01	0.04
	(0.02)	(0.02)	(0.05)
$SMSA_{72}$	2.51**	2.64**	3.56
	(0.72)	(0.78)	(3.25)
TNG_{72}	1.56**	1.31**	4.19**
	(0.67)	(0.74)	(1.73)
FT_{72}	2.13**	2.18**	4.94**
	(0.79)	(0.86)	(2.70)
Constant	20.67	23.08	9.49
R^2	0.18	0.17	0.19
F	14.07**	10.84**	3.70**
N	599	474	119
Mean (Y)	47.50	47.77	44.03
SD (Y)	8.67	8.50	10.02

[a]Reference group: *general* curriculum.

*Significant at 0.10 level (1-tailed t test except for curriculum variables).

**Significant at 0.05 level.

Table A4.23.   1969 full-year earnings in occupation of current
job, 1972: regression results for women with exactly
12 years of school, not enrolled, 1972, employed
for wages or salary, 1972
(Standard errors in parentheses)

Explanatory variables and statistics	Whites	Blacks
SA	10**	22**
	(5)	(8)
SEO	18	71
	(35)	(66)
VOC_{72}[a]	99	-879
	(377)	(629)
$B\&O_{72}$[a]	262**	-182
	(127)	(216)
CP_{72}[a]	198	-427
	(150)	(373)
$WEXP_{72}$	32	-3
	(26)	(46)
TNR_{72}	1	-5
	(3)	(6)
$SMSA_{72}$	255**	101
	(119)	(368)
TNG_{72}	-81	-17
	(112)	(196)
FT_{72}	130	528**
	(131)	(306)
Constant	3,256	1,948
R^2	0.03	0.07
F	2.29**	1.84**
N	474	119
Mean (Y)	$4,984	$4,787
SD (Y)	1,190	1,061

[a]Reference group: *general* curriculum.

*Significant at 0.10 level (1-tailed t test except for curriculum variables).

**Significant at 0.05 level.

Table A4.24. Hourly rate of pay, 1972: regression results for
women, all races, with 10–11 or 13–15 years of school,
not enrolled, and employed for wages or salary, 1972
(Standard errors in parentheses)

Explanatory variables and statistics	Completed 10–11 years	Completed 13–15 years		
		Basic model	Including	
			% FM, OCC_{72}	CB
SA	0.01 (0.01)	0.017 (0.014)	0.017 (0.014)	0.016 (0.013)
SEO	0.05 (0.05)	0.07 (0.08)	0.07 (0.08)	0.10 (0.08)
VOC_{72}[a]	b	b	b	b
$B\&O_{72}$[a]	b	b	b	b
CP_{72}[a]	b	0.23 (0.33)	0.22 (0.33)	0.21 (0.32)
$WEXP_{72}$	0.03 (0.02)	−0.04 (0.09)	−0.04 (0.09)	−0.04 (0.09)
TNR_{72}	−0.00 (0.00)	0.01 (0.01)	0.01 (0.01)	0.00 (0.01)
$SMSA_{72}$	0.29** (0.14)	−0.03 (0.30)	−0.04 (0.30)	−0.05 (0.29)
TNG_{72}	0.28** (0.14)	0.14 (0.27)	0.16 (0.28)	0.02 (0.27)
FT_{72}	0.93** (0.14)	−0.46* (0.30)	−0.46* (0.31)	−0.40 (0.30)
CB_{72}	c	c	c	0.78** (0.34)
%FM,OCC_{72}	c	c	0.00 (0.00)	c
Constant	0.38 (0.71)	0.84 (1.60)	0.73 (1.64)	0.66 (1.58)
R^2	0.40	0.00	0.01	0.02
F	5.75**	0.92	0.84	1.33*
N	80	171	171	171
Mean (Y)	$2.25	$3.35	$3.35	$3.35
SD (Y)	0.69	1.68	1.68	1.68

[a]Reference group: *general* curriculum.

[b]Based on less than 25 sample cases.

[c]Variable *not* included in the model.

  *Significant at 0.10 level (1-tailed t test except for curriculum variables).

**Significant at 0.05 level.

Table A4.25. Occupation (major group) on first job after leaving school 1966, current (or last) job 1966, and current (or last) job 1973, by highest year of school completed and high school curriculum (most recent) as of relevant year: men *not* enrolled but interviewed in year in question, who had completed exactly 12 years of school (N in thousands)

	Vocational			Commercial			General		
	1st job	Current (last) job 1966	1973	1st job	Current (last) job 1966	1973	1st job	Current (last) job 1966	1973
Whites (N)	373	401	564	128	136	194	1415	1481	2085
Prof, tech[a]	1%	4%	4%	3%	3%	0%	1%	4%	3%
Managerial	2	3	5	0	12	9	2	3	11
Clerical	5	6	3	27	25	12	11	12	7
Sales	*	3	3	4	8	8	5	3	4
Craftsmen	20	31	36	0	11	22	13	23	31
Operatives	36	35	31	29	29	32	33	35	28
Service	5	2	4	6	6	7	6	5	6
Farm	7	10	6	9	0	2	9	5	4
Laborer, nonfarm	23	6	7	22	6	6	20	10	6
Armed forces	0	*	0	0	0	0	*	1	0
Blacks (N)	52	54	77	9	9	13	217	224	252
Prof, tech[a]	0%	0%	2%	b	b	b	2%	0%	4%
Managerial	0	0	3	b	b	b	0	1	4
Clerical	26	17	3	b	b	b	4	7	6
Sales	0	0	0	b	b	b	0	0	4
Craftsmen	2	8	22	b	b	b	6	10	22
Operatives	15	55	51	b	b	b	29	42	44
Service	32	8	5	b	b	b	26	18	8
Farm	14	0	0	b	b	b	2	2	2
Laborers, nonfarm	10	13	15	b	b	b	30	18	7
Armed forces	0	0	0	b	b	b	0	2	0

[a]Detail may not add to 100 percent due to rounding.
[b]Percentages not shown; base less than 25 sample cases.
*Less than 0.5 percent.

Table A5.1. Reason hurt (or not hurt) by not having more education, by highest year of school completed, high school curriculum (most recent), and race: men (1966) *not* enrolled in school (N in thousands)

	Hurt				Not Hurt				
	N	Can't get as good a job	Difficult to get a job	Other	N	Have job; no trouble getting job	Wouldn't be making as much money	Don't need more for job	Other
					Whites				
10-11, total (or average)	373	63%	25%	12%	382	75%	3%	15%	7%
Voc/com	64	a	a	a	54	a	a	a	a
General	278	62	27	12	306	78	4	10	9
College preparatory	30	a	a	a	22	a	a	a	a
12, total (or average)	996	80	10	10	1,357	75	3	13	9
Voc/com	155	77	5	18	332	77	4	10	8
General	606	82	10	9	788	75	3	12	10
College preparatory	235	76	15	8	237	71	0	21	7
13-15, total (or average)	279	80	11	9	276	70	3	14	14
Voc/com	20	a	a	a	24	a	a	a	a
General	122	81	12	7	102	51	8	29	12
College preparatory	137	88	6	6	150	80	0	5	14
10-15, total (or average)	1,671	75	14	10	2,064	74	3	14	9

					Blacks				
10-11, total (or average)	150	81%	14%	5%	72	52%	1%	15%	32%
Voc/com	30	81	16	3	7	a	a	a	a
General	107	78	16	6	63	52	0	13	34
College preparatory	12	a	a	a	2	a	a	a	a
12, total (or average)	186	87	8	5	116	78	1	10	12
Voc/com	43	100	0	0	15	a	a	a	a
General	120	84	9	7	88	81	0	10	9
College preparatory	22	a	a	a	12	a	a	a	a
13-15, total (or average)	33	76	4	20	10	a	a	a	a
Voc/com	1	a	a	a	3	a	a	a	a
General	14	a	a	a	4	a	a	a	a
College preparatory	18	a	a	a	3	a	a	a	a
10-15, total (or average)	376	84	10	6	208	71	1	10	17

aPercent *not* reported; less than 25 sample cases.

Table A5.2 Perceived change in financial position, by highest year of school completed, high school curriculum (most recent), sex, and race: men (1970-71) *not* enrolled 1971, and women (annual average 1968-69, 69-70, 70-71, and 71-72) *not* enrolled in relevant years
(N in thousands)

	Whites			Blacks		
		Percent[a]			Percent[a]	
	N	Better off now	Worse off now	N	Better off now	Worse off now
Men						
10-11, total (or average)	905	54%	15%	222	34%	23%
Vocational	129	55	18	34	43	28
General	662	53	15	163	31	20
12, total (or average)	3,640	53	14	487	42	11
Vocational	581	59	13	86	37	13
Commercial	209	58	15	25	47	7
General	2,164	53	13	321	42	12
College preparatory	686	47	19	56	48	5
13-15, total (or average)	1,453	58	14	90	61	9
Vocational	107	51	11	10	b	b
General	540	55	13	44	62	16
College preparatory	776	61	16	35	52	2
Women						
12, total (or average)	3,213[c]	60%	10%	396	54%	8%
Vocational	111[d]	60	17	15	b	b
Business and office	1,168[c]	62	8	99	58	8
General	1,214[c]	56	8	225	51	8
College preparatory	715[c]	59	11	54	65	3

[a]Middle category, "about the same," not included in percentaging.
[b]Percent *not* reported; less than 25 sample cases or observations.
[c]Weighted average for the four years.

Table A6.1. Hourly rate of pay, 1971: regression results for selected groups of men, not enrolled, employed as wage or salary workers 1971 (Standard errors in parentheses)

Explanatory variables and statistics	Completed exactly 12 years				Completed 10–11 years (all)
	Total (all races)	Blacks only	Health limits work (all)	Foreign language in home, age 15 (all)	
SA	0.01** (0.004)	−0.004 (0.007)	0.07** (0.02)	0.01 (0.01)	0.01 (0.01)
SEO	0.06** (0.03)	0.12** (0.06)	0.05 (0.14)	0.26** (0.08)	0.002 (0.05)
VOC_{71}[a]	0.05 (0.13)	0.19 (0.25)	−0.40 (0.53)	−0.54 (0.78)	0.13 (0.28)
COM_{71}[a]	−0.30 (0.21)	−0.34 (0.45)	−0.25) (1.63)	−0.05 (0.71)	0.61 (0.65)
CP_{71}[a]	−0.20 (0.14)	−0.50 (0.31)	−0.19 (0.50)	0.26 (0.43)	0.18 (0.35)
$WEXP_{71}$	0.20** (0.02)	0.10** (0.04)	0.30** (0.11)	0.13** (0.06)	0.10** (0.04)
$MLSVC_{71}$	−0.02 (0.10)	0.17 (0.12)	−0.39 (0.44)	0.43 (0.37)	−0.02 (0.22)
$SOUTH_{71}$	−0.66** (0.11)	−0.60** (0.20)	0.05 (0.44)	−0.30 (0.39)	−0.75** (0.20)
$SMSA_{71}$	0.13 (0.11)	0.30* (0.21)	−0.33 (0.50)	0.36 (0.33)	0.19 (0.20)
$TNG(IM)_{71}$	0.39** (0.10)	0.24* (0.18)	−0.15 (0.47)	0.88** (0.34)	0.43** (0.20)
Constant	0.10	1.74	−5.92	−1.42	1.94
R^2	0.20	0.22	0.31	0.28	0.20
F	20.13**	4.02**	2.74**	3.48**	3.89**
N	803	157	71	98	167
Mean (Y)	$3.60	$3.04	$3.60	$3.81	$3.37
SD (Y)	1.48	1.22	1.75	1.75	1.31

[a]Reference group: *general* curriculum

*Significant at 0.10 level (1-tailed t test except for curriculum variables and $MLSVC_{71}$).

**Significant at 0.05 level.

Table A6.2. Wage or salary earnings in past year, 1971: regression results
for selected groups of men, not enrolled 1970 or 1971,
employed as wage or salary workers 1971
(Standard error in parentheses)

Explanatory variables and statistics	Completed exactly 12 years				Completed 10-11 years (all)
	Total (all races)	Blacks only	Health limits work (all)	Foreign language in home, age 15 (all)	
SA	32** (11)	14 (20)	106* (75)	-10 (33)	24 (22)
SEO	144* (83)	181 (161)	-223 (493)	475** (253)	7 (132)
VOC_{71}[a]	324 (368)	-376 (631)	-1,034 (2,154)	-263 (2,362)	415 (706)
COM_{71}[a]	256 (565)	-234 (1,267)	-2,032 (7,036)	-2,422 (1,085)	20 (1,683)
CP_{71}[a]	502 (382)	-236 (833)	-4,715* (2,578)	1,418 (1,393)	1,613* (927)
$WEXP_{71}$	585** (58)	217** (108)	353 (537)	175 (188)	366** (95)
$MLSVC_{71}$	-122 (288)	385 (556)	-771 (2,202)	-1,041 (1,178)	-315 (574)
$SOUTH_{71}$	-893** (300)	-1,366* (536)	27 (2,016)	-45 (1,227)	-1,300** (514)
$SMSA_{71}$	-214 (301)	-89 (546)	-1,321 (2,224)	953 (1,008)	-381 (522)
$TNG(IM)_{71}$	603** (284)	417 (484)	-2,583* (1,919)	2,322** (1,088)	637 (516)
Constant	-1,959	2,217	-2,012	1,087	1,426
R^2	.17	0.07	0.17	0.17	0.20
F	14.71**	1.91	1.03	1.46**	3.58**
N	724	130	60	81	153
Mean (Y)	$7,296	$5,999	$6,515	$7,796	$6,794
SD (Y)	3,820	2,774	4,742	4,386	3,190

[a]Reference group: *general* curriculum.

*Significant at 0.10 level (1-tailed t test except for curriculum variables and $MLSVC_{71}$).

**Significant at 0.05 level.

Appendix B

Average Size of Employing Establishments, by Industry

Listed below are the number of employees per establishment in mid-March 1973, as reported to the Social Security Administration on Treasury Form 941. Excluded from the count are self-employed persons, government workers, and employees of the nation's railroads.

Employees per unit[1]	1960 Census 3-digit industry code[2]	Standard Industrial Classification (SIC) Title[2]
6	016)	
10	017)	Agriculture, forestry, and fisheries
5	018)	
107	126)	
56	136)	Mining
16	146)	
23	156)	
11	196	Construction
		Manufacturing-Durable:
7	206	Logging
34	207	Sawmills, planing mills, and millwork
29	208	Miscellaneous wood products
52	209	Furniture and fixtures
141	216	Glass and glass products

[1]Source: U.S. Bureau of the Census (1974), Table 1B, pp. 14–27.

[2]Equivalencies reported in Freedman (1976), pp. 156–161.

Employees per unit	1960 Census 3-digit industry code	Standard Industrial Classification (SIC) Title
		Manufacturing-Durable: (continued)
25	217	Cement and concrete, gypsum, and plaster products
72	218	Structural clay products
77	219	Pottery and related products
49	236	Miscellaneous nonmetallic mineral and stone products
537	237	Blast furnaces, steel works, and rolling and finishing mills
171	238	Other primary iron and steel industries
115	239	Primary nonferrous industries
100	246	Cutlery, hand tools, and other hardware
43	247	Fabricated structural metal products
75	248	Miscellaneous fabricated metal products
55	249	Non-specified metal industries
100	256	Farm machinery and equipment
250	257	Office, computing, and accounting machines
44	258	Miscellaneous machinery
152	259	Electrical machinery, equipment, and supplies
299	267	Motor vehicles and motor vehicle equipment
473	268	Aircraft and parts
106	269	Ship and boat building and repairing
86	276	Railroad and miscellaneous transportation equipment
72	286	Professional equipment and supplies
182	287	Photographic equipment and supplies
154	289	Watches, clocks, and clockwork-operated devices
32	296	Miscellaneous manufacturing industries
		Manufacturing-Nondurable:
78	306	Meat products
43	307	Dairy products
78	308	Canning and preserving fruits, vegetables, and sea food
42	309	Grain-mill products
68	316	Bakery products
83	317	Confectionary and related products
60	318	Beverage industries

Employees per unit	1960 Census 3-digit industry code	Standard Industrial Classification (SIC) Title
		Manufacturing-Nondurable: (continued)
39	319	Miscellaneous food preparations and kindred products
160	326	Not specified food industries
185	329	Tobacco manufactures
100	346	Knitting mills
134	347	Dyeing and finishing textiles, except wool and knit goods
126	348	Floor coverings, except hard surface
190	349	Yarn, thread, and fabric mills
172	356	Miscellaneous textile mill products
61	359	Apparel and accessories
32	367	Miscellaneous fabricated textile products
288	368	Pulp, paper, and paperboard mills
78	387	Paperboard containers and boxes
83	389	Miscellaneous paper and pulp products
49	396	Newspaper publishing and printing
25	398	Printing, publishing, and allied industries, except newspapers
934	406	Synthetic fibers
132	407	Drugs and medicines
45	408	Paints, varnishes, and related products
68	409	Miscellaneous chemicals and allied products
158	416	Petroleum refining
31	419	Miscellaneous petroleum and coal products
165	426	Rubber products
54	429	Miscellaneous plastic products
50	436	Leather: tanned, curried, and finished
180	437	Footwear, except rubber
47	438	Leather products, except footwear
32	459	Non-specified manufacturing industries
		Transportation and public utilities:
—	506	Railroads and railway express service
61	507	Street railways and bus lines
20	508	Taxicab service
16	509	Trucking service
14	516	Warehousing and storage
37	517	Water transportation
72	518	Air transportation
20	519	Petroleum and gasoline pipe lines

Employees per unit	1960 Census 3-digit industry code	Standard Industrial Classification (SIC) Title
		Transportation and public utilities: (continued)
11	526	Services incidental to transportation
30	536	Radio broadcasting and television
174	538	Telephone (wire and radio)
47	539	Telegraph (wire and radio)
99	567	Electric light and power
56	568	Gas and steam supply systems
199	569	Electric-gas utilities
7	576	Water supply
12	578	Sanitary services
8	579	Other and not specified utilities
		Trade:
14	606	Motor vehicles and equipment
15	607	Drugs, chemicals, and allied products
13	608	Dry goods and apparel
16	609	Food and related products
11	616	Farm products-raw materials
15	617	Electrical goods, hardware, and plumbing equipment
14	618	Machinery, equipment, and supplies
11	619	Petroleum products
15	626	Miscellaneous wholesale trade
12	629	Not specified wholesale trade
15	636	Food stores except dairy products
12	637	Dairy products stores and milk retailing
42	638	General merchandise retailing
27	639	Limited price variety stores
10	646	Apparel and accessories stores, except shoe stores
8	647	Shoe stores
8	648	Furniture and housefurnishings stores
7	649	Household appliance, TV, and radio stores
14	656	Motor vehicles and accessory retailing
5	657	Gasoline service stations
11	658	Drug stores
12	659	Eating and drinking places
7	666	Hardware and farm equipment stores
11	676	Lumber and building material retailing
4	678	Liquor stores
5	679	Retail florists

Employees per unit	1960 Census 3-digit industry code	Standard Industrial Classification (SIC) Title
		Trade: (continued)
7	686	Jewelry stores
8	687	Fuel and ice dealers
7	689	Miscellaneous retail stores
5	696	Not specified retail trade
		Finance, Insurance and Real Estate:
26	706	Banking and credit agencies
16	716	Security and commodity brokerage and investment companies
15	726	Insurance
5	736	Real estate (including real estate, insurance, law offices)
		Other Services:
13	806	Advertising
19	807	Miscellaneous business services
6	808	Automobile repair services and garages
5	809	Miscellaneous repair services
—	816	Private households
17	826	Hotels and lodging places
10	828	Laundering, cleaning, and dyeing services
3	829	Dressmaking shops
3	836	Shoe repair shops
4	838	Barber and beauty shops
8	839	Miscellaneous personal services
17	846	Theaters and motion pictures
12	848	Bowling alleys and billiard and pool parlors
13	849	Miscellaneous entertainment and recreation services
7	867	Medical and other health services, except hospitals
377	868	Hospitals
4	869	Legal services
26	876	Educational services, government and private
10	879	Welfare and religious services
10	888	Nonprofit membership organizations
12	896	Engineering and architectural services
7	897	Accounting, auditing, and bookkeeping services

Employees per unit	1960 Census 3-digit industry code	Standard Industrial Classification (SIC) Title
		Other Services: (continued)
30	898	Miscellaneous professional and related services
—	906	Postal service
—	916	Federal public administration
—	926	State public administration
—	936	Local public administration

Appendix C

Selected Characteristics of Occupations and of Occupational Incumbents, 1969

Listed below for each 1960 Census three-digit occupation are: (1) education and training opportunities or requirements; (2) general educational development (GED) and specific vocational preparation (SVP) scores; and (3) median earnings in 1969 of full-year workers in the 1970 experienced civilian labor force.

Pre-employment training (1, 2, or 3)[1]	GED	SVP	Median full-year earnings, 1969		Occupation:
			Men	Women	
					Professional, technical
1	16.00	5.00	$12,511	$ 6,841	000 Accountants
2	14.00	3.00	12,839	9,662	010 Actors
2	—	—	19,398	a	012 Airplane pilots
1	—	—	16,848	10,506	013 Architects
2	14.80	4.95	11,307	7,185	014 Artists
3	—	—	10,188	4,611	015 Athletes
1	17.33	1.50	13,235	7,564	020 Authors
1	16.35	3.16	12,678	9,888	021 Chemists
1	16.00	3.00	15,932	7,276	022 Chiropractors
1	—	—	6,819	4,302	023 Clergymen
1	17.20	6.40	12,784	7,721	030 College presidents and deans
1	17.20	6.40	13,468	a	031 Agricultural instructors
1	17.20	6.40	13,583	8,628	032 Biological instructors
1	17.20	6.40	14,343	9,483	034 Chemistry instructors
1	17.20	6.40	15,916	a	035 Economics instructors
1	17.20	6.40	15,642	a	040 Engineering instructors
1	17.20	6.40	13,827	a	041 Geology and geophysics instructors
1	17.20	6.40	13,204	8,787	042 Mathematics instructors
1	17.20	6.40	21,998	9,394	043 Medical sciences instructors
1	17.20	6.40	13,925	a	045 Physics instructors
1	17.20	6.40	15,642	9,843	050 Psychology instructors
1	17.20	6.40	13,204	8,787	051 Statistics instructors
1	17.20	6.40	12,821	9,631	052 Natural sciences instructors, n.e.c.
1	17.20	6.40	14,849	10,623	053 Social sciences instructors, n.e.c.
1	17.20	6.40	12,821	9,631	054 Nonscientific subjects instructors

1	17.20	6.40	12,784	7,721	060 Subject not specified instructors
2	13.00	3.88	9,642	4,879	070 Dancers
1	18.00	7.00	23,817	14,101	071 Dentists
2	15.60	4.90	12,496	8,055	072 Designers
2	16.00	3.00	8,271	5,961	073 Dietitians and nutritionists
2	12.68	2.68	9,430	6,601	074 Draftsmen
1	15.67	4.65	12,830	7,151	075 Editors and reporters
1	15.20	4.60	15,444	12,088	080 Aeronautical engineers
1	15.20	4.60	15,069	9,116	081 Chemical engineers
1	15.20	4.60	13,858	11,816	082 Civil engineers
1	15.20	4.60	13,992	11,061	083 Electrical engineers
1	15.20	4.60	13,245	9,349	084 Industrial engineers
1	15.20	4.60	14,292	12,110	085 Mechanical engineers
1	15.20	4.60	12,678	9,388	090 Metallurgical engineers
1	15.20	4.60	13,407	a	091 Mining engineers
1	15.20	4.60	14,643	a	092 Sales engineers
1	15.20	4.60	13,759	11,309	093 Engineers, n.e.c.
2	7.00	.38	12,642	7,185	101 Entertainers, n.e.c.
1	14.67	2.06	11,017	8,176	102 Farm and home management advisors
1	10.58	1.50	9,135	5,600	103 Foresters and conservationists
2	12.00	3.00	12,318	9,505	104 Funeral directors and embalmers
1	18.00	6.35	23,365	13,946	105 Lawyers and judges
1	16.00	5.00	10,694	7,004	111 Librarians
2	16.00	8.67	9,118	3,274	120 Musicians and music teachers
1	17.20	3.18	10,860	9,474	130 Agricultural scientists
1	17.20	3.18	11,867	8,154	131 Biological scientists
1	17.20	3.18	15,528	a	134 Geologists and geophysicists
1	17.20	3.18	15,256	9,686	135 Mathematicians

aInformation not available.

1"1" designates occupations for which four or more years of college is required or preferred; "2" means that other pre-employment training opportunities, including apprenticeship, exist; "3" is a residual category.

Source: GED and SVP scores on the NLS public-use tapes were derived from Scoville (1969); 1969 earnings from U.S. Bureau of Census (1973); information in column 1 is authors' estimates based on a series of U.S. Bureau of Labor Statistics pamphlets (1976a through 1976e).

Pre-employment training (1, 2, or 3)[1]	GED	SVP	Median full-year earnings, 1969		Occupation:
			Men	Women	
					Professional, technical
1	17.20	3.18	15,731	11,058	140 Physicists
1	17.20	3.18	15,540	a	145 Miscellaneous natural scientists
2	12.00	2.50	9,374	6,585	150 Nurses
2	—	—	4,519	2,213	151 Nurses, student
1	16.00	3.00	18,590	9,939	152 Optometrists
1	18.00	7.00	29,969	15,344	153 Osteopaths
1	16.80	4.08	12,819	7,770	154 Personnel and labor relations workers
1	16.00	3.00	13,475	7,897	160 Pharmacists
2	12.67	2.01	10,047	5,307	161 Photographers
1	17.78	7.00	29,969	15,344	162 Physicians and surgeons
1	16.80	4.08	13,420	7,908	163 Public relations and publicity writers
2	11.60	.74	8,432	5,830	164 Radio operators
1	16.00	5.00	8,654	5,709	165 Recreation and group workers
1	—	—	7,439	4,207	170 Religious workers
1	15.50	3.92	9,495	7,405	171 Social and welfare workers
1	17.33	3.00	15,813	9,268	172 Economists
1	17.33	3.00	15,373	10,789	173 Psychologists
1	17.33	3.00	12,675	8,132	174 Statisticians and actuaries
1	17.33	3.00	11,646	7,481	175 Miscellaneous social scientists
1	—	—	9,642	4,879	180 Sports instructors and officials
2	15.00	2.62	8,604	6,933	181 Surveyors
1	16.40	5.00	9,091	7,072	182 Teachers, elementary
1	16.40	5.00	9,798	7,417	183 Teachers, secondary

	Code	Occupation				
1	184	Teachers, n.e.c.	4,879	9,642	5.00	16.40
2	185	Technicians, medical and dental	6,008	8,979	1.80	12.36
2	190	Technicians, electrical and electronic	6,871	9,908	1.65	12.27
2	191	Technicians, other engineering, and physical sciences	6,190	9,250	1.65	12.27
2	192	Technicians, n.e.c.	5,661	8,047	1.76	12.25
1	193	Therapists and healers, n.e.c.	6,656	13,283	2.12	14.00
1	194	Veterinarians	9,455	19,112	5.67	16.00
1	195	Professional, technical and kindred workers, n.e.c.	8,093	11,936	2.55	14.91

Farmers and farm managers

	Code	Occupation				
2	200	Farmers (owners and tenants)	3,578	6,505	7.00	16.00
2	222	Farm managers	5,490	8,520	7.00	16.00

Managers and administrators, except farm

	Code	Occupation				
2	250	Buyers and department heads, store	6,380	11,835	7.00	16.00
2	251	Buyers and shippers, farm products	a	10,205	1.00	8.00
3	252	Conductors, railroad	a	10,739	5.00	11.00
2	253	Credit personnel	5,894	10,400	—	—
1	254	Floor men and floor managers, store	a	9,303	—	—
3	260	Inspectors, public administration	a	9,397	2.16	11.46
2	262	Managers and superintendents, building	4,474	9,756	—	—
2	265	Officers, pilots, pursers, and engineers, ship	a	12,171	3.53	11.40
1	270	Officials and administrators, n.e.c., public administration	7,928	12,695	3.26	13.20
3	275	Officials, lodge, society, union, etc.	7,673	12,805	.04	11.00
3	280	Postmasters	6,608	10,212	—	—
2	285	Purchasing agents and buyers, n.e.c.	7,399	11,628	7.00	12.00
1	290	Managers, officials, and proprietors, n.e.c.	7,458	15,446	3.54	12.50

Pre-employment training (1, 2, or 3)[1]	GED	SVP	Median full-year earnings, 1969 Men	Women	Occupation:
					Clerical and kindred
2	11.73	1.48	13,515	6,178	301 Agents, n.e.c.
3	14.00	3.88	4,901	4,416	302 Attendants and assistants, library
2	9.50	1.58	6,451	4,180	303 Attendants, physician's and dentist's office
3	—	—	7,916	a	304 Baggagemen, transportation
3	—	—	6,770	4,574	305 Bank tellers
2	10.33	.44	8,487	5,144	310 Bookkeepers
3	10.67	.53	5,714	3,880	312 Cashiers
3	12.00	.04	7,715	4,871	313 Collectors, bill and account
3	11.50	1.97	8,810	4,927	314 Dispatchers and starters, vehicle
3	7.00	.10	6,608	4,527	315 Express messengers and railway mail clerks
3	10.22	.79	6,699	4,694	320 File clerks
3	11.73	1.48	9,898	5,820	321 Insurance adjusters, examiners, and investigators
3	8.50	.10	8,127	5,819	323 Mail carriers
3	7.50	.10	5,183	4,075	324 Messengers and office boys
2	8.42	.23	8,286	5,209	325 Office machine operators
3	10.22	.79	8,252	5,632	333 Payroll and timekeeping clerks
3	10.22	.79	8,440	5,910	340 Postal clerks
2	10.22	.79	6,961	4,343	341 Receptionists
2	10.91	.58	9,148	5,161	342 Secretaries
3	10.00	.75	6,956	4,687	343 Shipping and receiving clerks
2	10.91	.58	12,352	5,726	345 Stenographers
3	10.22	.79	7,057	5,235	350 Stock clerks and storekeepers

3	351	Telegraph messengers	8.50	.04	a	a
3	352	Telegraph operators	9.10	1.06	8,771	5,860
3	353	Telephone operators	10.86	.63	8,612	5,035
3	354	Ticket, station and express agents	10.00	.56	8,972	6,441
2	360	Typists	10.91	.58	7,078	4,858
3	370	Clerical and kindred workers, n.e.c.	10.22	.79	8,322	4,997

Sales workers

1	380	Advertising agents and sales personnel	10.00	.04	13,473	6,585
2	381	Auctioneers	—	—	14,000	a
3	382	Demonstrators	12.00	.16	10,367	3,786
2	383	Hucksters and peddlers	6.00	.08	8,991	2,167
2	385	Insurance agents, brokers, and underwriters	10.70	1.19	12,430	6,308
3	390	Newsboys	8.50	.04	3,035	2,615
2	393	Real estate agents and brokers	—	—	13,749	7,401
1	394	Salesmen and sales clerks, n.e.c.	9.12	.82	19,830	9,045
2	395	Stock and bond salesmen	—	—	10,346	3,711

Craftsmen & kindred

2	401	Bakers	9.25	1.54	7,410	3,921
2	402	Blacksmiths	11.18	2.18	7,554	a
3	403	Boilermakers	11.78	2.29	9,287	a
2	404	Bookbinders	8.33	3.56	8,377	4,688
3	405	Brickmasons, stonemasons, and tile setters	9.73	1.92	8,796	6,027
2	410	Cabinetmakers	12.00	3.00	7,310	4,561
2	411	Carpenters	11.67	2.70	8,042	6,236
3	413	Cement and concrete finishers	11.50	2.62	7,949	6,551
2	414	Compositors and typesetters	12.00	4.38	8,651	5,146
3	415	Cranemen, derrickmen, and hoistmen	9.11	.74	8,855	7,770

Pre-employment training (1, 2, or 3)[1]	GED	SVP	Median full-year earnings, 1969		Occupation:
			Men	Women	
					Craftsmen & kindred
2	9.38	.83	8,094	4,567	420 Decorators and window dressers
2	11.14	1.73	9,751	7,452	421 Electricians
2	11.00	5.00	10,099	a	423 Electrotypers and stereotypers
2	11.46	4.08	8,142	5,556	424 Engravers, except photoengravers
3	8.88	.82	8,069	7,140	425 Excavating, grading, and machinery operators
3	11.70	3.90	10,473	6,174	430 Foremen, n.e.c.
3	10.33	1.50	8,763	6,012	431 Forgemen and hammermen
2	10.67	2.50	8,153	a	432 Furriers
3	10.00	2.50	8,627	5,015	434 Glaziers
3	10.50	2.13	8,678	a	435 Heat treaters, annealers, and temperers
3	10.64	1.55	6,740	4,088	444 Inspectors, scalers, and graders, log and lumber
3	11.88	3.58	8,724	4,920	450 Inspectors, n.e.c.
3	11.53	3.63	8,135	4,857	451 Jewelers, watchmakers, goldsmiths and silversmiths
3	10.67	3.00	8,830	7,113	452 Job setters, metals
3	10.61	2.18	9,288	6,339	453 Linemen and servicemen, telegraph, telephone, and power
3	10.00	2.02	11,441	11,078	454 Locomotive engineers
3	10.00	.75	9,801	a	460 Locomotive firemen
3	10.00	3.00	6,815	a	461 Loom fixers
2	11.69	3.32	8,640	5,952	465 Machinists
2	12.00	3.00	8,886	8,131	470 Mechanics and repairmen, air conditioning, heating, and refrigeration
2	10.71	2.34	9,279	15,376	471 Mechanics and repairmen, airplane

	Code					Occupation
2	472	6,285	7,493	1.66	10.80	Mechanics and repairmen, automobile
2	473	6,199	8,168	3.00	11.00	Mechanics and repairmen, office machine
2	474	5,789	7,923	3.00	12.00	Mechanics and repairmen, radio and television
3	475	a	7,984	.75	10.00	Mechanics and repairmen, railroad and car shop
2	480	4,725	8,390	2.83	11.44	Mechanics and repairmen, n.e.c.
3	490	a	7,018	.97	9.22	Millers, grain, flour, feed, etc.
3	491	9,049	9,910	3.00	12.00	Millwrights
3	492	4,966	7,856	1.71	9.17	Molders, metal
3	493	a	8,623	3.00	12.00	Motion picture projectionists
2	494	4,996	9,125	1.49	8.67	Opticians, and lens grinders and polishers
3	495	5,949	7,509	1.78	10.90	Painters, construction and maintenance
3	501	a	8,560	—	—	Paperhangers
3	502	7,351	10,501	3.64	11.47	Pattern and model makers, except paper
2	503	6,109	10,744	4.46	10.53	Photoengravers and lithographers
2	504	a	7,445	3.00	12.00	Piano and organ tuners and repairmen
3	505	a	8,998	2.62	10.50	Plasterers
2	510	8,174	9,559	3.83	11.23	Plumbers and pipe fitters
2	512	5,274	8,956	4.19	10.90	Pressmen and plate printers, printing
3	513	6,102	9,627	1.02	7.90	Rollers and roll hands, metals
3	514	6,660	7,410	—	—	Roofers and slaters
2	515	3,955	5,950	2.40	12.40	Shoemakers and repairers, except factory
3	520	6,970	9,104	2.08	11.11	Stationary engineers
3	521	a	6,964	3.23	9.89	Stone cutters and stone carvers
3	523	10,600	10,007	1.47	9.88	Structural metal workers
2	524	4,052	9,288	1.62	10.67	Tailors and tailoresses
2	525	7,198	9,041	2.57	11.60	Tinsmiths, coppersmiths, and sheet metal workers
2	530	7,489	10,365	3.78	11.62	Toolmakers, and die makers and setters
2	535	4,225	6,671	1.59	9.00	Upholsterers
3	545	4,864	8,733	2.32	10.83	Craftsmen and kindred workers, n.e.c.
3	555	7,490	4,304	—	—	Members of the Armed Forces, and former members of the Armed Forces

Pre-employment training (1, 2, or 3)[1]	GED	SVP	Median full-year earnings, 1969		Occupation:
			Men	Women	
					Operatives and kindred workers
2	11.36	.16	5,357	a	601 Apprentice auto mechanics
3	11.36	.16	8,113	a	602 Apprentice bricklayers and masons
2	11.36	.16	6,236	a	603 Apprentice carpenters
2	11.36	.16	7,330	a	604 Apprentice electricians
2	11.36	.16	6,815	a	605 Apprentice machinists and toolmakers
2	11.36	.16	7,469	a	610 Apprentice mechanics, except auto
2	11.36	.16	6,961	a	612 Apprentice plumbers and pipe fitters
3	11.36	.16	7,509	a	613 Apprentices, building trades, n.e.c.
2	11.36	.16	7,469	a	614 Apprentices, metalworking trades, n.e.c.
2	11.36	.16	6,092	a	615 Apprentices, printing trades
2	11.36	.16	a	a	620 Apprentices, other specified trades
3	11.36	.16	a	a	621 Apprentices, trade not specified
3	12.00	2.25	9,756	a	630 Asbestos and insulation workers
3	8.56	.98	7,339	4,904	631 Assemblers
2	11.00	1.69	5,096	3,776	632 Attendants, auto service and parking
3	10.50	2.92	7,850	a	634 Blasters and powdermen
3	9.67	2.51	7,781	a	635 Boatmen, canalmen, and lock keepers
3	4.00	.00	9,337	a	640 Brakemen, railroad
3	12.00	.75	7,667	3,477	641 Bus drivers
2	7.40	.70	6,150	a	642 Chainmen, rodmen, and axmen, surveying
3	11.88	3.58	8,344	4,960	643 Checkers, examiners, and inspectors, manufacturing
3	—	—	8,890	a	645 Conductors, bus and street railway
3	10.75	1.78	7,529	4,936	650 Deliverymen and routemen

	Code	Occupation				
2	651	Dressmakers and seamstresses, except factory	3,463	6,408	2.44	9.25
3	652	Dyers	4,662	6,074	.96	8.86
2	653	Filers, grinders, and polishers, metal	5,732	7,788	1.16	8.67
3	654	Fruit, nut, and vegetable graders and packers, except factory	3,135	5,687	.21	7.00
3	670	Furnacemen, smeltermen, and pourers	5,981	8,227	1.42	9.94
3	671	Graders and sorters, manufacturing	4,281	6,643	.98	8.56
3	672	Heaters, metal	a	9,607	—	—
3	673	Knitters, loopers, and toppers, textile	4,041	6,661	.98	8.56
3	674	Laundry and dry cleaning operatives	3,370	6,744	.63	8.42
2	675	Meat cutters, except slaughter and packing house	4,775	7,922	2.51	10.00
2	680	Milliners	4,838	a	1.01	8.71
3	685	Mine operatives and laborers, n.e.c.	5,110	7,606	1.02	7.89
3	690	Motormen, mine, factory, logging camp, etc.	a	7,671	.93	9.75
3	691	Motormen, street, subway, and elevated railway	a	8,890	—	—
3	692	Oilers and greasers, except auto	5,326	7,757	.33	5.60
3	693	Packers and wrappers, n.e.c.	4,381	6,328	.98	8.56
3	694	Painters, except construction and maintenance	4,588	7,282	.75	7.15
2	695	Photographic process workers	4,938	8,189	1.27	9.40
3	701	Power station operators	6,304	9,993	1.55	10.30
3	703	Sailors and deck hands	a	7,890	1.68	7.14
3	704	Sawyers	4,535	5,898	1.08	8.70
2	705	Sewers and stitchers, manufacturing	3,853	6,124	.98	8.56
3	710	Spinners, textile	4,307	5,582	1.25	8.00
3	712	Stationary firemen	4,341	8,017	2.25	11.00
3	713	Switchmen, railroad	7,178	8,885	.21	7.00
3	714	Taxicab drivers and chauffeurs	4,259	6,211	3.52	9.50
3	715	Truck and tractor drivers	3,785	7,966	.25	8.50
3	720	Weavers, textile	4,772	5,719	3.00	12.00
2	721	Welders and flame-cutters	5,462	8,079	.61	9.85
2	775	Operatives and kindred workers, n.e.c.	4,589	7,440	.98	8.56

Pre-employment training (1, 2, or 3)[1]	GED	SVP	Median full-year earnings, 1969 Men	Women	Occupation:
					Private household workers
3	8.90	.96	2,021	1,397	801 Baby sitters
3	12.00	.94	5,021	1,850	802 Housekeepers
3	7.00	.04	a	1,146	803 Laundresses
3	8.90	.96	2,985	1,678	804 Private household workers, n.e.c.
					Service workers, except private household
2	9.50	.10	5,299	3,751	810 Attendants, hospital and other institutions
3	8.00	.10	5,558	4,268	812 Attendants, professional and personal service, n.e.c.
3	7.00	.03	6,270	3,780	813 Attendants, recreation and amusement
2	11.00	.94	6,563	4,651	814 Barbers
3	7.00	.16	6,787	4,122	815 Bartenders
3	4.00	.04	2,494	a	820 Bootblacks
3	12.00	.94	6,894	4,886	821 Boarding and lodging housekeepers
3	6.00	.40	5,209	2,841	823 Chambermaids and maids, except private households
3	6.00	.40	5,226	3,967	824 Charwomen and cleaners
2	11.33	3.58	6,057	3,274	825 Cooks, except private household
3	7.75	.12	4,493	3,032	830 Counter and fountain workers
3	7.00	.04	5,572	3,691	831 Elevator operators
3	11.90	2.23	7,817	3,582	832 Housekeepers and stewards, except private household
3	8.29	1.21	5,674	3,324	834 Janitors and sextons
3	7.11	.26	4,229	3,037	835 Kitchen workers, n.e.c., except private household
2	—	—	a	a	840 Midwives
3	4.75	.04	5,226	3,067	841 Porters
2	10.00	1.50	6,420	4,772	842 Practical nurses

					Code	Occupation
2	11.00	.94	8,587	4,155	843	Hairdressers and cosmetologists
2	10.50	1.26	9,588	8,730	850	Firemen, fire protection
2	9.17	.14	6,851	5,215	851	Guards, watchmen, and doorkeepers
2	–	–	7,641	a	852	Marshals and constables
2	11.33	.19	9,223	6,774	853	Policemen and detectives
2	–	–	7,927	6,522	854	Sheriffs and bailiffs
3	5.50	.02	6,473	2,680	860	Watchmen (crossing) and bridge tenders
3	6.00	.04	3,994	4,457	874	Usher, recreation and amusement
3	7.00	.61	4,966	2,905	875	Waiters and waitresses
3	7.11	.26	6,224	2,812	890	Service workers, except private household, n.e.c.

Farm laborers and foremen

					Code	Occupation
3	12.00	3.00	6,973	5,358	901	Farm foreman
3	8.47	1.20	4,011	2,634	902	Farm laborers, wage workers
3	6.87	.80	a	a	903	Farm laborers, unpaid family workers
3	9.00	1.06	a	a	905	Farm service laborers, self-employed

Laborers, except farm and mine

					Code	Occupation
3	6.46	.46	5,320	3,924	960	Carpenters' helpers, except logging and mining
3	8.10	.60	6,877	a	962	Fishermen and oystermen
3	2.67	.04	5,678	4,081	963	Garage laborers, and car washers and greasers
3	7.50	.37	5,672	3,670	964	Gardeners, except farm. and groundkeepers
3	7.20	.25	8,586	a	965	Longshoremen and stevedores
3	6.71	.52	5,837	4,188	970	Lumbermen, raftsmen, and woodchoppers
3	8.50	.24	6,206	a	971	Teamsters
3	6.46	.46	5,108	3,743	972	Truck drivers' helpers
3	6.46	.46	6,896	5,354	973	Warehousemen, n.e.c.
3	6.46	.46	4,276	4,714	985	Laborers, n.e.c.
					995	Occupation not reported